MANORIAL DOMESTIC BUILDINGS IN ENGLAND AND NORTHERN FRANCE

Manorial Domestic Buildings in England and Northern France

Edited by Gwyn Meirion-Jones and Michael Jones

VOLUME 15 OF OCCASIONAL PAPERS FROM
THE SOCIETY OF ANTIQUARIES OF LONDON

THE SOCIETY OF ANTIQUARIES OF LONDON
BURLINGTON HOUSE, PICCADILLY, LONDON W1V 0HS

FRONT COVER: *Bien Assis, Erquy, Côtes-d'Armor, rebuilt in stone by Geoffroy de Quelennec between c. 1412 and 1434*
Photograph: Gwyn Meirion-Jones

British Library Cataloguing-in-Publication Data.

A catalogue record for this book is available from the British Library

1004799352

© Society of Antiquaries of London, 1993
ISBN 0-85431-263-3
ISSN 0953-7155

Contents

LIST OF ILLUSTRATIONS

Notes sur l'habitat noble rural dans le nord et l'est de l'Ile-de-France du XIIe au XVe siècle, *by* Jean Mesqui

Les manoirs du Perche, *by* Elisabeth Gautier-Desvaux

The seigneurial domestic buildings of Brittany, 1000–1700, *by* Gwyn Meirion-Jones, Michael Jones and Jon R. Pilcher

Acknowledgements

The Colloquium from which these collected papers result had its origins in informal discussions between Dr John Blair, F.S.A., Professor Michael Jones, F.S.A., and Professor Gwyn Meirion-Jones, F.S.A. They felt that there was a need to look anew at manorial domestic buildings and, in particular, to re-appraise the plan-development of the ground-floor hall, the free-standing chamber-block and the so-called 'first-floor' hall. Recent renewed interest in the subject in England could only be stimulated by discussion with colleagues working on related topics in northern France. A one-day Colloquium was proposed and the Society of Antiquaries of London generously agreed to sponsor the event which was held on 24 November 1990.

The originators of the Colloquium are immensely grateful to the late Dr Hugh Chapman, F.S.A., General Secretary of the Society of Antiquaries from 1988 until his untimely death in 1992, for his support and encouragement and for overseeing the organization of the Colloquium; in this he was considerably aided by the Society's staff in Burlington House and by Miss Elizabeth Nichols, Editor, who has been responsible for seeing this volume through the press. Dr Michael Robbins, C.B.E., F.S.A., presided over the occasion. The Society is indebted to French colleagues for taking the time and trouble to support the Colloquium and for contributing papers based upon their current researches. Dr Elisabeth Lorans kindly assisted by translating the Abstracts into French. It is hoped that this volume will serve to stimulate further work on a subject of which the potential is far from being exhausted.

Introduction

Gwyn Meirion-Jones, Michael Jones, John Blair and Philip Dixon

Of the eight papers presented at the Colloquium and printed here, three are concerned with the English seigneurial dwelling and five with French *châteaux* and *manoirs*. The geographical range of the research reported in this volume extends from the Scottish Borders southwards through midland and southern England to Brittany, the Perche and the Ile-de-France. Although several authors touch on the Renaissance, all contributions have the medieval period in common and all but one are concerned with the central Middle Ages from *c.* 1000 onwards; this is a period when relations between England and northern France were particularly close and it will not come as a surprise to find sometimes strong similarities in the form and function of manorial domestic buildings, and parallels in their development within the Anglo-Norman world.

Among the contributors only Julian Munby confines himself to a particular type of building construction, that of the timber-frame so important in the building tradition of England. John Blair and Joseph Decaëns begin their respective studies about AD 1000; Edward Impey studies the period 1050–1350 so crucial to an understanding of the transition from the free-standing—and sometimes loosely arranged—buildings of the central Middle Ages to the unified late medieval seigneurial residence; Jean Mesqui takes the subject as far as the fifteenth century in the Ile-de-France, a region of formative influences; Elisabeth Gautier-Desvaux describes the numerous late medieval and Renaissance *manoirs* of the Perche; and for Brittany the authors attempt an evolutionary sequence covering some seven hundred years. What emerges is a core of common time-span in the central and later Middle Ages and a degree of cultural homogeneity in the essentials of the design of the seigneurial residence.

Joseph Decaëns elucidates the transition from the motte-and-bailey castles of the eleventh century to stone-built structures. He emphasizes the all-important fact that mottes and ringworks built of earth and wood, or castles constructed of stone, are military works and aristocratic residences functioning as the economic and political centres of a lordship, symbols of seigneurial authority. In his examination of a very large number of sites in north-west France he is able to distinguish subdivisions according to type: strongholds where a military function is paramount and strategic importance clear; others where the function is primarily political, economic and social, the military aspect being subordinate; in a third category are those castles associated with a town and the development of a market and commerce.

From the beginning of the eleventh century, earth and stone are both used as building materials for castles, but earth defences were then in the majority. A gradual transition resulted, stone buildings becoming preponderant, even though earth fortifications continued to exist, by the thirteenth century. There is no difference of function between earth and stone castles; in most cases they express only a difference in the social level of their builders. Texts firmly attest the presence of mottes in the middle Loire valley by 1020–40 and in Normandy by *c.* 1050. Thereafter mention becomes very frequent in the whole of northern France from the Loire to the Rhine. It has recently been shown that many mottes were in use by the middle of the eleventh century.

If mottes are found in large numbers, so too are ringworks; the former probably originating by the infilling of smaller ringworks. Many mottes make partial use of a natural eminence or rocky outcrop. One or more baileys are usual. Recent excavations have shown the residential and military character of the motte-and-bailey castle. A wooden tower, which might be either a seigneurial residence or merely a simple look-out post, stood on the motte. The bailey housed the domestic, agricultural and other dependent buildings. In most cases a hall, chapel and the private apartments—the three essential elements of contemporary aristocratic houses—are located in the bailey. The motte-and-bailey castle was the political, social and economic centre of a lordship.

John Blair centres his account on the functions of 'hall and chamber' in English domestic planning, 1000–1200. He argues cogently that the storeyed ranges of *c.* 1150–1220, which English historians have termed 'first-floor halls', are in fact chamber-blocks, originally accompanied by free-standing open halls. Descriptions of English houses written between *c.* 900 and *c.* 1200 generally assume the existence of both components (termed *aula* and *camera* in Latin, *heall* and *bur* in Old English). In a series of aristocratic houses, some standing and others known from excavation, it can be proved that both an open hall and a chamber-block existed on one site. Royal and manorial houses often have buildings arranged on linear axes, whereas bishops' palaces (influenced by monastic planning) are generally laid out around courtyards. Architecturally-ambitious aisled halls only became common in England after *c.* 1150. The typical late medieval arrangement at the lower end of the hall, with a cross-passage, two service rooms and secondary chambers above, developed *c.* 1180–95. From the early thirteenth century it was increasingly common for the main chamber-block to be attached to the upper end of the hall, producing the standard late medieval English house.

This theme is continued by Edward Impey in his account of seigneurial architecture in Normandy, 1050–1350, based on the study of a small but significant group of standing buildings. He outlines the basic design of medieval seigneurial dwellings in Normandy as it developed during the period. An interpretation of important buildings, surviving in part, indicates that twelfth-century seigneurial builders shared a common tradition with those of England. The three ensembles subjected to detailed study included ground-floor halls, while in two cases detached storeyed buildings of the so-called 'first-floor hall' type were recorded; the survival of these elements in association substantiates the re-interpretation of the 'first-floor hall' (here referred to as 'chamber-block') as adjuncts to ground-floor halls, their upper floors containing private seigneurial chambers. The thirteenth century saw the replacement of the 'hall and chamber-block ensemble' by self-contained structures, the *logis,* in which upper and lower floors served the combined functions of hall and chamber for socially-differentiated sections of the household. As this was the direct antecedent of the typical late medieval *manoir,* early examples were still acceptable to later medieval occupants and have survived in substantial numbers; in contrast, the comparative rarity of 'hall and chamber-block' ensembles can be attributed to their unsuitability for conversion to *logis*. The origins of the new design are far from clear. It may have been introduced from elsewhere, or it may have been an innovation without structural antecedents in Normandy; it might also have been a development of the hall or chamber-block alone. Evidence from two other buildings—which may be interpreted as 'transitional'—suggests that the emergence of the *logis* was preceded by an integration of the hall and chamber within a single axial block, the *logis* being a further development.

In the borderlands of England and Scotland more than three centuries of intermittent warfare resulted in the construction of some five hundred fortified houses, sufficiently strongly built for later generations to preserve and incorporate them into new buildings. In his account of the region Philip Dixon shows that the central Middle Ages was a period in which feudal lordships developed slowly, and involved the construction of relatively few castles, belonging in the main to the new baronies imposed on the existing system of estates during the reign of Henry I. During the later twelfth and early thirteenth centuries, the region displayed a complex pattern of Norman and native lordships whose manor-houses included timber halls and stone *camerae* of two or three storeys. Simple stone ground-floor halls, built without aisles and with service rooms at their lower ends, form a distinct regional style during the first part of the thirteenth century. The first-floor hall appears in the Borders soon after the middle of that century. Some of the early examples may be *camerae* whose halls have been lost; where the type is certain, the arrangement of the accommodation provides us with two superimposed halls, not normally connected together, attached to a chamber block of two or more storeys, access to which was obtained from the upper hall, and not from the lower hall.

The storeyed chamber-block at the end of the ground-floor or first-floor hall might take the form of a tower, and the outbreak of open war between England and Scotland at the end of the thirteenth century led to the introduction of stronger solar towers at the end of or beside the earlier halls. During the ensuing century, rebuilding of the manor houses of the region continued rapidly, with the development of distinctive tower-houses at the end of the fourteenth century. The owners of these halls and the towers which succeeded them were of high status, and the buildings formed the capital messuages of the lesser baronies and the manors of the region.

During this period few stone buildings were constructed in the Scottish uplands, but during the later Middle Ages, and in particular during the sixteenth century, this pattern was reversed, and new stone towers were built in the Scottish dales in very large numbers. Their occupants included men of high social standing, but the characteristic of the period was the fortification of the houses of relatively minor lairds. Towards the end of the sixteenth century a still lower class, the crown tenants of the Border uplands, began to build stone-defended houses of sub-manorial status, during a phase in which the older feudal aristocracy of the region was removed by the policy of the central governments, leaving little authority in the area to replace them.

Jean Mesqui studies the rural noble habitat in the north and east of that crucially-important region, the Ile-de-France, from the twelfth to the fifteenth centuries. Whilst the fortified castles of France have long been studied—although not necessarily in the depth and to the detail now expected of such studies—this is not true of the rural noble dwellings. Dr Mesqui's aim is to define a typology, starting from surviving rural noble dwellings, and based on the main palatial or castral structures. Three elements emerge as being of great importance:

the *salle* (hall), the *chambre* (the chamber or solar), and the *chapelle* (private chapel). In each dwelling these three elements are fundamental to an understanding of the architecture; it is also very interesting to consider, however, the variation in the combination of these three basic elements, depending of the social position of the owner.

In complete contrast, the approach of Julian Munby is to trace and discuss, in manorial and related contexts, the development of building in timber in central and southern England between the thirteenth and sixteenth centuries. Regional variations in building types in England are considered in relation to the highland/lowland zones, wealth and agricultural practices, and the availability of timber and stone. Status and range of carpentry are briefly discussed together with its place in surviving manorial buildings. The aisled hall and its derivatives are described, from the varieties of roof-structures and decorative elements, to the means by which aisle-posts were replaced with new types of construction. The development of plan-types is considered including the relationship of jetties to the H-plan and the gradual evolution of a unified three-part plan on a rectilinear base, culminating in the plan of the late medieval Wealden house. The possible influence of carpentry techniques on ground-plans is liable to be overlooked; it is an important theme to which Julian Munby rightly draws our attention.

As Elisabeth Gautier-Desvaux shows, the *manoirs* of the Perche—on the margins of the Armorican massif and the Paris Basin—survive in remarkably large numbers, a characteristic shared with other regions of western France, notably Brittany, both regions which long retained their administrative autonomy. The custom of the Perche reserves to the eldest son, not only the woodland, but the manorial *pourpris*—the courtyards and all dependent buildings including the enclosing walls and moats—by which the whole manorial ensemble is protected, including those buildings closely linked to seigneurial prerogative, the chapel and the dovecot. Place-name evidence demonstrates the antiquity of many sites: names that testify to defence, to the building of earthworks, to the activities of a knightly class or of a military vocation. The permanence of the seigneurial habitat and continuity of site is borne out by documentary evidence; it is also evident in the reuse and adaptation of earlier buildings. The Hundred Years' War was responsible for much destruction of the fabric of buildings; it also contributed to the decline and extinction of many an ancient family, its aftermath saw the rebuilding to which we owe most of the extant *manoirs*. The advent of Renaissance ideas led to change. Symmetry of plan and a move to greater comfort begin to appear. Economic factors, with the proper ordering and management of the estate, are highlighted by the publication of influential manuals; the maintenance of the economic and symbolic integrity of the *manoir* remains paramount. The seventeenth and eighteenth centuries brought change as estates were rationalized. Many *manoirs* were razed to make way for larger structures in the new styles of the period; others were simply adapted and enlarged. Many were reduced to the status of a farm in which form they have survived to the present day.

In Brittany the evolution of the seigneurial residence is traced from the earliest known sites, the motte-and-bailey castles, to the late Renaissance, a span of some seven hundred years. Many of the elements known in adjacent parts of western Europe are found also in Brittany: the free-standing ground-floor hall, the chamber-block, the inhabited tower with its ascending hierarchy of rooms, both undefended and in its fortified form, the *donjon*. Hall and chamber are the recurring common elements which, together with the kitchen and *cave,* form the 'seigneurial minimum' accommodation. The *chambre* is always raised above ground level. Emphasis on height—and domination—is a recurring theme. From the thirteenth century multiple halls become common, stacked above each other; two superimposed halls are frequent, four not unknown. Veritable apartments appear—each with hall and chamber—on several levels. Although the open hall is ubiquitous, no evidence of a former open hearth has yet come to light in the buildings studied. Many of the smaller *manoirs* retain their open roofs until the fifteenth century or later. The period 1500–1660 is one of modernization of medieval halls by the insertion of ceilings, rationalizing internal communication.

Renaissance styles appear towards the end of the fifteenth century as Flamboyant-Gothic ornament becomes noticeably decadent in its expression; it is in the sixteenth century that the Renaissance idiom makes its impact. By mid-century it is in full flood. Superficially, the sixteenth century marks the advent of classical motifs and detail. The appearance of a degree of symmetry, albeit imperfect, may be noted. The century saw the complete rebuilding of some houses; new houses were sometimes built alongside the old residence. Long before the dawn of the seventeenth century, Gothic mouldings and details have been superseded by the classical idiom. There is ever increasing evidence of symmetry, although at the beginning of the century the eccentric juxtaposition of Renaissance dress and medieval plan forms is still to be found. Peace, greater wealth and prosperity following the Union with France lead to much new building and the rebuilding of earlier residences. Evolution of the domestic life of the seigneurial household symbolizes the turning away from the noise, smells and distractions of the workaday courtyard in front of the old house; new *pavillons* were built so that the family might enjoy direct access to garden and orchard, with views across the countryside. Greater prosperity was accompanied by new building, the search for a better quality of life and more leisure. These developments, with the accompanying romanticization of the countryside, are evidence of the pervasive influence of Renaissance culture among the Breton *noblesse*.

The common core in all this recent research is the highlighting of the presence in the earliest surviving buildings of a free-standing ground-floor hall, of either timber or stone or both, with a detached chamber-block providing private seigneurial accommodation at first-floor level. As Jean Mesqui has pointed out, the essential elements of the seigneurial residence are the (ground-floor) hall, the seigneurial chamber and the private chapel. To this we might follow Madame Gautier-Desvaux and add the dovecot.

Initially-detached units so evolved that they eventually came to be united in such a way that there was direct access from one to the other, frequently under a single roof. Whilst in the motte-and-bailey castles the *donjon* on the motte might, in its simplest form, be no more than a simple lookout, it soon took the form of a habitable tower. Other domestic buildings might be found in the *basse-cour,* but the seigneurial chambers, and in the grander examples no doubt a private hall too, were sometimes, but not always, provided in the tower. The residential or solar tower, defended, undefended or only lightly defended, is a recurring theme in later medieval European domestic architecture. It occurs on a grand scale at Dinan in the late fourteenth century, where a complete and sophisticated ducal residence is so contrived. Simpler forms, usually with only one chamber per storey, are found in larger Breton *manoirs,* in the towers of the Scottish borders and elsewhere.

In thirteenth-century northern France there begins a process by which an upper hall was built over the ground-floor hall; examples come into existence by the end of the Middle Ages where three, and occasionally four, such superimposed halls are found, with associated chambers provided on the same axis and usually at the same level, except that a seigneurial chamber—coupled with the ground-floor hall—is frequently at mezzanine level over a part-sunken cellar. Here we have a veritable hierarchy of halls which, with their accompanying chambers, comprise a series of superimposed apartments. These upper halls take on the function of the private hall and the social implications for the hierarchy of apartments is considerable. In some Breton *châteaux* the lower of the two suites is reserved for the master of the house, the upper for the mistress.

At the humblest seigneurial level, that of the multitude of tiny *manoirs* of northern France, the late medieval and early Renaissance house expresses the 'seigneurial minimum' accommodation; a ground-floor hall is accompanied by a seigneurial chamber set over either a kitchen or a semi-sunken cellar. These minor lords were lucky to have twenty hectares of land and the domaine consisted of no more than the *manoir* itself and a *métairie,* or home farm.

These papers range widely across the world of the Anglo-Normans and their neighbours. They bring out both similarities and differences between regions. Economic factors are clearly significant, but at this high social level these are less important than the attitude of medieval lords to the types of buildings suitable for their status. A uniting theme in all these papers is change: changes in fashion in the royal courts were reflected in the design of the houses of their vassals; changes in the scale and variety of accommodation, first found in the greatest houses, led to the replacement or rebuilding of manorial buildings of more humble standing, and changes in the houses of prestigious regions were imitated by the lords of more remote districts. To chart in detail the stages of these changes by field survey, documentary search, and structural analysis is a massive task which is only now being undertaken: to this task these papers are offered as a contribution.

Hall and Chamber: English Domestic Planning 1000–1250

John Blair

The study of domestic planning in medieval England has been dominated by two scholars whose formative works were published in the 1950s and 1960s: the late Margaret Wood, and Patrick Faulkner. Interpretations of individual buildings are heavily influenced by the models of development which they proposed, and by one model above all: that the main component of a normal twelfth-century manor-house was a stone-built block containing a *first-floor hall* raised over a basement, and that this was a direct alternative to the open *ground-floor hall* of earlier and later houses. Thus Faulkner wrote in 1958:

> The earliest form of dwelling house of a purely domestic character that remains and which forms a basic type already developed in the late 12th century is the Upper Hall house. Essentially, this form of plan is arranged on two floors each of which is provided with a greater and lesser chamber. The residence within these limits appears to be self-contained . . . Covering somewhat the same period as the upper hall house but with a tendency to a later average date is a second fundamental plan form that may be called the end hall type. The most striking characteristic of this form is the domination by a ground floor hall of both plan and elevation. This type of house shows a development through the period from the late 12th century, when it first appears, to the 14th century . . . Its basic form is that of a structurally independent hall with a domestic block attached to one end. The type is perhaps of greater importance than the upper hall type, as from it stems the main stream of subsequent English domestic planning.[1]

Thirty years ago, this was a reasonable conclusion from the available architectural evidence. Numerous manor-houses have been excavated since then, and it is the archaeologist rather than the architectural historian who has come to realize that things are not quite so simple as they once seemed.[2] Furthermore, scrutiny of contemporary documents shows the terminology evolved by modern architectural historians to be anachronistic and misleading in some crucial respects. It is time to make explicit the simple message which has implicitly been emerging from recent work: that the 'first-floor hall' model is inappropriate to normal manorial buildings in England between the eleventh and thirteenth centuries, because the storeyed stone buildings usually called first-floor halls are in fact chamber-blocks which were once accompanied by detached ground-floor halls of the normal kind. Thus the lineal descendant of the so-called 'first-floor hall' was not the open hall, but the solar wing.

This is not to deny the existence of halls at first-floor level in specific places and contexts. The ubiquity of the storeyed house in many parts of France from the thirteenth century onwards is clear from other papers in this volume. In Normandy, as Edward Impey shows (see below pp. 82–120) the ground-floor aisled hall was probably common until superseded by the storeyed house in the thirteenth century. In England the ancient tradition of the ground-floor hall proved more resilient, but some buildings reflect French practice. The halls of the great Anglo-Norman keeps functioned exactly like normal ground-floor halls but were raised at an upper level, while in some other castles (notably Castle Acre and Eynsford)[3] the main component was a massive two-storey block which must have contained the hall on its first floor. The word *aula* was occasionally used for exceptional storeyed buildings, notably the 'new hall' by the precinct gate at Canterbury Cathedral Priory.[4] Urban houses, despite their obvious similarity to manorial *camerae*, developed special forms which may have included raised halls analogous to the *grandes salles* of French town-houses.[5] But these are byways from the main course of development in rural England, which was directed by the almost universal survival of the ground-floor hall.

The first aim of this paper is to clear the ground by redefining normal arrangements in English royal, manorial and episcopal houses: abnormalities, including genuine first-floor halls, can then be better understood. Also reconsidered, in the light of the new model, are two innovations between the mid-twelfth and mid-thirteenth centuries which brought into being the stereotyped late medieval English house: the development of the services and cross-passage at the lower end of the open hall, and the attachment to its upper end of the previously free-standing chamber-block.

AULA CUM CAMERA: THE DOCUMENTARY EVIDENCE

By 1100 there was already a literary convention of defining any substantial residence in terms of two main components: one communal, public and official, used for activities such as the holding of courts and the eating of formal meals, and the other private and residential: in Latin *aula* and *camera* (or *thalamus*), in Old English *heall* and *bur*, in modern English *hall* and *chamber*. We may begin with King Alfred. In his paraphrase of St Augustine's soliloquies, Alfred describes the descending order of accommodation at any royal palace: 'some men are in the chamber, some in the hall, some on the threshing-floor, some in prison' *(sume on bure, sume on healle, sume on odene, sume on carcerne).*[6] Alfred's biographer Asser praises him for his 'royal halls and chambers *(de aulis et cambris regalibus)* marvellously constructed of stone and wood', and in other contexts we encounter Alfred sitting talking to Asser 'in the royal chamber' *(in regia cambra),* and issuing a judgement while washing his hands 'in the chamber *(bur)* at Wardour'.[7]

A number of excavated late Anglo-Saxon manor-houses had private apartments detached from the hall.[8] A particularly clear case is the early eleventh-century phase at Goltho (Lincolnshire), where the hall and bower were juxtaposed but not actually touching (fig. 1).[9]

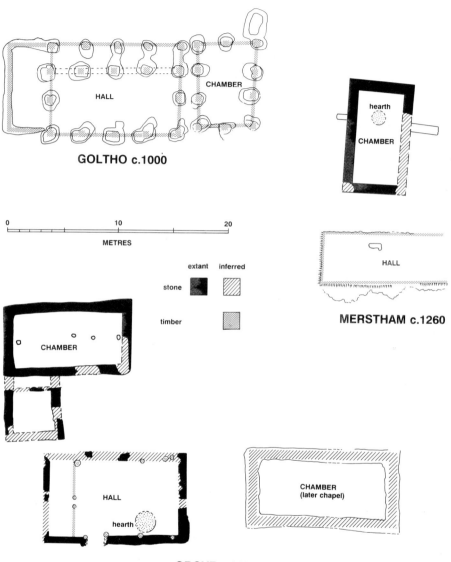

GOLTHO c.1000

CHAMBER

hearth

CHAMBER

MERSTHAM c.1260

HALL

	extant	inferred
stone		
timber		

CHAMBER

HALL

hearth

CHAMBER
(later chapel)

GROVE c.1180

1. *Three simple houses with free-standing halls and chambers: Goltho (after Beresford 1987); Grove (based on site archive by permission of Mrs E. Baker); Alsted, Merstham (after Ketteringham 1976)*

No rural example hitherto known from archaeology has been shown to have had an upper floor. But in 978 the Anglo-Saxon Chronicle describes the collapse of a timber floor under the weight of the royal council, assembled in the king's house at Calne in what the Latin version calls a *solarium*, [10] while the Bayeux Tapestry (which also depicts open halls) shows Harold's feast at Bosham and King Edward's death occurring in upper chambers. Texts of the late eleventh and twelfth centuries continue to juxtapose the terms hall and chamber: William II's reputed comment that his vast new hall at Westminster was 'too big for a chamber, not big enough for a hall'; [11] works on the *nova aula et camera regine* at Westminster in the 1167 pipe roll; [12] St Hugh of Lincoln dining in hall and then withdrawing to his chamber with a few distinguished people *(in aula . . . finito . . . prandio, . . . sumptis vero secum viris honestioribus . . . in cameram secedebat);* [13] and numerous similar phrases.

If such sources are rather imprecise, the more specific descriptions of manor-houses in some estate surveys and leases reveal the continuance of the planning conventions displayed by late Anglo-Saxon houses such as Goltho. The following six examples have been chosen as particularly clear illustrations of the norms suggested by others: [14]

> *Horstead, Norfolk, 1106* x *1130:* A house with a bower *(domum i cum buro);* a kitchen. [15]
> *Ardleigh, Essex, 1141:* A good hall and chamber *(halla et camera);* a tresance *(trisanta);* a pentice *(appenditium)* against the hall on the south; a privy next to the chamber and another in the courtyard; a kitchen. [16]
> *Kensworth, Hertfordshire, 1152:* A hall *(halla)* 35 feet long, 30 feet wide and 22 feet high (11 below the beams *(sub trabibus)* and 11 above); a chamber *(thalamus)* 22 feet long, 16 feet wide and 18 feet high (9 below the beams and 9 above); a house *(domus)* between the hall and the chamber, 12 feet long, 17 [*sic*] feet wide and 17 feet high (10 below the beams and 7 above). [17]
> *Thorp, Essex,* c. *1160:* A hall *(aula);* a chamber *(camera);* a tresance *(tresantia);* two privies; a kitchen. [18]
> *Oxford,* c. *1195:* A great house *(domus magna)* of stone, a cellar with solar above *(cellarium cum solario desuper)* of stone, a tiled privy, a chamber *(thalamus)* of stone, a house *(domus)* of stone and earth. [19]
> *Cuxham, Oxfordshire:* In the later thirteenth century an existing building was known as the 'great chamber' or 'lord's chamber' *(magna camera, camera domini)*. It was stone-built, and reached by wooden steps; a new timber hall was built up against it in 1331-2. [20]

These descriptions suggest four general conclusions. First, there is no indication that any of the halls was a storeyed building. The hall at Kensworth in 1152, 30 feet wide and 11 feet high from floor to tie-beam, was clearly open and almost certainly aisled. Secondly, the chambers at the early to mid-twelfth-century rural manors were also apparently single-storey buildings, and sound like later versions of the tenth- and eleventh-century bowers known from excavation; the Horstead survey actually uses the word *burum*. Thirdly, there were often ancillary buildings called 'houses', 'pentices' and 'tresances'; although *domus* can sometimes mean 'hall' (as at Horstead), the *domus* at Kensworth was evidently a connecting passage of some kind between the hall and the chamber. The impression is one of disparate buildings which might be linked by covered ways. [21] Fourthly, the group at Oxford in the 1190s, which stands for numerous urban descriptions of this sort, had a *solarium* over the cellar, not an *aula;* it looks as though the *domus magna* served as a hall. The Cuxham account (admittedly a century later) describes as a *camera* a free-standing stone building which had an important room on its upper floor.

From these archival sources we may turn to a literary one, Alexander Neckam's treatise *De Utensilibus.* This was written in about the late 1190s—in other words in the supposed *floruit* of the 'first-floor hall'—and refers to an aristocratic milieu: here, if anywhere, we should find a reflection of contemporary habits in domestic planning.[22] The following components of the ideal house are described:[23]

> *Hall (corpus aule, cors le sale):* its features include a lobby (or screens-passage?) *(vestibulum, porch),* a porch *(porticus honeste).* and posts *(postes, posz)* spaced at suitable intervals.
> *Chamber (camera, thalamus, la chaumbre):* contains curtains, drapes, a bed and bed-clothes.
> *Cellar (promptuarium, celarium, celer):* contains barrels, leather wine-bottles, coffers, baskets, beer, wine, etc.
> *Spense (dispensa, dispensatorium):* contains cloths, towels, knives, salt-cellar, cheese-bin, candlesticks, carrying-baskets etc.
> *Kitchen (coquina, quisine):* contains cooking equipment.

While Neckam does not state explicitly that his *camera* is on the first floor, he clearly assumes the existence of an open aisled hall. Thus the hall was certainly not above the *celarium,* which can hardly be other than the sort of cellar normally found at semi-basement level under so-called 'first-floor halls'. *De Utensilibus* reinforces the conclusions, suggested by the other written sources, that the open hall remained ubiquitous throughout this period and that the word. *aula* was not normally applied to an upper room.

Royal and Manorial Houses

Can the norms of domestic planning revealed by these written sources be observed in the standing and excavated remains of aristocratic houses? The answer to this question may be sought by considering sites where the overall layout and inter-relationship of component buildings can be recovered. The best starting point is a group of royal houses which are rooted in traditional English planning (notably the practice of aligning the buildings axially, used centuries earlier in the Northumbrian palace at Yeavering), and all of which include a larger and a smaller domestic component reasonably interpreted as the hall and the chamber.

Biggest by far was the palace of Westminster (fig. 2), dominated by William Rufus's vast hall. Aligned on the south end of this hall was a twelfth-century building containing a large and elaborate chamber over a vaulted undercroft; by the 1260s it was known as the 'little hall', but its twelfth-century designation is unknown.[24] Although this building was substantially larger than the ordinary chamber-blocks of the period, its juxtaposition with Westminster Hall is reminiscent of the juxtapositions of chamber-blocks with open halls at other sites. In its pairing of an open and public with a storeyed and more private building, Westminster displays traditional patterns of domestic planning articulated to the special needs of the main royal palace.

The Anglo-Saxon and Norman palace at Cheddar (Somerset) is probably more typical, and thanks to Philip Rahtz's excavations its successive phases can be traced much more

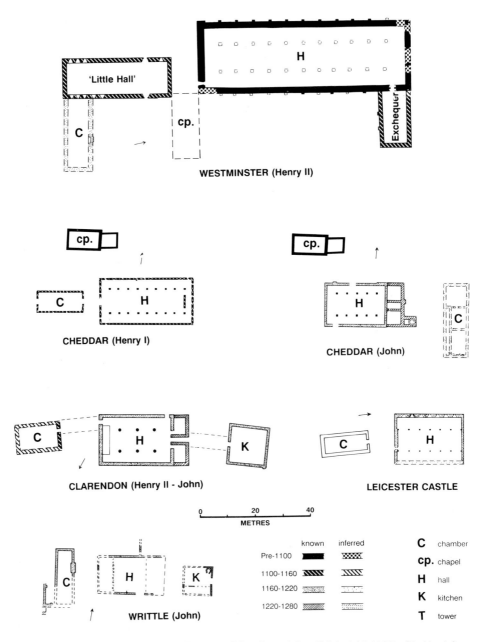

2. *Royal and baronial houses on linear alignments: Westminster (after Colvin (ed.) 1963); Cheddar (after Rahtz 1979); Clarendon (after James and Robinson 1988); Writtle (after Rahtz 1969); Leicester (after Toy 1954, with further information from a survey by Edward Impey, 1992)*

clearly (fig. 2). At the end of the eleventh century, an aisled hall (termed by the excavator 'East Hall I') was built axially to the east of a small late Anglo-Saxon structure ('West Hall III'), rebuilt at the same time. It seems extremely likely that the 'West Hall', from which an end dais was removed at this stage, was adapted to serve as a *camera* or *bur* associated with the new 'East Hall', henceforth the hall proper.[25] In the early thirteenth century the 'East Hall' was itself rebuilt; a long building to its east, divided on the ground floor into four compartments, can be interpreted as a chamber-block replacing the old 'West Hall' which had now disappeared.[26] In any case it is clear that throughout the twelfth and thirteenth centuries, the main domestic building was an open ground-floor hall.

A third and rather later royal house is Henry II's at Clarendon (fig. 2). Although many of the buildings on the site date from Henry III's grandiose enlargements, some idea of the late twelfth-century plan can be recovered. Dominating the site is the aisled hall of the 1180s, with the kitchen to its west. A group of buildings east of the hall can be identified as the royal apartments of Henry III's time, and they include an earlier storeyed rectangular building which is reasonably interpreted as the *camera regis* mentioned in the 1160s.[27] This building was aligned roughly on the axis of the hall.

The alien priory of Grove (Bedfordshire) originated as a royal manor-house given to the order of Fontevrault by Henry II (fig. 1).[28] At the time of this gift, in the 1150s, the main buildings consisted of an unaisled hall (apparently with a partitioned-off bay at its west end), to the east of which, and axially aligned on it, was a stone chamber-block later converted to a chapel. In the late twelfth century, an earlier timber structure north of the west end of the hall was rebuilt as a second chamber-block, evidently with an upper floor supported on a row of posts.

Latest in this sequence of axially-planned royal houses is King John's hunting-lodge at Writtle (Essex) (fig. 2). The excavated early thirteenth-century buildings comprised an open hall (apparently with two internal screens), a detached kitchen to the east, and a long, narrow building (somewhat reminiscent of the early thirteenth-century compartmentalized range at Cheddar) to the west. This last stood where a chapel, a great chamber and two other chambers are recorded in 1419, and it may have been more complex in its internal arrangements than the imperfectly-surviving footings indicate.[29] It is at all events in a directly comparable position to the *camera regis* at Clarendon, at the end of the hall furthest from the kitchen.

Each of these five sites had both a hall and another major domestic building, in axial juxtaposition to each other. Although the identification of the second building as a *camera* is never (except perhaps at Clarendon) conclusive, a correlation with the written references to halls associated with *camerae* is too obvious to be resisted. The *camerae* were storeyed and solidly built at the grander sites (Westminster and Clarendon), but lighter and simpler elsewhere; this again is consistent with the conclusions already drawn from the documents.

Only a few excavations of ordinary secular manor-houses have produced coherent plans of a similar date. The house at Alsted, Merstham (Surrey) (fig. 1) comprised a small early thirteenth-century stone chamber-block alongside the platform of a timber building, and can be interpreted as a simple version of the detached hall and chamber plan.[30] Clearer to read is the moated courtyard house at Penhallam, Jacobstow (Cornwall) (fig. 5). Here the earliest recorded building is a late twelfth-century storeyed block, with a row of post-bases in the undercroft and a plinth for what was presumably a fireplace heating the great chamber above. Enlargements in the 1220s included an open hall at right-angles to this

3. Boothby Pagnell (Lincs.): chamber-block, c. 1200 (from Turner 1851, between pp. 52-3)

earlier block, with an enclosed stair at its 'high' end leading up to the great chamber.[31] This archaeological evidence from an ordinary manorial site tells the same story as the evidence discussed above: the two main components are the chamber-block and the open hall.

These documented and excavated sites provide a context for the beautifully preserved two-storey house at Boothby Pagnell (Lincolnshire), long celebrated as the paradigm of the 'first-floor hall' (fig. 3): they leave little room for doubt that contemporaries would have described such a building as *camera* rather than *aula*. In the light of this new model, several examples can now be recognized in twelfth-century castles, for instance Framlingham (Suffolk) and Great Chesterton (Oxfordshire).[32] The so-called 'solar tower', exemplified in a sequence of buildings between the late eleventh and mid-thirteenth centuries such as Chilham (Kent), Witney (Oxfordshire), Greenhythe (Kent) and Old Soar (Kent),[33] may be defined as a version of the chamber-block which is squatter and often has more than one storey above the basement: in essence it is a chamber-block adapted to the needs of a defensive or semi-defensive site.

Most surviving houses of the Boothby Pagnell type date from *c.* 1170–1220 rather than earlier. As is clear from the texts quoted above, many *camerae* on ordinary twelfth-century manorial sites were simple single-storey buildings. The wide diffusion of the chamber-over-basement type may be a distinctively late twelfth-century phenomenon, an elaboration of the traditional timber bower influenced by strong-houses and keeps of earlier decades and a higher social level. In Alexander Neckam's up-to-date house of the 1190s, the chamber and cellar would surely have been contained within a building such as this.

Both more adaptable and more durable, stone *camerae* have survived better than the timber open halls which would once have stood near them, and which by definition would have lacked substantial chambers attached to either end. Small manorial halls of this type from

4. *Barnack (Northants): two-bay aisled hall,* c. *1200 (now demolished; from Turner 1851, between pp. 52-3)*

the early to mid-thirteenth centuries are, however, being recognized in increasing numbers, as at Barnack (Northamptonshire) (fig. 4), Sandal Castle (Yorkshire), Fyfield (Essex), Temple Balsall (Warwickshire), Harwell (Berkshire) and Chalton (Hampshire).[34] The obvious reason why these, like much grander halls, seem to have such scanty private accommodation is that they were accompanied by free-standing chamber-blocks which have disappeared.

Sadly, no ordinary English manor-house with substantial and unambiguous remains of both components has yet been discovered. At Leicester Castle (fig. 2), however, a cellar axially aligned on the aisled hall has walls which are clearly older than the late medieval vaulting and may well survive from a twelfth-century chamber undercroft. Much clearer are two of the French cases discussed by Impey (below): Beaumont-le-Richard, where the hall and chamber-block are loosely aligned as at Westminster, Cheddar and Clarendon, and the rather later and more developed Bricquebec (fig. 5) where they meet corner-to-corner as at Jacobstow. As well as hinting that high-status domestic planning in England and northern France may have developed along much closer lines than is usually supposed, these buildings reveal with particular clarity the problems inherent in the traditional model. If the storeyed ranges at Beaumont and Bricquebec had stood in England, and had happened to survive in isolation, English architectural historians would unhesitatingly have classified them as 'first-floor halls'.

BISHOPS' PALACES AND THE COURTYARD PLAN

The royal and manorial houses derive the main features of their planning from traditional insular practice, albeit translated into grander and more modern forms. But the palaces of twelfth-century bishops form a distinct group: they are distinguished by a predilection for courtyard rather than axial layouts, they are more tightly integrated, and they are more exotic in some of their details.[35] Several have two main components, one open and the other raised over a basement, which are usually described as 'double halls'. But in fact the model of hall and chamber is as applicable to these palaces as it is to aristocratic houses of other kinds.

The two fortified houses built by Roger, bishop of Salisbury (1107–39), at Sherborne (fig. 5) and at Old Sarum Castle, are unique in their regularity and their integration.[36] The main ranges are set around square courtyards with covered walks like cloisters, and

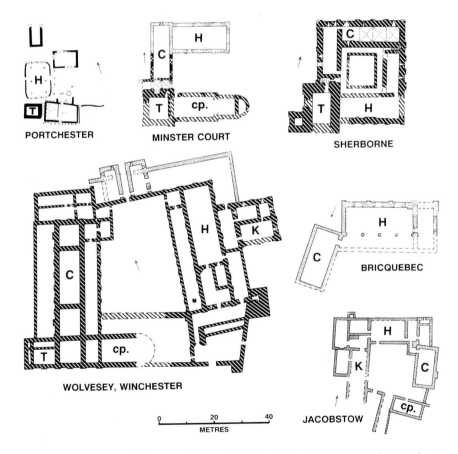

5. *The early development of the courtyard house: Portchester (after Cunliffe 1976); Minster Court (after Kipps 1929, with amendments by E. Impey); Sherborne (after White 1983); Wolvesey (after Biddle 1972); Bricquebec (after present vol. Impey, figs 13-18); Jacobstow (after Beresford 1974) (for key to conventions see fig. 2)*

in each case there is a corner tower. Halls probably occupied the south range at Sherborne and the west range at Old Sarum; the facing ranges, in other words the north at Sherborne and the east at Old Sarum, contained large upper rooms which are surely to be interpreted as the great chambers. The only essential difference between Roger's castles and a house such as Briquebec is that they are more integrated, the hall and chamber being linked by lesser ranges to form a completely enclosed courtyard.

The same applies to Wolvesey Palace at Winchester (fig. 5), the vast fortified house of the bishops of Winchester built during the first half of the twelfth century.[37] Wolvesey is less regular than Roger's houses, but much larger. There is a gatehouse in the north range, and a chapel in the south. The other ranges contain the two main elements: on the east the open hall and its annexes, including a kitchen designed in imitation of a stone keep, and on the west a long room raised over a solid basement with smaller flanking rooms and a corridor. Although usually called the 'west hall' this range is better interpreted as the main chamber-block.

Two smaller early twelfth-century houses of the bishops of Winchester echo features of Wolvesey. Bishop's Waltham (Hampshire) has a south-west corner tower from which a long storeyed range extends northwards; there are fragmentary remains of the south and east ranges, the latter including a chapel.[38] At Witney (Oxfordshire) the tower-lodging is at the south-east corner, but the east range again contains the chapel; there are fragments of the north range, including a gatehouse and lodgings, and later documentary evidence for a hall in the west range.[39]

These palaces of c. 1100–40 are a highly distinctive group, drawing on traditions of ecclesiastical as well as of domestic planning. Besides the obvious resemblance of Roger's houses to monastic cloisters, the corner towers (which at least at Sherborne and Witney functioned as lodgings) recall the massive west towers characteristic of major episcopal churches, derived ultimately from the Ottonian *Westwerk*.[40] It is instructive to compare Sherborne and Old Sarum with the monastic grange of c. 1100 at Minster Court, Thanet (fig. 5), where a hall, a lodging range and a church with a great west tower form three sides of a courtyard.[41] This arrangement is strikingly foreshadowed by a small early eleventh-century complex excavated at Portchester Castle (fig. 5), where a timber aisled hall and two domestic ranges formed three sides of a courtyard which had a stone tower at its south-west corner.[42] In the mid-eleventh century, a rich priest of Abingdon built himself a house said in the Abingdon Chronicle to resemble a monastic cloister, comprising a church with two ranges at right-angles containing the hall, kitchen and lodgings.[43] The true context of episcopal courtyard houses may be a lost group of eleventh-century establishments on the borderline between secular and monastic, perhaps including the dwellings of unreformed minster clergy and cathedral canons.[44]

From the 1170s onwards, episcopal palaces planned on a simpler and more open version of the courtyard layout appear in increasing numbers (fig. 6). The format of a large hall, a chamber-block either at right-angles or parallel, and a range closing one of the two remaining sides of the courtyard, occurs at Old Sarum (the house adjoining the cathedral, not to be confused with the castle), at Hereford, at Lincoln and at Canterbury, the chamber ranges at Canterbury and Old Sarum being reused early Norman buildings.[45] Several decades into the thirteenth century, the palace at Wells perpetuates this arrangement in its sumptuous storeyed chamber-block, linked by a chapel to the aisled hall.[46] It was doubtless in emulation of these palaces that early thirteenth-century manorial gentry started to build modest courtyard

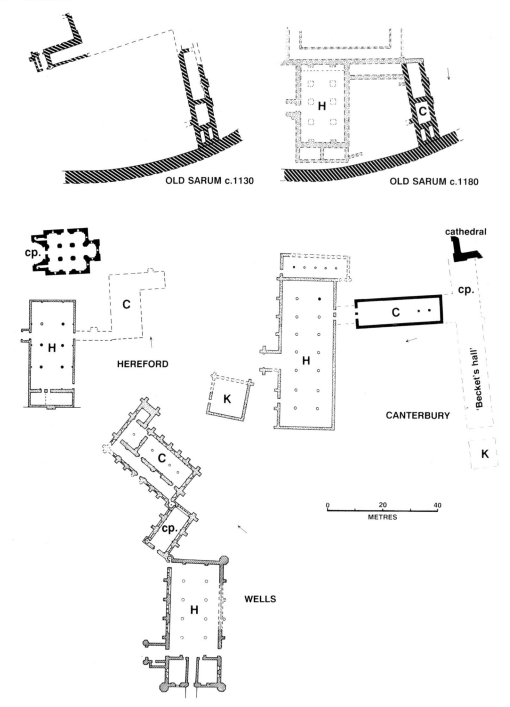

6. *Bishops' palaces, mid-twelfth to mid-thirteenth centuries: Old Sarum (after Hawley 1914-15 and Hawley 1915-16, with new phasing); Hereford (after Blair 1987); Canterbury (after Rady, Tatton-Brown and Bowen 1991); Wells (after Wood 1965) (for key to conventions see fig. 2)*

houses such as Jacobstow, which were in turn to influence manor-house planning in the late Middle Ages.

The Development of Halls and Services in the Later Twelfth Century

In England the grand secular aisled hall is a feature of the later twelfth century, influenced by the architecture of great churches and, perhaps more immediately, by monastic infirmaries such as those at Canterbury and Ely. Pre-1150 aisled halls so far known in England (such as Goltho, Portchester and Cheddar 'East Hall I') are of a supra-vernacular character, modest in conception and simple in construction. A supposed early twelfth-century example on a grander scale, the hall of the house beside Old Sarum cathedral, has clearly been misdated: it overlies the east range of a courtyard apparently laid out c. 1100, and should be ascribed to a reconstruction in c. 1160-80 which retained the existing west range as its chamber-block (fig. 6).[47] Even the most elaborate early twelfth-century complexes, such as Sherborne and Wolvesey, had halls which were unaisled and relatively narrow, with tall side walls. This form, also exemplified on a very grand scale by the 'Echiquier' at Caen (Impey, below) is an Anglo-Norman aristocratic fashion which may reflect the influence of monastic refectories.

The first evidence that architecturally ambitious halls were becoming at all common dates from the third quarter of the twelfth century, with the fragmentary timber arcades at Leicester (fig. 2) and Farnham castles.[48] In the Midlands and the South, the fashion was developed in halls of the 1170s and 1180s such as Hereford bishop's palace (in timber imitating stone) (fig. 6), Clarendon palace (fig. 2) and Oakham Castle.[49] In northern England, the tradition of grand aisled halls with stone arcades has been traced through Archbishop Roger's hall of c. 1170 at York[50] to Hugh du Puiset's halls at Durham and Bishop Auckland, and to their ecclesiastical analogue, his Galilee at Durham Cathedral.[51] The proliferation of sumptuous halls, like that of storeyed stone chamber-blocks, is less an early Norman phenomenon than a reflection of the growing personal wealth of Angevin England.

A feature of the grandest later twelfth-century halls was the development of cellarage at the 'lower' end with subsidiary chambers above. Chronologically isolated, and startlingly precocious, is Wolvesey Palace at Winchester, where the early twelfth-century 'east hall' included a three-storey chamber-block at its south end (fig. 5). Hereford (c. 1180) had a tall, narrow range of three storeys over a basement, in series with the hall, while a basement of similar proportions has been excavated at the end of the huge early thirteenth-century archiepiscopal hall at Canterbury (fig. 6).[52] Although these halls lacked the service doorways and screens-passage which were soon to become ubiquitous, they clearly foreshadow the developed service end.

The distinctive elements of fully-fledged services are (i) a buttery and pantry entered through separate doorways in the end wall of the hall; (ii) a main hall entrance at the lower end of one of the side walls, at right-angles to these doorways; and (iii) a facing entrance in the opposite wall, allowing the formation of a screens-passage. There is thus a critical difference between houses of c. 1160–80 where the entrance or porch is in the centre of the side wall (notably Old Sarum and Hereford, fig. 6),[53] and houses of c. 1190 onwards where it is usually placed at the lower end. This change is the clearest signal of the advent of the screens-passage, the first well-attested case of which is in the 1190s at Bishop Auckland Castle.[54] Neckam's prescription of a *vestibulum* adjoining the hall porch (above, p. 5) may well refer to this newest of innovations. Permutations occur, however, over several decades. As already noted, the early thirteenth-century archbishop's hall at Canterbury had a single undercroft rather than service-rooms, and accordingly still had a centrally-placed porch (fig. 6). The juxtaposition of service-doors and main entrance can also occur where there is no opposed entrance, as at Oakham in the 1180s,[55] or a century later at Stokesay (Shropshire) where the moat precludes a through-passage.

Continuing the precedent of Wolvesey and Hereford, large houses of *c.* 1190–1230 normally had a subsidiary chamber above the services, reached from the hall by a timber stair such as still survives (albeit a century later) at Stokesay. Bricquebec (Impey, below), where the chamber over the services was entered from the hall by a grand high-level doorway, is again an important parallel, suggesting that the arrangement was well known in Anglo-Norman aristocratic society by the end of the twelfth century. At Oakham, the lower end wall of the hall retains service doorways in conjunction with a first-floor doorway approached from the north aisle. In the small manor-house at Appleton (Berkshire) the service doors (one slightly larger than the other) are flanked, on the side furthest from the main entrance, by a full-height quoined opening which probably contained a straight stair from the hall to the chamber above.[56] At Warnford (Hampshire), slightly later than Appleton but more complete, one entrance to the cross-passage survives and the other appears on a plan of 1779. Two service doorways lead to basements of unequal size; above these was a single chamber, entered from the hall through a high-level doorway.[57]

A further sophistication, the separation of the two service rooms by a passage allowing direct access from the hall to the kitchen, occurs at Clarendon, Old Sarum and Cheddar East Hall II (figs. 2 and 6), but in all three cases the service-blocks are additions of unknown, probably thirteenth-century date.[58] This plan may be used *c.* 1180 at Farnham Castle (Surrey) and at Oakham, though in neither case is the function of the three doorways entirely clear;[59] it survives intact in the thirteenth-century episcopal halls at Lincoln and Wells (fig. 6), and is documented in royal works at Guildford in 1244.[60]

THE INTEGRATION OF HALLS AND CHAMBER-BLOCKS

It is a curious fact that although the aristocratic houses discussed above were made up of free-standing components, integrated all-timber houses are known from an early date. The late tenth-century house at Sulgrave (Northamptonshire) consisted of a long range with complex internal divisions, including a pair of opposed doorways associated with a screen.[61] The twelfth-century houses at Ellington (Huntingdonshire) and Brooklands (Surrey) each had a pair of rooms separated by a cross-passage and with a screened-off compartment in the larger room.[62] It might be argued that these are more akin to the long-house than to the late medieval hall-house. But in 1183 the tenants of Bishop Auckland (Co. Durham) were obliged to build a hunting-lodge which sounds like a fully-integrated house of a century later: *faciunt aulam episcopi in foresta, longitudinis lx pedum et latitudinis infra postes xvj pedum, cum butilleria et dispensa, et cameram et privatam; preterea faciunt capellam longitudinis xl pedum et latitudinis xv pedum.*[63] It appears that in the twelfth century, as much later, the grandest houses were often the least compact. Aspects of the planning conventions adopted from the 1180s onwards may thus have drawn on an established vernacular tradition.

In great houses the integration of the main chamber-block with the upper end of the hall lagged somewhat behind the development of services at its lower end, as is clear from the plans of palaces in figure 6. In lesser houses too, the separation of *aula* and *camera* remained common well after 1200. The thirteenth-century manor-house at Harwell had a detached chamber-block, as well as a compartment at the end of the hall called the 'wardrobe' or *extrema camera*.[64] As late as *c.* 1300 the house built at Eltham (Kent) by Bishop Bek had a cellared chamber-block separated by a four-metre gap from the high end of the hall, while the hall at Nurstead (Kent) was linked to a slightly older chamber-block corner-to-corner.[65] But starting probably in about the 1220s or 1230s, and increasingly common thereafter, are surviving or excavated houses in which the main chamber-block is attached directly to the upper end of the hall. This development, not surprisingly, is often seen in the upgrading of old houses: replacement halls were built up against the sides of existing chamber-blocks, and chamber-blocks were added to existing halls. On three quasi-monastic sites, the alien priory of Cogges (Oxfordshire) and the Templars' *camerae* at Strood (Kent) and Harefield (Middlesex), halls were built against older chamber-blocks at dates between the mid-thirteenth and early fourteenth centuries, a sequence which is also recorded in the manorial accounts for Cuxham (Oxfordshire).[66] A more integrated example (though even here the two elements may not be exactly coeval) is the manor-house at Burmington (Warwickshire), where the two-bay (or three-bay) aisled hall and the storeyed solar wing are both of the early thirteenth century.[67] At Woodstock palace in the 1230s the 'king's high chamber' was at one end of the hall, and was entered by a flight of stone steps from the courtyard.[68] After 1300, the addition of spacious chamber-blocks to existing halls became ubiquitous practice.[69]

Terminology in the first half of the thirteenth century was fluid, as it so often is at times of rapid change. Some descriptions are ambiguous to the extent that they list 'chambers' at both ends of the hall. Thus a farm at Thorpe or Egham (Surrey) in 1241 included *aula et duobus talamis eidem aule adiunctis,* while a monastic grange at Addington (Surrey) in the late thirteenth century comprised a hall with a *maior solarium* and a *minor solarium.*[70] Perhaps because the *camera* basement had always been a service room, the services in some of these earlier small integrated houses were not at the 'lower' end of the hall but under the main chamber, which increasingly is called the *solarium.* The early thirteenth-century chamber-blocks at Little Chesterford (Essex) and Hambledon (Hampshire) have service-doors in their side walls at basement level, presumably once communicating with attached halls.[71] The manor-house at Sandon (Hertfordshire) described in a text of *c.* 1258, apparently built within the previous twenty years, consisted of a hall with a wardrobe *(warderoba)* at one head and a 'spense' with a solar *(spenseriam cum solario),* at the other; the 'spense' was presumably a service-room under the solar.[72]

But the pattern was about to crystallize. In 1268 the monks of Eynsham made a contract for a house to be built at Histon (Cambridgeshire). It was to contain a hall with a 'spense' *(dispensa)* at one end and a suitable chamber with a privy *(unam cameram competentem cum necessariis camere)* at the other, all of which were to be under one roof *(erunt sub eodem tecto).*[73] This defines, in essence, the classic three-part house of later medieval England: at the upper end of the hall the great chamber, perhaps over a parlour, and at the lower end the services, either with or without a lesser chamber above them. For the next three centuries, English houses at all levels but the lowest were to approximate to this type.

ACKNOWLEDGEMENTS

For their comments on an earlier draft the author is extremely grateful to Sarah Blair, Edward Impey, Gwyn Meirion-Jones, Derek Renn and John Steane.

ABSTRACT

HALL AND CHAMBER: ENGLISH DOMESTIC PLANNING 1000–1250

The storeyed ranges of *c.* 1150–1220 which English historians have termed 'first-floor halls' are in fact chamber-blocks, originally accompanied by free-standing open halls. Descriptions of English houses written between *c.* 900 and *c.* 1200 generally assume the existence of both components (termed *aula* and *camera* in Latin, *heall* and *bur* in Old English). In a series of aristocratic houses, some standing and others known from excavation, it can be proved that both an open hall and a chamber-block existed on one site. Royal and manorial houses often have buildings arranged on linear axes, whereas bishops' palaces (influenced by monastic planning) are generally laid out around courtyards. Architecturally ambitious aisled halls only became common in England after *c.* 1150. The typical late medieval arrangement at the lower end of the hall, with a cross-passage, two service rooms and secondary chambers above, developed during *c.* 1180–95. From the early thirteenth century it was increasingly common for the main chamber-block to be attached to the upper end of the hall, producing the standard late medieval English house.

RÉSUMÉ

LE HALL ET LA CHAMBRE: LES PLANS DES RÉSIDENCES SEIGNEURIALES
EN ANGLETERRE, 1000–1250

Les bâtiments pourvus d'un étage construits dans les années 1150–1220, que les historiens anglais ont qualifiés de *first-floor halls,* sont en fait des *chamber-blocks* (c'est-à-dire qu'ils abritent les chambres de la famille seigneuriale), accompagnés à l'origine par un édifice distinct, le *hall,* grande salle basse, en général de plain-pied et à charpente apparente. Des descriptions de résidences anglaises, rédigées entre environ 900 et 1200, révèlent l'existence de deux éléments, désignés par les termes de *aula* et de *camera* en latin, de *heall* et de *bur* en vieil anglais. A travers un certain nombre de résidences encore en élévation, ou connues par des fouilles, on peut prouver que ces deux édifices ont coexisté sur un même site.

Les demeures royales et seigneuriales présentent souvent des bâtiments organisés selon un axe unique, tandis que les palais épiscopaux, influencés par le modèle monastique, sont généralement disposés autour d'une cour. Quel que soit leur statut, les *halls* à bas-côtés, qui font partie des formes architecturales les plus ambitieuses, se répandirent en Angleterre seulement après 1150. Le plan caractéristique du bas Moyen Age pour le *lower end* (c'est-à-dire l'extrémité du *hall* proche des pièces de service), qui comprend un passage à travers tout le bâtiment ainsi que deux pièces de service et, au-dessus, des chambres d'importance moindre, est né pendant les années 1180–95.

A partir du début du XIIIᵉ siècle, il devint de plus en plus courant que le *chamber-block* soit attaché à l'autre extrémité du *hall,* produisant ainsi l'archétype de la demeure du bas Moyen Age en Angleterre.

NOTES

1. Faulkner 1958, 151, 163-4. Cf. Wood 1965, 16-34, for a detailed discussion of surviving examples which assumes the 'first-floor hall' hypothesis.

2. Thus the excavators of Wharram Percy are now careful to describe their two-storey stone house as a *camera* rather than a first-floor hall: J. C. Thorn in Hurst (ed.) 1979, chapter V. Cf. the uneasy comment by Beresford 1974, 105: 'It is at times difficult to distinguish the archaeological remains of a camera from those of a first-floor hall'.

3. Coad and Streeten 1982; Rigold 1971.

4. This building is shown on the famous 'waterworks' plan of the 1150s, where it is unambiguously captioned *aula nova*. One top-rank late thirteenth-century English house which seems closer to contemporary French planning is Acton Burnell Castle, where the hall with its chambers and services is raised over a ground floor containing offices and a 'lower hall': West 1981, 85-92. This should be contrasted with the grand fourteenth- and fifteenth-century houses in which the hall has a low undercroft, such as St David's, Kenilworth and South Wingfield, for these merely exhibit a new elaboration of the ground-floor hall.

5. A clear but very special case is Chester, where the height of the 'rows' above street-level produced almost inevitably a standard house-plan including a raised hall: Brown, Howes and Turner 1986. I am grateful to Mr Turner for clarifying some points.

6. T. A. Carnicelli (ed.), *King Alfred's Version of St. Augustine's Soliloquies* (Cambridge, Mass., 1969), 77.

7. *Asser's Life of Alfred,* ed. W. H. Stevenson (Oxford, 1904), chs. 91, 88; Keynes 1992, 73.

8. Beresford 1987, 52-4.

9. *Ibid.* 74-81.

10. *The Anglo-Saxon Chronicle,* trans. G. N. Garmonsway (London, 1953), 123.

11. Colvin (ed.) 1963, I, 45.

12. *Pipe Roll 13 Henry II,* 1.

13. Adam of Eynsham, *Magna Vita Sancti Hugonis,* v. 17 (ed. D. L. Douie and H. Farmer, 2 vols., 1961-2, II, 202).

14. The following summaries list only the domestic buildings mentioned, not the agricultural ones.

15. *Charters and Custumals of the Abbey of Holy Trinity Caen,* ed. M. Chibnall (London, 1982), 36.

16. *The Domesday of St. Paul's,* ed. W. H. Hale (Camden Soc., old ser., 69, 1858), 136.

17. *Ibid.* 129.

18. *Ibid.* 132.

19. *The Cartulary of Oseney Abbey,* ed. H. E. Salter, II (Oxford Hist. Soc., 90, 1929), 283. I owe this reference to David Sturdy.

20. Harvey 1965, 32-4.

21. Several thirteenth-century references to 'pentices', making it clear that they were external corridors, are given by Turner 1851, 181-201.

22. Wright 1857, 96-119.

23. Words in brackets are Neckam's Latin and the near-contemporary French glosses.

24. For the thirteenth-century references see Colvin (ed.) 1963, I, 491-3; Lethaby 1906, 142; Binski 1986, 15, 22, 35. There is no clear evidence that the 'little hall' was the *nova aula* mentioned in 1167 (see note 12), though this building is otherwise unknown. I am grateful to Paul Binski for discussing this problem with me.

25. Rahtz 1979, 60-2. The present interpretation of the functions of these buildings differs from the one published, but Philip Rahtz informs me (pers. comm.) that he does not consider it incompatible with the excavated evidence.

26. Rahtz 1979, 62-4; again this is my interpretation, not the excavator's. The position of the 'South-east Building' near the service end of the hall is at first sight an obstacle to regarding it as a chamber-block; this may not, however, have applied in the early thirteenth century, since the service rooms were almost certainly added later. The limits of the excavation leave open the possibility that other, more peripheral chamber-blocks existed.

27. James and Robinson 1988, 4-7, 64 fig. 10, 99-103.

28. The complex sequence of excavated buildings is currently being assessed by Mrs Evelyn Baker, to whom I am extremely grateful for permission to cite her latest thoughts and to use the plan reproduced in figure 1. This interpretation is radically different from the summaries hitherto published.

29. Rahtz 1969 (where the western building is interpreted as a chapel). I am grateful to Howard Colvin for the following description of the buildings in a survey of 1419 (Essex Record Office D/DP.M.546): 'una magna aula, et ad finem occidentalem eiusdem aule una capella bassa, et ad finem occidentalem eiusdem capelle una magna camera cum duabus aliis cameris

eidem camere annexis, et ad finem orientalem eiusdem magne aule, supra panetriam et buteleriam, una camera qua dividitur in duas cameras'.

30 Ketteringham 1976, 8.

31 Beresford 1974, 90-127. Unfortunately nothing survived of the other late twelfth-century buildings which must have accompanied the chamber-block in its first phase.

32 Raby and Reynolds 1989; Blair 1984.

33 Clapham 1928; Durham 1984; Gravett and Renn 1981; Wood 1950, 36-8.

34 Turner 1851, 52-3; Michelmore 1983, 73-5 (end aisles partitioned off leaving a small service bay at one end and a still smaller space at the other); Smith 1955, figs. 1-2; Alcock 1982; Fletcher 1979 (though this house is now known to have been misidentified); Cunliffe 1969.

35 For another recent survey of this group see James 1990, 42-7.

36 RCHM 1952, 64-6 and plan; RCHM 1980, 6-11 and plan; Stalley 1971, 65-70; White 1983. Both Stalley and White interpret the grand upper room in the north range as Sherborne as a chapel, but on no more substantial evidence than that it is elaborately decorated. At Old Sarum castle, the change in levels by the height of a full storey renders ambiguous the relationship between the ranges, and it is unclear whether the main chamber was in the east range, over cellarage, or in the north range which stands on solid ground.

37 Biddle 1972, 125-31.

38 Publication of the late S. E. Rigold's excavations at Bishop's Waltham is in progress. I am grateful to Jane Geddes and John Hare for advice, though my interpretation does not necessarily agree with theirs.

39 Durham 1984.

40 For a recent survey of some English examples, with references, see Blair 1989, 68-70.

41 Kipps 1929.

42 Cunliffe 1976. There is no documentary evidence that the site was ecclesiastical, but the small cemetery established in the eleventh century on the site of the hall provides a strong suggestion that it was.

43 Chronicon Monasterii de Abingdon, 2 vols., ed. J. Stevenson, (Rolls Ser., Chronicles and Memorials, 2, London 1858), I, 474: 'ecclesiam . . . fabricavit, cuius in lateribus dextrorsum et sinistrorsum claustralibus ad monachorum formam habitaculorum, cum domibus edendi, victusque coquendi, quiescendique, et ceteris conversationi virorum necessariis mirifice

coaptatis'.

44 The first phase of the house by Old Sarum cathedral (fig. 6) is worth considering in the light of the last suggestion: was it originally built for the canons?

45 Note 47 below for Old Sarum; Blair 1987, 67-9; Chapman, Coppack and Drewett 1975; Rady, Tatton-Brown and Bowen 1991. The chamber-block at Canterbury was a building of Lanfranc's time, connected to the north-west corner tower of the cathedral. At Lincoln the chamber-block is known as the 'east hall', a name resulting from the same wrong premise as that of the 'west hall' at Wolvesey.

46 Wood 1965, 23-4. Once again, the storeyed range is usually conceived as an earlier hall, but is clearly a direct descendant of the main chamber-blocks in twelfth-century palaces.

47 Interim reports are Hawley 1913-14, Hawley 1914-15 and Hawley 1915-16; Hawley's phasing is substantially followed by RCHM 1980, 15-22. The latrine-block at the north end of the west range is contemporary with, or earlier than, the early twelfth-century curtain wall. However, Hawley's 1915 season revealed a substantial building, at right-angles to the west range but on a different alignment from the hall, which partly underlay the cloister. Hawley's diaries (now in Salisbury Museum) make it clear that his excavations were innocent of stratigraphy, and there seem to be no grounds for preferring his interpretation to the one proposed here in figure 4.

48 Alcock 1987. His dating of the Leicester arcades is perhaps too early, and the Farnham arcades are associated with high-quality masonry of c. 1180.

49 Blair 1987, 63; James and Robinson 1988, 5-7, 90-6; Turner 1851, 28-31, Wood 1974, 47-9, and James 1990, 60-3.

50 Gerald of Wales, De Vita Galfridi Archiepiscopi Eboracensis, in Giraldi Cambrensis Opera, 8 vols., ed. D. S. Brewer (Rolls Ser., Chronicles and Memorials, 21, London 1873), IV, 367n: et columnis sublimibus erectam, pariisque structuris et marmore distinctam.

51 Halsey 1980, 67. Cf. James 1990, 52.

52 Biddle 1972, 127-8; Blair 1987, 63-7; Rady, Tatton-Brown and Bowen 1991.

53 cf. Blair 1987, 65-7. Both halls had service doorways, but they were later at Old Sarum (note 58 below) and of unknown date at Hereford.

54 Cunningham 1990, 87-8.

55 VCH Rutland, 2 (1935), 8-10 (showing the

original position of the entrance, moved since 1730), and references in note 49.

[56] Wood 1974, 21-2 and Pl. IA; the quoined opening (identified in a new survey by J. Blair, C. Currie and E. Impey, *Oxoniensia*, 57 (1992), 100-2) is not shown on Wood's plan but can be seen indistinctly in the plate. It is unknown whether this house had a cross-passage, since the hall entrance now faces a later oriel window. A pair of service doorways very similar to those at Appleton has recently been identified by J. Blair at Maunds Farmhouse, Deddington (Oxfordshire).

[57] Wood 1950, 27-9.

[58] James and Robinson 1988, 90-4 and fig. 23 (showing the services at Clarendon butt-jointed to the late twelfth-century hall), 236; Hawley 1914-15, 234 and plan facing p. 232; Rahtz 1979, 178-86.

[59] *VCH Surrey*, 2 (1905), 600 and facing plan; Nairn and Pevsner 1971, 233. See note 55 above for Oakham, where the three doorways are not, however, arranged symmetrically.

[60] Colvin (ed.) 1963, II, 950.

[61] Davison 1977, 109-11.

[62] Tebbutt *et al.* 1971, 31-73; Rigold 1977, 55-8. Rigold perceptively notes: 'Perhaps it is better to adduce the three requirements in the 12th century leases of St. Paul's . . ., *camera* or *thalamus*, *aula* and *domus* . . ., and to find themprecociously forced into a single building

but thought of as separate.'

[63] *Boldon Buke*, ed. W. Greenwell (Surtees Soc., 25, 1852), 26.

[64] Fletcher 1979, 176, 187-9.

[65] Woods 1982, 218-27; Cherry 1989, 458-60.

[66] Blair and Steane 1982, 69-84; Rigold 1965. For Cuxham see above, p. 4.

[67] Cooper 1985, 27-30; Brodie 1990, 92. The likelihood of a third hall bay was suggested by a small excavation in 1993.

[68] Colvin (ed.) 1963, II, 1011. The arrangement must have been very similar to Stokesay.

[69] Examples are Faccombe, Hampshire (Fairbrother 1975), Bisham, Berkshire (Fletcher and Hewett 1969), Chalgrove, Oxfordshire (excavation by the Oxford Archaeological Unit, report in progress) and Harwell, Berkshire (Fletcher 1979, 176-9).

[70] PRO, CP25(i)/226/11(247); Blair 1978. The stated dimensions of the *solarii* at Addington suggest that they were cross-wings.

[71] Wood 1950, 19-22, 106. Little Chesterford still has remains of a later thirteenth-century hall in this position.

[72] St Paul's Cathedral inventory: Guildhall Library MS 25,324. The house had apparently not existed, at least in this form, at the time of the previous lease in 1239: MS 25,122/1220.

[73] *The Cartulary of the Abbey of Eynsham*, 2 vols., ed. H. E. Salter (Oxford Hist. Soc., 49, 51, 1906-7, 1908), I, 260.

BIBLIOGRAPHY

ALCOCK, N. W. 1982. 'The hall of the Knights Templars at Temple Balsall, W. Midlands', *Medieval Archaeol.*, 25, 155-8

——, 1987. 'Leicester Castle: the great hall', *Medieval Archaeol.*, 31, 73-9

BERESFORD, G. 1974. 'The medieval manor of Penhallam, Jacobstow, Cornwall', *Medieval Archaeol.*, 18, 90-145

——, 1987. *Goltho: the Development of an Early Medieval Manor c. 850-1150*, HBMC(E) Archaeol. Rep., 4, London

BIDDLE, M. 1972. 'Excavations at Winchester, 1970: ninth interim report', *Antiq. J.*, 52, 93-131

BINSKI, P. 1986. *The Painted Chamber at Westminster*, Soc. Antiq. London Occ. Pap., new ser., 9, London

BLAIR, W. J. 1978. 'A late thirteenth-century survey of buildings on estates of Southwark Priory',

Antiq. J., 58, 353-4

——, 1984. 'Great Chesterton, Manor House', *Medieval Archaeol.*, 28, 235-6

——, 1987. 'The twelfth-century bishop's palace at Hereford', *Medieval Archaeol.*, 31, 59-72

——, 1989. 'The early church at Cumnor', *Oxoniensia*, 54, 57-70

BLAIR, W. J. and STEANE, J. M. 1982. 'Investigations at Cogges, Oxfordshire, 1978-81', *Oxoniensia*, 47, 37-125

BRODIE, A. M. 1990. 'The sculpture of Burmington Manor, Warwickshire', in *Medieval Architecture and its Intellectual Context: Studies in Honour of Peter Kidson* (eds. E. Fernie and P. Crossley), 91-101, London

BROWN, A.N., HOWES, B., and TURNER, R.C. 1986. 'A medieval stone townhouse in Chester', *J. Chester Archaeol. Soc.*, 68, 143-53

CHAPMAN, H., COPPACK, G. and DREWETT, P. 1975. *Excavations at the Bishop's Palace, Lincoln, 1968-72*, Occ. Pap. Lincolnshire Hist. Archaeol., 1, Lincoln

CHERRY, M. 1989. 'Nurstead Court, Kent: a reappraisal', *Archaeol. J.*, 146, 451-64

CLAPHAM, A. W. 1928. 'An early hall at Chilham Castle, Kent', *Antiq. J.*, 8, 350-3.

COAD, J.G. and STREETEN, A.D.F. 1982. 'Excavations at Castle Acre Castle, Norfolk, 1972-77: country house and castle of the Norman earls of Surrey', *Archaeol. J.*, 139, 138-301

COLVIN, H.M. (ed.), 1963. *The History of the King's Works: I: The Middle Ages*, HMSO, London

COOPER, N. 1985. 'Burmington Manor, Warwickshire: the thirteenth-century building', *RCHM (England) Annual Review 1985*, London

CUNLIFFE, B.W. 1969. 'Hampshire: Chalton', *Medieval Archaeol.*, 13, 269-71.

——, 1976. *Excavations at Portchester Castle. II: Saxon*, Soc. Antiq. London Res. Rep., 33, London

CUNNINGHAM, J. 1990. 'Auckland Castle: some recent discoveries', in *Medieval Architecture and its Intellectual Context: Studies in Honour of Peter Kidson* (eds. E. Fernie and P. Crossley), 81-90, London

DAVISON, B.K. 1977. 'Excavations at Sulgrave, Northamptonshire, 1960-76', *Archaeol. J.*, 134, 105-14

DURHAM, B.G. 1984. *Witney Palace: Excavations at Mount House, Witney, in 1984*, Oxford Archaeological Unit, Oxford

FAIRBROTHER, J.A. 1975. 'Hampshire: Faccombe, Netherton', *Medieval Archaeol.*, 19, 250-1

FAULKNER, P.A. 1958. 'Domestic planning from the twelfth to the fourteenth centuries', *Archaeol. J.*, 105, 150-83

FLETCHER, J.M. 1979. 'The bishop of Winchester's medieval manor-house at Harwell, Berkshire', *Archaeol. J.*, 136, 173-92

FLETCHER, J.M. and HEWETT, C.A. 1969. 'Medieval timberwork at Bisham Abbey', *Medieval Archaeol.*, 13, 220-4

GRAVETT, K.W.E. and RENN, D.F. 1981. 'The tower of Stone Castle, Greenhythe', *Archaeol. Cantiana*, 97, 312-15

HALSEY, R. 1980. 'The Galilee chapel', in *Medieval Art and Architecture at Durham Cathedral*, Brit. Archaeol. Assoc. Conference Trans., 3 (for 1977), 59-73

HAWLEY, W. 1913-14; 1914-15; 1915-16. Interim reports on the excavations at Old Sarum Cathedral, *Proc. Soc. Antiq. London*, 26, 100-19; 27, 230-9; 28, 174-84

HARVEY, P.D.A. 1965. *A Medieval Oxfordshire Village*, Oxford

HURST, J.G. (ed.) 1979. *Wharram: a Study of Settlement on the Yorkshire Wolds*, Soc. Medieval Archaeol. Monograph Ser., 8, London

JAMES, T.B. 1990. *The Palaces of Medieval England*, London

JAMES, T.B. and ROBINSON, A.M. 1988. *Clarendon Palace. The History and Archaeology of a Medieval Palace and Hunting-Lodge near Salisbury, Wiltshire*, Soc. Antiq. London Res. Rep., 45, London

KETTERINGHAM, L.L. 1976. *Alsted: Excavation of a Thirteenth-Fourteenth-Century Sub-Manor House*, Surrey Archaeol. Soc. Research Vol., 2, Guildford

KEYNES, S. 1992. 'The Fonthill Letter', in *Words, Texts and Manuscripts: Studies in Anglo-Saxon Culture Presented to Helmut Gneuss* (ed. M. Korhammer), 53-97, Cambridge

KIPPS, P.K. 1929. 'Minster Court, Thanet', *Archaeol. J.*, 86, 213-23

LETHABY, W. R. 1906. 'The palace of Westminster in the eleventh and twelfth centuries', *Archaeologia*, 60, 131-48

MICHELMORE, D.J.H. 1983. 'Interpretation of the buildings of the timber phase', in *Sandal Castle Excavations 1964-1973* (eds. P. Mayes and L.A.S. Butler), Wakefield Historical Publications, 73-5, Wakefield

RCHM 1952. *An Inventory of the Historical Monuments in Dorset*, 1, London

RCHM 1980. *Ancient and Historical Monuments in the City of Salisbury*, 1, London

RABY, F.J.E., and REYNOLDS, P.K.B. 1989. *Framlingham Castle*, revised reprint, English Heritage, London

RADY, J., TATTON-BROWN, T., and BOWEN, J.A. 1991. 'The Archbishop's Palace, Canterbury', *J. Brit. Archaeol. Assoc.*, 144, 1-60

RAHTZ, P.A. 1969. *Excavations at King John's Hunting Lodge, Writtle, Essex*, Soc. Medieval Archaeol. Monograph Ser., 3, London

——, 1979. *The Saxon and Medieval Palaces at Cheddar*, Brit. Archaeol. Rep. Brit. Ser., 65, Oxford

RIGOLD, S. E. 1965. 'Two camerae of the military orders', *Archaeol. J.*, 122, 86-132

——, 1971. 'Eynsford Castle and its excavation', *Archaeologia Cantiana*, 86, 109-71

——, 1977. 'Discussion of the medieval buildings', in *Brooklands, Weybridge: the Excavation of an Iron Age and Medieval Site 1964-5 and 1970-71* (R. Hanworth and D. J. Tomalin), Surrey Archaeol. Soc. Research Vol., 4, Guildford

SMITH, J. T. 1955. 'Medieval aisled halls and their derivatives', *Archaeol. J.* 112, 76-94

STALLEY, R.A. 1971. 'A twelfth-century patron of architecture: a study of the buildings erected by Roger bishop of Salisbury', *J. Brit. Archaeol. Assoc.*, 3rd ser., 34, 62-83

TEBBUTT, C.F. et al. 1971. 'Excavation of a moated site at Ellington, Huntingdonshire', *Proc. Cambridge Antiq. Soc.*, 63, 31-73

TOY, S. 1954. *The Castles of Great Britain*, 2nd edn., London

TURNER, T.H. 1851. *Some Account of Domestic Architecture in England from the Conquest to the End of the Thirteenth Century*, Oxford

WEST, J. 1981. 'Acton Burnell Castle, Shropshire', in *Collectanea Historica: Essays in Memory of Stuart Rigold* (ed. A. Detsicas), Kent Archaeol. Soc., 85-92, Maidstone

WHITE, P. 1983. 'Sherborne Old Castle', *Archaeol. J.*, 140, 67-70

WOOD, M. 1950. *Thirteenth-Century Domestic Architecture in England: Archaeol. J.*, 105, supplement, London

——, 1965. *The English Mediaeval House*, London

——, 1974. *Norman Domestic Architecture*, Royal Archaeol. Inst., London

WOODS, H. 1982. 'Excavations at Eltham Palace, 1975-9', *Trans. London Middlesex Archaeol. Soc.*, 32, 215-65

WRIGHT, T. 1857, *A Volume of Vocabularies*, Liverpool

Mota, Aula et Turris:
The Manor-Houses of the
Anglo-Scottish Border

Philip Dixon

The Anglo-Scottish Border is an area famous for its castles, an area in which private fortifications abound, and in which, it has been said, 'nearly all men of any wealth at all occupied bastle-houses', that is to say, fortified farmhouses.[1] The common picture of the society and its architecture is one in which the rough and conservative North preserved Norman or even earlier habits to the end of the Middle Ages. The types of buildings, too, are seen as backward-looking: the towers of the fourteenth century and later which are so distinctive a feature of the area were based on Norman keeps: 'By this time [1386] the days of castle building in England were virtually over . . . by this time the castle has yielded pride of place to the mansion house. But in the North of England, along the Scottish border where warlike conditions persisted, the old Norman tradition of a square keep or tower-house was never forgotten'.[2] Even Allen Brown followed this line: 'Northern fortification in the later Middle Ages shows a remarkable conservatism. Etal . . . is essentially a lesser keep-and-bailey castle after the twelfth-century manner . . . and Edlingham in Northumberland . . . consists merely of a simple, walled enclosure with a square keep at one end and perhaps a gatehouse at the other'.[3] This echoes a view long held by students of the architecture of the Middle Ages, summed up by Hamilton Thompson: 'The pele-tower may be regarded as a direct survival of the rectangular keep in a simplified form'.[4] In this military society, therefore, there is for the student little prospect of tracing the progressive changes to be found in southern England. '[Yanworth Hall, Westmorland] shows little development from the Norman keeps of a date two hundred years earlier. This fact alone indicates the still disturbed state of the Border country, which stifled progress towards that comfort in house design which the more settled South was already beginning to enjoy; peace and security have ever been necessary to house development.'[5]

These views are fundamentally misguided. It is true that there are many castles, towers and lesser fortified buildings on the Borders, and true, too, that these range in date from the eleventh to the seventeenth century. But a close examination shows that the building of them falls into distinct phases, and that, particularly in the thirteenth century, the seigneurial buildings of the Borders differed little from those outside the region: the history of manorial building in the region is a story of the recurrent ebb and flow of styles. It is the purpose of this paper to present a summary of the current results of a long-term survey of the medieval secular and military architecture of the Borders, and to draw out some conclusions about the social and economic context in which these structures were built.

Periods of construction

1. From about 1080 to about 1130 was a phase of earthwork castles, of both motte-and-bailey and ringwork type; in addition to earthwork castles whose buildings, now gone, were of timber, surviving structures in the region include castles with stone curtain towers on earthen banks, and stone halls and chambers within ringworks. After the first quarter of the twelfth century stone donjons were built on some of these sites, and the construction of great towers continued into the thirteenth century.

2. From about 1220 until the early fourteenth century almost all the new building on manorial sites took the form of stone halls inside courtyards most of which can have been scarcely stronger than the moated sites of contemporary Midland and Eastern England.

3. During the second and third quarters of the fourteenth century we see the construction of new houses with solar towers of great strength, and curtain walls creating small but very defensible castles. These led, by the later fourteenth century, to the building of freestanding tower-houses.

4. The tempo of building slackened during the fifteenth century. From about 1500 until the early seventeenth century there was a second phase of the building of towers, which were distinguished from the earlier examples by their smaller size, and by the lower status of most of their builders.

5. These towers overlapped in date, from about 1550 to about 1620, with a remarkable group of very small, and often roughly built, fortified houses whose owners were normally customary tenants. During this period unfortified manor-houses similar in their design to those built outside the Border region were introduced into the area.

THE FIRST PHASE: THE EARLY CASTLES

In strong contrast to the density of early castles in Midland England or the Welsh Borders, the Anglo-Scottish frontier was, it seems, poorly protected. Considering the size of the region, remarkably few castles can be identified. Bamburgh, the seat of the Anglian kings and earls, was fortified as early as the sixth century, and may have had continuously maintained defences thereafter.[6] The bishop's castle at Durham belongs to the first years of the Conquest, and contains masonry of the 1070s in its chapel. The king's castle of Newcastle upon Tyne was begun as a ringwork with at least one tower of stone after 1080.[7] During the reign of William Rufus another castle was begun at Carlisle on the western border, and at least by 1095 further castles stood at Tynemouth and perhaps at Morpeth, where the earthworks of the existing castle may be the *munitiuncula* referred to by Symeon of Durham.[8]

The archives of the North during these years are comparatively sparse, and some of the undated motte-and-bailey castles of the uplands may belong to this period. The creation

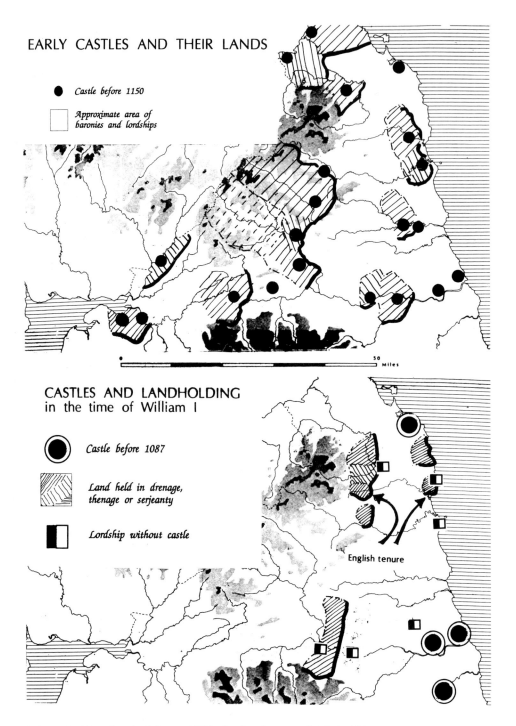

1 (upper). *Map of castles before c. 1150, showing the extent of their lordships*
   (lower). *Map of eleventh-century castles, English tenure, and lordships without castles*

of few indeed of the baronies and lordships of the area, however, can with confidence be placed before the very end of the eleventh century, or even later,[9] and it seems likely that the castles which formed their *capita* belong to the period following the extinction of the earldom in 1095, perhaps after the settlement of 1106, when Henry I established his followers in forfeited estates.[10] The major castles at Prudhoe, Wark on Tyne, Wark on Tweed, Elsdon, Norham and Alnwick all probably belong to the first third of the twelfth century, and so too, perhaps, the less well known mottes at Wooler (Northumberland), Liddel (Cumberland), and the colonizing earthwork castles of Dumfries.[11] This pattern of early baronial castles seems to have become fixed by the 1150s or 1160s. This at any rate is the likely period for the building of the motte-and-bailey castle at Harbottle in Coquetdale, or perhaps just its refortification, since Harbottle received the service of the territorial unit long known as The Ten Towns of Coquetdale, and so is likely to have been the centre of a pre-Conquest estate, and also therefore the location of an early Norman *caput*.[12]

It is significant that even by this stage, nearly a century after the Conquest, there were proportionately fewer castles in the region of the Anglo-Scottish border than, for example along the Welsh border, or even in central England between Oxford and Leicester.[13] The distribution of these castles, too, is interesting. Figure 1 (upper) shows the pattern of known early castles, with an approximation of their territories. Together they occupied a broad belt of uplands, agriculturally somewhat poor, which surrounded the much more fertile manors of the central Northumberland plain, and separated that area from the Scottish border. A similar pattern in the central uplands of Cumbria has been claimed to have been linked to the organization of pre-feudal multiple estates, in which lordships shared in lowlands and highland transhumance areas.[14] The same may be true in these lordships on the Borders, for transhumance farming was the norm in the agricultural strategies of the Border uplands when documents survive, late in the Middle Ages.[15] A second distribution, however, suggests alternative reasons for the pattern. On figure 1 (lower) are shown the very early castles, and two interestingly odd phenomena: in the first place the map shows a pattern of manors and baronies the *capita* of which, to the best of our knowledge, were never fortified, and secondly some lordships whose tenure, by thenage, drenage, and serjeanty, sets them apart from the norms of feudal holding, together with the lands belonging to the ancient centre of Corbridge, some of which were subsequently detached and amalgamated with the feudal baronies of Bolam and Styford. We can see a discrete pattern in which the fortified *capita* surrounded areas containing lands with pre-Conquest tenures and manors that were never castellaries. Their occupiers were perhaps the survivors of the Anglian nobility discussed by Kapelle,[16] some of whom, at any rate, later claimed descent from Earl Gospatric,[17] and whose descendants gradually merged with the lesser Norman landlords, perhaps at a date too late to adopt the fashion of motte-and-bailey castles for their *capita*. It is likely enough that the manorial seats in these unfortified lordships were timber halls, such as the *aula* of the rich man of Tughall, burnt down by heavenly fire in 1069.[18] None is so far known to have survived, or has been excavated, in this area; the existence of stone chamber-blocks, today without any sign of a contemporary attached hall, suggests the former presence of such wooden buildings at a number of sites such as Aydon, Shield Hall, Heaton or Cresswell.[19]

Stone towers were built during the twelfth century at the most important of these early castles. The first were probably those at the two principal seigneurial *foci* of the early Borders, the castles of Carlisle and Bamburgh; both *donjons* share many features in common, and

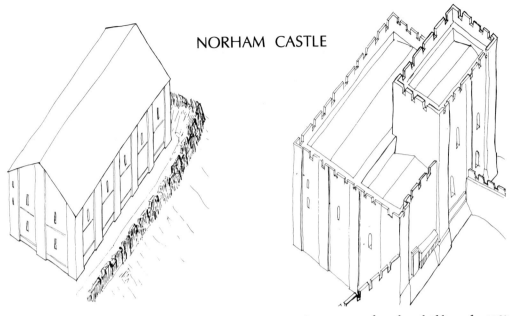

NORHAM CASTLE

First phase of great tower, c.1120

Great tower after the rebuilding of c.1160

2. *The development of the great tower at Norham Castle, Northumberland, from 1120 to* c. *1170*

were perhaps built during the Scottish tenure of the North after the end of Henry I's reign. [20] Subsequent great towers at Newcastle, and then Brough and Brougham extend the date of the building of these structures into the thirteenth century. [21] One of the most striking examples is the great tower of the bishop of Durham's castle at Norham, a massive *donjon* considered to have been constructed as a great tower in the 1150s or 1160s, and then repaired during the fifteenth century. [22] Recent survey of this building, however, suggests a much more complicated development (fig. 2), in which the first phase, probably attributable to Bishop Ranulph Flambard *c.* 1121, was a first-floor hall raised on a vaulted basement, set within a ringwork which had a stone gatehouse, but which might have been simply fenced in timber. A second phase, perhaps the work of Bishop de Puiset in the 1150s, involved the construction of a chamber-block parallel to the hall (making a double-pile building), one end of which rose above a vault to create a small tower. A stone curtain of twelfth-century appearance may belong to this phase. It seems that this remarkable and irregular complex survived in this form through much of the Middle Ages, reaching its present form of a 'typical' rectangular great tower only as a result of massive rebuilding *c.* 1400. [23]

By the middle of the thirteenth century there is some evidence to suggest that these early castles were becoming obsolete. The decline of Wooler, a strategically significant place on the flank of Cheviot, is a particularly striking sign of the general good order of the Borders. In an inquisition held in 1255 it was noted that Isabella de Ford held one third of the capital messuage of Wooler, a derelict motte (*mota vasta*) worth nothing. [24] Similarly the castle which had been head of the barony of Bolam may have begun its decay as soon as the early thirteenth century, when Aline and John de Caux, coparceners of the barony, moved from Bolam to Harnham, setting up a new manor by subdivision, and built a hall at Shortflatt, abandoning the *caput*.[25] The alterations which were made to the motte at Mitford, Northumberland, may provide another example. The twelfth-century shell-keep was partially demolished, and a long rectangular building, with walls less than a metre thick, was built in place of the internal ranges within the shell. This hall-like structure was eventually replaced by the five-sided tower whose basement storey still stands on the motte. It seems likely that this sequence shows a partial demilitarizing of the castle, presumably not earlier than the later twelfth century, succeeded by a refortification.[26] During this period the greater castles, of course, remained occupied as seigneurial seats; it is, however, notable how many of them (for example Alnwick, massively rebuilt after 1310, Mitford, repaired *c.* 1300, or Warkworth, refurbished about 1330) were very substantially rebuilt during the fourteenth century, after the Anglo-Scottish wars began, suggesting that they too had not been kept in adequate repair.

THE SECOND PHASE: THE HALLS

The existence of stone halls in the region has long been known, at least since the first publication of Aydon in 1851.[27] What has emerged only in recent years is the wide range and the surprisingly large number of these buildings in an area generally thought to be dominated by towers. Surveys have now revealed at least twenty-six hall-houses in the Borders. The work continues, and more of these buildings may well await discovery.[28] The range of dates is wide, from the thirteenth to the fifteenth century, and there is more than one type of building represented, but the majority of these structures belong to the thirteenth century.[29]

The simplest of these buildings, and perhaps the earliest, is the hall which formed the first phase at Drumburgh, Cumbria. This was a long rectangular ground-floor hall, entered by a broad round-headed doorway of earlier thirteenth-century appearance. No internal divisions have been preserved, but the position of the door suggests that it gave access to the lower end of a hall at least eleven metres long, with a service room to its west and perhaps a small chamber at its upper end. A ground-floor hall of similar size survives as the core of Featherstone Castle, Northumberland. The entrance door here suggests a date of about 1260. Both ends of this hall have been rebuilt, but it may have contained services and chamber like Drumburgh. Other ground-floor halls, heavily rebuilt, form the earliest parts of the 'towers' at Rudchester (1285), Halton and Corbridge Low Hall (both *c.* 1300), and each may have contained at least services, and perhaps chambers, within a simple long rectangular plan.

Halls in which the principal accommodation lay on the first floor, raised above a basement storey, form a distinct regional type. Dally Castle in North Tyndale, the earliest known of these (apart, that is, from Bishop Flambard's hall at Norham Castle), was under construction in 1237, when Sir David de Lindesey, later Justiciar of Lothian, was said to be building a house with wonderfully thick walls like a tower.[30] Thirty years later, John Comyn the Competitor was granted licence to crenellate the manor-house at Tarset, two miles distant from Lindesey's manor. Both these structures were rectangular, with corner turrets, and the wording of the documents suggests that the first-floor defended hall was hard to classify, and perhaps was something of a novelty, since Dally was a *domum . . . ad modum turris*, and Tarset was called not a hall but a *camera*.[31] A clearer example of a first-floor hall has recently been excavated at Edlingham, where a ditched courtyard, looking like a typical moated site, and perhaps enclosed originally with a palisade, contained a large rectangular building with polygonal corner turrets, whose hall and chambers lay on its first floor, approached by an external stair.[32]

Few of these hall houses are sufficiently well preserved for the original arrangement of their accommodation to be certain. The clearest example is Aydon, of *c.* 1296 (fig. 3).[33] Here the appearance of an 'end-hall', that is to say a hall-and-chamber on two floor levels, is illusory. The recent restoration has shown that the lower hall had no communication with the lower chamber, but gave access solely to service and store rooms at the lower end of the house. The ground-floor chamber was almost certainly reached only from the first-floor solar, to which it provided a secluded and secure inner room, with the most elaborately decorated fireplace in the building. The chamber-block at Aydon was therefore conceived of as a separate three-storeyed tower, probably built against the gable end of an existing timber ground-floor hall, which was soon to be replaced by a new structure, containing an attendants' hall and stores on the ground floor, and a hall and kitchen on the floor above. In its first phase the hall excavated at Edlingham Castle appears to have had a similar arrangement of chambers in a three-storeyed block at the end of a two-storeyed hall;[34] in

3. *Aydon Castle (Northumberland): the first-floor hall and the chamber block from the North*

this case a separate chamber lay at the lower end of the hall, while the kitchen was below, next to the lower hall; kitchen and lower hall had access only from the courtyard, and food must have passed by the external stair to the hall. Unless the lower hall was used for service and storage, these functions must have been relegated to a separate building. During the fourteenth-century rebuilding, this arrangement with an integral, vertically-set suite of chambers was abandoned, and a new strong chamber was added in a massive solar tower (fig. 4). Access to this was contrived through an anteroom at the lower end of the hall. The provision of this new accommodation led to a reworking of the chamber block at the upper end of the hall. Its ground-floor chamber seems now to have been separated from

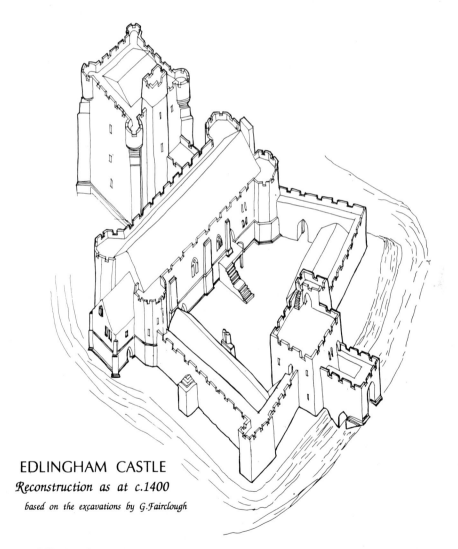

EDLINGHAM CASTLE
Reconstruction as at c.1400
based on the excavations by G.Fairclough

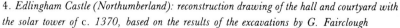

4. *Edlingham Castle (Northumberland): reconstruction drawing of the hall and courtyard with the solar tower of c. 1370, based on the results of the excavations by G. Fairclough*

5. *Edlingham Castle (Northumberland): interior of the solar tower, showing the lower chamber, and the vaulted great chamber with its fireplace. An inner chamber lay on the second floor above the vault*

the upper storeys, and was connected by a new door with what had been an independent single room, to make a two-room set, with its own door to the courtyard. A similar set was also provided in the lowest storey of the new solar tower by the creation of an independent access through the end of the old lower hall. The result was to provide a series of separate apartments: the great hall now gave access to three family (or perhaps guest) rooms at its upper end and to a strong and grandly appointed set in the new tower (fig. 5), important rooms called in 1572 the "Parlar' and 'the Brode chambre'. Separately-entered suites of heated chambers lay on the ground floor of both hall and tower. Their use is uncertain, but it is interesting to note that similar chambers, perhaps intended for occupation by a steward or constable, occur at the nearly contemporary great houses of Markenfield, Yorkshire, and Tulliallan, Fife.[35]

The complexity of the accommodation and the elaboration of the decoration in these halls indicates clearly enough the high status of their builders, a point which is demonstrated by the inventories and inquisitions of the thirteenth and fourteenth centuries. The lords who built and occupied the Border halls belonged at least to the minor nobility of Northumberland and Cumberland. Many, of course, were substantial lords who had lands elsewhere, such as David de Lindesey of Dally Castle, who was Justiciar of Lothian, or John Comyn of Tarset Castle, competitor for the Scottish throne, and brother-in-law to John Balliol. Others held baronies (Langley, Aydon) or substantial manors (Haughton, Edlingham).[36]

The *Inquisitiones post mortem* of the early fourteenth century demonstrate the devastation which followed the uprising against Edward I's nominee in Scotland.[37] Tarset, once worth £246, was in 1314 only worth £5. 7s. 4d., while Aydon was valued at no more than 14s. 7d. in 1322, and in 1326 Chirdon in North Tyndale was worth 'nothing on account of the poverty of the country and want of beasts' and the neighbouring manor of Snabdough 'worth nothing for want of tenants'.[38]

During these years fortifications were added to the hall-houses: the hall at Aydon was rebuilt with battlements and a small courtyard by 1305; by 1315 a larger crenellated wall cut off the manor-house from the level ground to the north. A round tower commanding the approach may have been added after 1346.[39] The hall with solar tower at Haughton in North Tyndale was rebuilt twice during the fourteenth century. In the first stage a barrel vault was inserted over the ground floor, and a second floor, carried on broad arched machicolations, was built above the hall; subsequently these arches were blocked in a thickening of the walls of the first storey (see fig. 6). At Edlingham a new solar tower was built at the side of the hall, perhaps about 1380, and perhaps in the same decade at Halton a small solar tower was built at a little distance from the hall of c. 1300. Few indeed of the old halls remained without fortifications during these years. Unfortified examples may

Haughton Castle

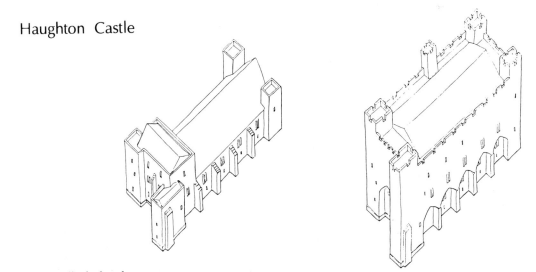

As originally built, about 1270

As reconstructed, about 1370

6. *Haughton Castle (Northumberland): the first two stages in the development of the castle from a first-floor hall and solar tower to a three-storeyed fortified hall block*

7. Old Hollinside (County Durham): a thirteenth-century hall with chambers and services in attached wings, later fortified by the addition of a small tower over the ground-floor entrance

perhaps include the *camera* at Heaton beside Newcastle or the solar-block at Proctor's Stead near Embleton, both some distance from the border line itself. Even in these cases, however, protection of the site by curtain walls and ditches cannot be ruled out: we know that the old hall at Drumburgh was fortified in 1307, but the surviving remains show no traces of defences, which were thus presumably outworks. Far from the Border, at Old Hollinside in County Durham, the entrance to the hall was protected by a raised tower (fig. 7). In an exposed position close to the frontier the manor-house of Burgh, a first-floor hall which about 1260 had replaced an earthwork castle, was abandoned and in ruins by 1362.[40]

THE THIRD PHASE: THE TOWERS

The attached solar towers, or the chamber-blocks with their rooms arranged in a vertical series at the end of a ground-floor or first-floor hall, bridge the gap between the hall-house and the tower-house of the later Middle Ages. During the course of the fourteenth century nearly one hundred of the manor-houses of the Border area were rebuilt as towers. To understand how these buildings fit into the rapidly changing politics of this period, it is clearly important to establish the precise date of these structures, but this has attracted a measure of controversy, with dates proposed in the early fourteenth or even the thirteenth century for such buildings as Corbridge, Chipchase and Belsay in Northumberland, or, among others, Drum and Hallforest in Aberdeenshire.[41] For none of these early dates is there good evidence. A *mansum* at Newlands by Belford was crenellated by licence in 1310; this was called a *turris* in the great list of Northumbrian fortifications of 1415,[42] and may therefore represent an early example of the type, but no trace now remains of the building. One cannot therefore judge either whether the house fortified in 1310 included a tower, or, if it did, whether it was no more than a solar tower such as are known at this date elsewhere in England.[43] The same is true of Eslington, whose fortification was licensed in 1335, which was called a *turris* in 1415, and a *toure with a barmekyn* [courtyard] in 1541.[44] During the period of the worst Scottish attacks between the death of Edward I in 1307 and the recovery after the battle of Halidon Hill (1333) old castles were put into order, but there is little sign of new fortifications in the Borders. An exception, the construction of a large new castle at Dunstanburgh after 1313, was probably due to the ambitions of Thomas, earl of Lancaster, and was not a response to local conditions. It is presumably no coincidence that Earl Thomas' conflict with his cousin Edward II, which saw the king and Gaveston making good use of the coastal castles at Tynemouth and Scarborough during their flight from the North in 1312, was followed within months by the earl's beginning the building of his own coastal castle at Dunstanburgh.[45] The earliest surviving new structures of this period in the region are the great towers at Etal (licensed in 1341) and Crawley (licensed in 1343).[46] Neither was certainly a tower-house: Crawley, which lacks any evidence for an internal hall, was probably a massive solar-tower attached to less well protected buildings, whose foundations can still be traced as mounds inside the large ditched courtyard which surrounds the main building, and the tower at Etal (fig. 8), despite Knowles's description of the site as consisting of a keep and gatehouse,[47] seems to have been an elaborate accommodation block at one end of the principal range of a courtyard castle. It seems, then, that during the first part of this phase some of the new buildings were continuing the pattern of hall and solar-tower which had been established during the thirteenth century.

During these years, however, we can see some transitional types. The castle of Thirlwall near Gilsland, first referred to in 1369, has the rectangular plan with angle towers to be seen in thirteenth-century halls, but its accommodation was arranged vertically like a tower, in three low storeys, without the tall principal room to be found in the earlier buildings. At Blenkinsopp the castle of 1340 seems to have been a thick walled square-set building no more than 16m long, set within a tight rectangular chemise.[48] The structure appears to have been much more like a tower than a hall, but the surveyors of 1415 chose to use the term *castrum,* glossed by the less precise word *fortalicium* for the site, rather than *turris.*[49]

The last of the Northumbrian licences was that of 1378 for Fenwick Tower, but Fenwick was in fact the first licensed fortification in Northumberland for over thirty years. Bates, indeed, suggested that after the Scottish invasion of 1346 it was crown policy to encourage the erection of fortified houses, which therefore needed no special licence.[50] It is not clear whether this or some administrative change was responsible for the hiatus: in Cumberland at any rate licences were being granted as late as 1399, though mostly for buildings far to the south of the Border; here too there is a very noticeable decline in numbers of licences after the early 1350s.

But can it be assumed that all or even most of the fourteenth-century towers which received no licence were therefore built after about 1350? Two considerations make this more plausible:

8. *Etal Castle (Northumberland): tower built at the end of a range of buildings in the 1340s*

the builders of the unlicensed towers were of similar social status to those whose fortifications received licence; there are therefore no grounds for suggesting that the former group of buildings were of small size or were built by men of lesser pretensions, or who hoped by their insignificance to escape notice. Secondly, though charters and similar sources occasionally refer to fortified buildings, none shows that any unlicensed structure predates 1350, and the earliest reference to the existence of a building for which no licence was issued is as late as 1365,[51] nearly twenty years after the end of the main Northumbrian series of licences. The implications of this negative evidence are shown graphically in figure 9, which indicates a rapidly mounting tempo in building during the later fourteenth century. These implications are striking: after the pause during the earlier part of the century, between *c.* 1350 and 1415 some seventy substantial towers were completed in Northumberland, and about half as many in Cumbria, a massive expenditure of resources in a period in which recovery from the crisis of the 1310s and the Black Death was still slow.[52]

Recognizable fragments of half of these fourteenth-century towers still survive. Fifteen are small rectangular buildings, averaging about 10m by 8m in size, best exemplified by

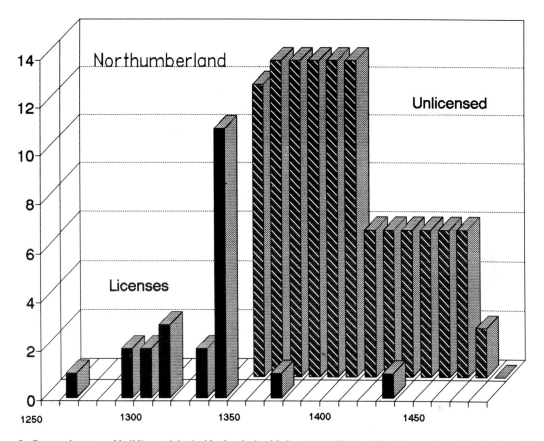

9. *Suggested pattern of building activity in Northumberland before 1415, distinguishing between licensed and unlicensed fortifications*

the vicar's towers at Corbridge (*c.* 1390) and Ford, or the little chamber block at Halton, also of *c.* 1390. Ten large rectangular towers (about 15m by 10m) were built with finer masonry details, corresponding to the greater resources of their builders. In other respects the layout of the large and small towers is similar: where evidence survives the entry was at ground-floor level beside a stair which led to the upper storeys. The ground floor, normally barrel vaulted, shows little sign of use as accommodation, and may have been used for storage. The first floor, normally a little loftier than the others, was presumably the hall: in two fifteenth-century examples (Newark on Yarrow and Comlongon) the entrance stair led to a screens passage and kitchen, partitioned off in timber from the hall itself. The upper storeys contained chambers, in the larger examples sometimes subdivided by partitions, with mural chambers including garderobes at the upper levels. The arrangements are so regular that a unique variant, at Chipchase (*c.* 1400?) is particularly noteworthy: here the kitchen, and the screens passage from the newel stair, is on the top storey, and so the hall seems to have been built above the chambers.

Chipchase, and the similar great tower at Belsay,[53] are members of a small group of towers, including Cessford in Roxburghshire, in which extra accommodation was obtained by the construction of a wing or jamb, projecting from the main body of the building, and containing suites of private chambers. They belong, it seems, to the late fourteenth and fifteenth centuries, a date in keeping with their occurrence elsewhere, for example at Craigmillar near Edinburgh of *c.* 1370. These are the first of the towers that can be considered true tower-houses, self-contained buildings enclosing kitchen, services, hall and sufficient chambers to accommodate a household. The extent to which in fact they were independent houses, however, remains very doubtful, and even Belsay seems to have been built to respect the end of an earlier hall.

The Fifteenth Century

With the exception of the great gatehouse at Bywell, built about 1430, perhaps as a replacement for the old earthwork castle of Styford,[54] and the new great gatehouse at Morpeth Castle, the new fortifications on the English side of the border were all minor works. At Cocklaw (fig. 10), Branxton, Dilston, and at the earlier halls of Low Hall, Corbridge and

10. *Cocklaw Tower (Northumberland): a fifteenth-century tower-house with first-floor hall and mural chambers*

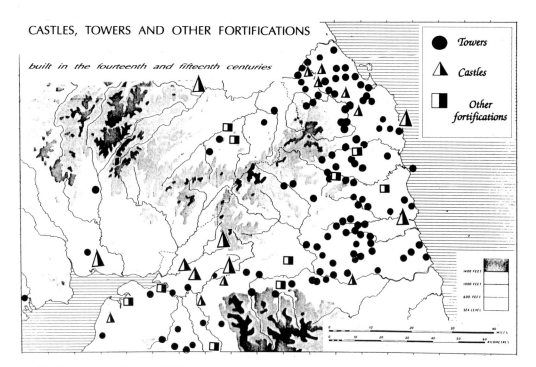

11. *Distribution map of the fortified houses of the Border region belonging to the fourteenth and fifteenth centuries*

Cresswell, towers were built by small landowners; where the builder can be identified, the other towers of this period were built by more significant lords, Percies, Nevilles or Ogles, not as principal houses, but as outliers on scattered portions of their estates, for example at Cockle Park (after 1461), Hefferlaw (after 1470), or Hulne (1488). Because of the lack of good documentation during most of this period, what is known of the buildings comes mostly from surviving structures, and no estimate is possible of how many buildings have vanished without record, but it seems clear that many fewer tower houses were now being built. The distribution pattern (fig. 11) closely resembles that of the preceding century, and the majority of the surviving buildings are of relatively small scale: thus they should be seen as the final stage of the major burst of building during the later fourteenth century.

The major fortifications on the Scottish side of the border date to the period before the outbreak of the wars of Independence. During the period of intensive building in England little may be found across the border, except the tower of Torthowald (?fourteenth century) and the English-built castle at Hermitage of *c.* 1360. Numerous earth and timber 'towers' have been alleged,[55] but none survives, and the evidence is as flimsy as the supposed structures. There could hardly be a greater contrast between these and the sophisticated towers of England. The erection during the fifteenth century of a group of major towers in the Scottish side of the border indicates a change. The Douglases, with their seat at Threave, with its massive tower of *c.* 1390, had before 1388 remodelled the courtyard castle at Hermitage to form a great tower,[56] and by 1423 they had begun a second great tower at Newark-on-Yarrow at the other end of the central uplands. Towers of similar size were founded by the influential Kers at Cessford and by the Murrays at Comlongon, both perhaps during the second quarter of the century. About the same time the powerful family of the lairds Johnstone built at Lochwood the tower which was to remain the principal house of the surname.

By 1485 by far the largest number of fortified houses lay on the coastal plain and in the adjacent uplands of Cumberland and Northumberland. Few indeed lay in the central border uplands. The builders of all were almost entirely landed men of considerable wealth, and most of the towers formed their principal houses, or the *capita* of substantial manors. In Scotland far fewer fortifications are known: in general their distribution was in the valleys below the uplands, and they formed the *capita* of the Norman baronies, or of the feudal magnates whose power increased at the expense of the crown during the later fourteenth century and the fifteenth century.[57] During the sixteenth century the picture changed radically. The majority of the new buildings lay within the central uplands. The interesting characteristic of the fourth and fifth phases of border fortification must therefore be seen as the massive development of stone buildings in this hitherto barren region (fig. 16).

THE FOURTH PHASE: THE LATER TOWERS

The survival of late medieval fortified houses in the border zone is striking. In all, at least some structural traces can be found of about 250 houses which can be dated to the sixteenth century, and the names and descriptions of an even greater number, now demolished, may be found in documentary sources. During this period towers were constructed in every part of the region, from the outskirts of Newcastle to the furthest recesses of the upland dales. A few, such as Hoddam in Dumfriesshire, were massive structures, as large as the great seigneurial tower houses of the late fourteenth century. Most, however, were comparatively small, on average not much more than 15m by 10m in plan, and only three or four storeys high (fig. 12). The number of surviving examples is sufficient to allow us to see distinct regional types. Despite the widespread distribution of these towers, no single architectural style unites the whole of the Borders, but the variations in design and decoration do not conform to the internal political zones of the region, and on occasion can be seen to cut across the Border line itself. To demonstrate the patterns, figure 13 shows a selection of architectural features: the design of gunports and the treatment of the parapets of towers.

Few roofs survive from this period: the eighteen at present identified in the survey fall into three clear groups. To the west, in northern Cumbria, all have heavily jowled king-posts on cambered tie-beams, supporting side purlins. Examples range from the elaborate roof of Askerton Castle, with a dendrochronological date of 1497, to the simple roof of the stonehouse at Cote House, perhaps of the later sixteenth century. In Northumberland, in contrast, king-posts of this date have not been observed, and the surviving roofs are simple principal-rafter trusses (sometimes with curved feet) with a cambered tie and a collar. A roof of this sort at Aydon Castle has a dendrochronological date of 1543, and others belong to the end of the sixteenth and the early seventeenth century. Raised crucks have also been noted in late sixteenth-century stonehouses. In Scotland, however, where surviving roofs are still rarer, all the known roofs of towers belong to the early seventeenth century, and have braced common rafters with collars but without longitudinal stiffening.

The distribution of the types of gunports used in these towers, in contrast, show two separate centres of distribution. The more sophisticated of these, the wide-mouthed oval

12. *Kirkandrews Tower (Cumberland): small tower-house of the later sixteenth century, built by one of the unruly members of the Graham surname*

version, is concentrated in the Tweed valley. In Dumfriesshire, on the other hand, examples of this style are confined to the major work at Caerlaverock Castle, to building of the same period nearby at Bankend Tower, to the elaborate work at Amisfield of 1600, and to a lone example in the north, that of Lochhouse Tower, near Moffat. The shot-holes of the other West Marches towers are either the starker wide-mouthed rectangular type, or one of the more elaborate keyhole or dumb-bell patterns. This rectangular variety, however, is comparatively rare in the Tweed region. Both types allow a similar field of fire, and have no apparent functional difference, nor are there distinctions in date or in social status between the buildings concerned. The difference between the two schools emphasizes local variations in building practice which cut across the Border line into England, where the western designs are similar to those of Dumfriesshire, while those few in Northumberland are similar to those of the Tweed. A similar pattern is shown by the distribution of styles of wall-head (fig. 13, lower), for the richly decorated blind machicolations of the Scottish West March spread into northern Cumberland, but not elsewhere in the Borders, and the rounds at the wall-head (and the rare turrets in the re-entrant angle) of Northumberland are matched most frequently in the Tweed valley. This cross-Border linking of schools of masons towards the end of the sixteenth century has been identified in the case of the Buckholm school of Roxburghshire, with its links in north Northumberland. [58]

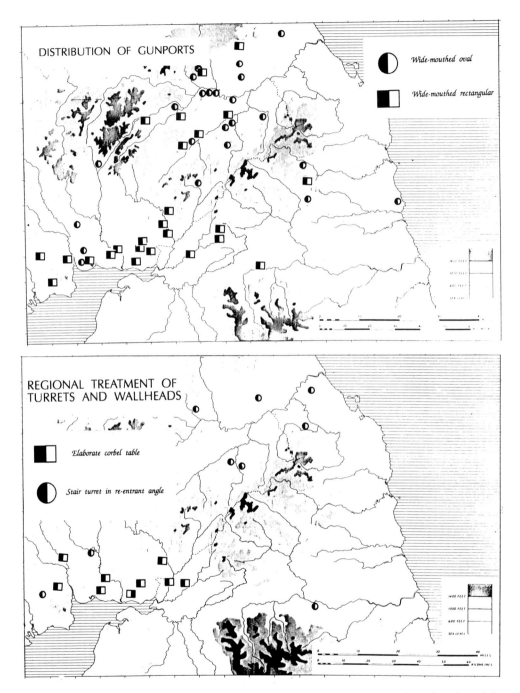

13 (upper). *Distribution map of gunports, distinguishing between the rectangular and the oval versions of the wide-mouthed type*
(lower). *Variations in the treatment of the wall-heads of towers, showing a division between styles of the West March and those of the Middle March*

The dating of the towers within the sixteenth century requires further discussion. In a synthesis of the Scottish tower-houses the period from about 1480 to 1560 has been described as 'the long pause' during which 'few tower houses of any consequence were built'.[59] An analysis of the architectural details of the border tower-houses suggests that the normal use of these features belongs to the second half of the sixteenth century:[60] wide-mouthed oval gunloops were apparently introduced by Italian engineers at Dunbar about 1520,[61] and are first found in the Borders between 1530 and 1540, and became common after 1560; four-centred doorhead and machicolated corbel-tables may be found in the fifteenth century, but occurred only rarely before c. 1570; edge rolls and pilaster mouldings are datable to the second half of the century, and trace their origin to the major works at Stirling (1538 x 1541). This tends to confirm the 'long pause' in the Scottish Borders. In England at least the pause is less obvious: in the area covered by the 1541 survey four towers had been built during the previous generation, and two more, and a number of 'bastells' were still under construction.[62] This seems to be a continuation, on a smaller scale, of the fifteenth-century pattern. Furthermore, the use of datestones, which underlies Cruden's chronology, is hazardous, since almost all bear dates of the second half of the sixteenth century or later; indeed, more than half belong to the period from 1590 to 1618. This is a common phenomenon: few of the hundreds of datestones collected by MacGibbon and Ross are earlier than 1560.[63]

THE FIFTH PHASE: THE STONE HOUSES, BASTLES AND PELEHOUSES

All the structures discussed so far have been at least of manorial status. During the sixteenth century, however, we find for the first time the survival of fortified buildings built by less important people. There is a greater variety of forms during this period, and a much wider range of contemporary records about the construction and their appearance: in consequence the written sources become of even greater significance in forming a picture of the fortified houses of the Border. This leads to problems, since the structures were described by contemporaries under a variety of names: tower, pele or peel, bastle-house, stronghouse, stonehouse, and pelehouse.[64] These are terms which are not used consistently.[65] During the sixteenth century a stone tower could be called a pele: Helefyld Peel in Yorkshire, for example, had a gate and garrets,[66] and the phrase 'castle or pele' or 'tower or pele' is not uncommon.[67] This rather loose usage is found in the borders in the brief survey of 1561,[68] but at the beginning of the century in this region, a pele was still regarded as an earth and timber fortification, as it had been during the thirteenth-century conquests of Edward I. In this way, in the Debateable Land of the West March in 1528, a 'strong pele of Ill Will Armistraunges' was 'buylded after siche maner that it couth not be brynt ne distroyed unto it was cut down with axes'.[69] The headsmen of North Tyndale in 1541 had similar buildings, described as 'very stronge houses whereof for the most parte the utter sydes or walles be made of greatt sware [square] oke trees stongly bounde & Joyned together with great tenons of the same so thyck mortressed that yt wylbe very harde withoute greatt force & laboure to breake or caste down any of the said houses the tymber as well of the said walles as rooffes be so great & covered most parte with turves & earthe that they wyll not easyly burne or be sett on fyere'[70]

None of these structures is now preserved, but they were familiar in Scotland even towards the end of the sixteenth century, when Bishop Leslie described the houses of the chieftains [*potentiores*] as pyramidal towers built of earth alone, which they call 'pailes'.[71] In England at this period slightly different terms were used: we find 'stone house', 'a lytle stone house or pyle', 'bastell house', 'stone houses or bastells', 'a stronge pele house of stone', or 'a lylte pele house or bastell'.[72]

The buildings themselves display wide a variation between elegant tall towers, six or seven storeys in height (fig. 14), and squat, rough, gabled buildings little different from the unfortified single-storeyed houses of the region. Though no classification of these structures can be clear cut, three types stand out: the tower, discussed in the previous section; the bastle, a large and normally well-built stone house; and the pele-house, a similar but smaller structure (fig. 15). It is the last which is now customarily designated 'bastle'.

These three types of fortified house show significant variations in the periods during which they were built, and interestingly separate distribution patterns. Towers are found throughout the period, perhaps more frequently after the middle of the century. Their distribution (fig. 16) shows a marked concentration in the upland valleys, in particular of western and central Scotland, in Dumfriesshire and Roxburghshire, and the density within the thin-soil uplands of Liddesdale and Eskdale is very striking. In England they are rare in the East March,

14. *Ferniehurst Castle (Roxburghshire): chamber-block and side of the hall of a very large late sixteenth-century L-shaped tower*

15. *Low Cleughs Field (Northumberland): pele-house built c. 1600 by customary tenants of the Crown lands*

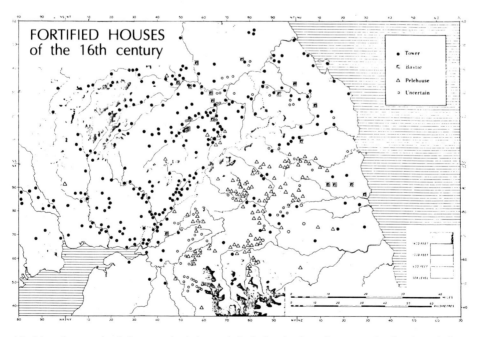

16. *Map of towers, bastle-houses and pele-houses built during the sixteenth century, showing the variations in the patterns of distribution of each type*

and are found in only limited numbers in the Middle March, except for those in the upland dales of Tyne, Rede and the headwaters of the Aln and Coquet. The distribution of bastle-houses, on the other hand, avoids these upland areas. Most common in the more fertile middle Tweed valley, they extend into the lowlands of Northumberland, ringing the Border uplands. Documentary sources name over seventy buildings which no longer survive, which may have been what we would recognize as bastle-houses. Their distribution suggests an extension of the pattern across the somewhat higher land between the lowland plain and the Border dales, and in Gilsland, in northern Cumberland. The distribution of pele-houses is in stark contrast to that of the other types. These rougher buildings have a dense distribution pattern[73] in Gilsland, Bewcastledale and the Northumbrian uplands.

LORDS AND REIVERS

In consequence of this sudden upsurge in building, fortified houses were built and owned by men of a social level far below that normally associated with private castellation. The occupants have been described as men 'not noticeably wealthier than their neighbours', and their society 'while far from being an egalitarian democracy, was extremely homogeneous', while 'all but the poorest families built for themselves a small fortified tower house'.[74] The situation, however, was somewhat different. The owners of tower-houses were likely to be cadets of the greater lords, or lairds and headsmen of their surnames, and to be worth at least £150 sterling at their deaths. Even the small and poorly-built pele-houses were occupied by relatively wealthy men—some of whom were as rich as the tower owners, though their formal status in society might seem lower, since most were customary tenants and not the freeholders or feu-holders of lordships. In short, the sixteenth-century tower-houses of England were built for members of the minor gentry, including the most substantial of the hereditary heads of surnames of the upland Borders. In Scotland the members of this social class were nationally even more significant, since a Border laird might be (like Scott of Branxholm) a Privy Counsellor. Within the Border dales on the English side, however, such chieftains as the Charlton of Hesleyside or the Heron of Chipchase (both families commonly including royal officials, and the occupants of towers) were uncharacteristic. In these dales the bulk of the society was organized in surnames under headsmen of considerably lesser standing, who lived in pele-houses.[75]

This remarkable Border society of thieves and riders has received considerable attention, chiefly by description of its final stages.[76] Its origins are less well known. There seem few grounds for claiming any great antiquity for the customs and social structure: indeed, during the thirteenth and the fourteenth centuries on both sides of the Border we can see a well developed feudal society, with a hierarchy of local lords, the greatest the occupants of castles, and the lesser lords inhabitants of halls and towers. During the fifteenth century and the early sixteenth century, however, national politics led to the removal or muzzling of the feudal principals, the Percies, the Douglases and the Dacres, and the imposition by the Crown of direct, inadequate, rule. While the minor gentry of the lowlands remained aloof, the vacuum in the Border uplands was filled by clan and kinship leaders, the Crown tenants who were headsmen of the Border surnames.

ABSTRACT

MOTA, AULA ET TURRIS: THE MANOR-HOUSES OF THE ANGLO-SCOTTISH BORDER

This paper surveys the seigneurial buildings of the Anglo-Scottish Border, and places the fortified buildings constructed between the eleventh century and the seventeenth century in their social and economic context. It shows that the development of these houses was a complex pattern in which the builders responded to changing needs of politics and lordship, which ended in a breakdown of the local feudal society in the late Middle Ages.

RÉSUMÉ

MOTA, AULA ET TURRIS: LES RÉSIDENCES SEIGNEURIALES DE LA FRONTIÈRE ANGLO-ÉCOSSAISE

Cet article passe en revue les constructions seigneuriales de la frontière anglo-écossaise et replace les sites fortifiés édifiés entre le XIe et le XVIIe siècle dans leur contexte social et économique. Le développement de ces résidences correspond à un schéma complexe, dans lequel les constructeurs ont répondu aux besoins changeants de la situation politique et de la seigneurie, processus qui localement s'acheva avec l'effondrement de la société féodale à la fin du Moyen Age.

NOTES

[1] Ramm *et al.* 1970, 65.

[2] Simpson 1940, 76.

[3] Brown 1953, 91.

[4] Thompson 1912, 316.

[5] Lloyd 1931, 186.

[6] Hope-Taylor 1977, 292 and note 339.

[7] Knowles 1926; Harbottle 1982, esp. fig. 1.

[8] Symeon of Durham, *Opera Omnia,* 2 vols., ed. T. Arnold (Rolls Ser., Chronicles and Memorials, 75, London 1882-5), II, 225; Bates 1891, 3, n. 11.

[9] Hedley 1968, 18-19.

[10] Kapelle 1979, 191-206.

[11] For a brief discussion see Simpson and Webster 1985.

[12] Bates 1891, 5; *NCH,* 15 (1940), 480: both of whom take a late date as likely; so, too, Blair 1944, 133-7.

[13] Renn 1968, map A; Cathcart-King and Alcock 1966.

[14] Winchester 1987, 3.

[15] For discussion of this see Dixon 1976, esp. 95-100.

[16] Kapelle 1979, 201-2.

[17] Hedley 1968, I. 12-14, 244-66.

[18] *Reginald of Durham,* ed. J. Raine (Surtees Soc., 1, 1835), chapter xvi, 30-1.

[19] For an excavated example elsewhere see Dixon *et al.* 1989, esp. 410-12; and for further discussion Dixon 1992.

[20] Colvin *et al.* 1963, 595-6, favour construction by David I; on the other hand McCarthy *et al.* 1990, 119-20, believe that Henry I was responsible: the argument turns in part on the use of the word *castellum,* and it should be noted that this is frequently used to refer to a town: see Coulson 1982.

[21] Simpson 1949a; Charlton 1979.

[22] For a sensible general discussion see Blair 1944, 137-41.

[23] Dixon and Marshall forthcoming.

[24] Inq. P. M. 39 Hen. III, no 40, printed in Bain, 1881-8, I, 374-5, cf. also *Cal. Inq. P. M.,* I, no. 341.

[25] Dixon 1988, 5; Dixon and Borne 1978, 234-9, esp. 235.

[26] The analysis is based on excavation, but these works (of the 1930s) were very unsatisfactory, and their publication includes no detailed plans or sections (Honeyman 1955).

27 Parker and Turner 1851, I, 148-9.

28 For the distribution of these buildings see Dixon 1988, 6. Surveys have been carried out by Philip Dixon, in association with Janet Sisson, Patricia Borne, and Leslie Milner. Parallel work by Peter Ryder has revealed early halls at Corbridge (Low Hall) and Blenkinsopp.

29 For a general account of the work on these buildings up to 1991 see Dixon 1992.

30 Bates 1891, 55-6, locates the house at Dally. Honeyman in *NCH*, 15 (1940), 274, is more cautious about this, since Lindesey was baron of Chirdon (about one mile to the north-east of the site), but he correctly confirms the ruin at Dally as of the earlier thirteenth century on the evidence of its architectural fragments, and is probably over-critical of the identification.

31 *NCH*, 15 (1940), 243-7. The term suggests that the foundations at Tarset (excavated in the 1880s) were the remains of a stone chamber block, and that the hall, and other buildings, lie undiscovered elsewhere in the moated site. The site at Dally, however, is too confined to allow room for other buildings.

32 For an interim account of the excavations see Fairclough 1982: the date of the hall itself is particularly uncertain, but it may be of the late thirteenth century.

33 For discussion of the internal arrangements see Dixon and Borne 1978, esp. 236.

34 The discussion is based on the planning diagrams in Fairclough 1982, 387.

35 Miller 1985, esp. 104 ('Undercroft C'); RCAHM Scotland, 1933, 275-9: I owe this reference to Mr John Dunbar. In its first phase Edlingham had a single independent chamber of this type at ground-floor level.

36 For a fuller discussion of the society and of the collapse in the early fourteenth century see Dixon 1992.

37 See in general Musgrove 1990, chapter 6; discussions of the collapse in Tuck 1971, and a modified view, emphasizing the resilience of the area, in Tuck 1985, esp. 36-42.

38 *NCH*, 15 (1940), 244-5; PRO, London, Chancery IPM, 25 Edward I (C133), file 81; 15 Edward II (C134), file 90 no. 2 (= *Cal. Inq. P. M.,* VI, no. 597); 19 Edward II (C134), file 96 no. 14 (= *Cal. Inq. P. M.,* VI, no. 693).

39 See Dixon 1988, 32.

40 Hogg 1954, 129.

41 Brown 1976, 131; Cruden 1963, 109-11; Wood 1965, 168, 175; Simpson 1938-9, I, xxix-xl; Simpson 1940, esp. 79-80.

42 Bates 1891, 8, 19.

43 For example at Stokesay, Shropshire (1305), or Longthorpe near Peterborough of *c.* 1300.

44 Bates 1891, 17, 43.

45 Simpson 1949b, 1-25, esp. 7-13, argues that the castle was built for reasons of patriotism and public spirit; Blair 1949, 25-8, disagrees on the grounds of Earl Thomas' character, surely rightly; see in general Maddicott 1970, and, for the immediately preceding events, Dixon 1990, esp. 126-8.

46 The great tower of Widdrington was licensed in 1341, and appears from the Buck engraving to have been an L-shaped tower house, but no trace of this building now remains.

47 *NCH*, 11 (1922), 467-9, followed by Brown 1976, 91.

48 The best interpretation of this much rebuilt (and now demolished) building is given in an unpublished survey report by Ryder (1986).

49 Bates 1891, 15. This is identical to their treatment of the moated site of Horton-iuxta-mare, but such arguments from medieval terminology are extremely tentative: see Coulson 1982.

50 Bates 1891, 11. For a more modern view of the significance of licences to crenellate, see Coulson 1993.

51 Bates 1891, 11, quoting *Cal. Inq. P. M.,* II. 270: this document refers, however, to the existence of a castle at Langley, which was a hall-house now refortified. The structure would require a licence less obviously than would a completely new building. For the date of the rebuilding of Langley (on architectural grounds *c.* 1340 x 1360) see Dixon 1976, 32.

52 For discussion of this see Dixon 1992.

53 Built *c.* 1370: here the kitchen is in the basement, apparently as an afterthought. See Middleton 1910, 15; Simpson 1940, esp. 81.

54 This is a motte-and-bailey castle in a wood at NGR NZ 027623, which seems to have escaped recognition. Styford was part of the barony of Bolbec, and Bywell a moiety of the barony of Balliol, but both baronies were held, from the late fourteenth century, by the Neville earls of Westmorland: *NCH*, 6 (1902), 75, 228.

55 For example by Simpson 1940.

56 RCAHM Scotland 1956, 83.

57 For discussion of this see Smout 1969, 37-8.

58 For discussion of this see Dixon 1975.

59 Cruden 1963, 144, 150-76.

60 For more detailed discussion of these points see Dixon 1976, 168-76.

61 I owe this point to discussion with Mr John Dunbar.

[62] Bates 1891, 49-50.

[63] MacGibbon and Ross 1887-92.

[64] The etymology of 'pele' and its forms are described by Nielson 1893, and his conclusions are generally accepted; Wood 1965, 168n.

[65] In view of the variation in terminology, strict adherence to sixteenth-century usage is thus neither possible nor desirable: It is, however, thoroughly regretable that the term 'bastle' now in common usage has been limited to the class of small, usually roughly built, fortified houses: only one now-surviving building, Akeld Bastle, was certainly called a bastle in the sixteenth century, but the authors of *Shielings and Bastles* are obliged to describe this house as 'not typical', as being 'of more superior character' than the other stone houses discussed in their book (Ramm *et al.* 1970, 67). For the problems connected with consistent terminology, and the mistaken use of 'bastle' in recent years compare Dixon 1972 and 1979.

[66] *Letters and Papers of Henry VIII*, 12 pt i, no. 1321, ed. J. Gairdner (1890).

[67] *Ibid.*, 18 pt ii, no. 455; 19 pt i, nos. 348; 19 pt ii. no. 664.

[68] Bates 1891, 52-3. The more detailed survey of 1541 has no such usage.

[69] British Library, Cotton MSS, Caligula B vii, fol. 28.

[70] *Ibid.*, Caligula B viii, fol. 856d.

[71] 'Pyramidales turres quas pailes vocant ex sola terra': Leslie, 1578, 61; Dalrymple's translation of this passage in his edition of Leslie (ed. 1596, I, 98) calls these towers 'four nuiked', that is, square. An Act of 1535 'for bigging of strenthis on the Bordouris' distinguishes between barmkins of stone and lime to be built by landed men of 'ane hundreth pund land' and 'big pelis' of unspecified but certainly poorer material, to be built by 'landit men of smallar rent': *APS,* ed. Thompson, II, 1424-1567, 346.

[72] British Library, Cotton MSS, Caligula B viii, fols. 636 ff: the descriptions of the buildings from this manuscript were transcribed by Bates 1891, 29-49; the whole document, with many errors of transcription, is published by Hodgson 1828, pt. 3, vol. 2, 171-242.

[73] In the Border area, at least: survey work in upper Clydesdale has recently revealed the ruins of several apparent pele-houses well away from the Border zone.

[74] Ramm *et al.* 1970, 65; Maxwell-Irvine 1970-1, esp. 217.

[75] For a full discussion of the range of wealth and the status of the builders and occupants of towers, bastles and pele-houses see Dixon 1979.

[76] For example, Fraser 1971; Tough 1927; Rae 1966; Watts and Watts 1975.

BIBLIOGRAPHY

BAIN, J. (ed.) 1881-8. *Calendar of Documents Relating to Scotland*, 4 vols, Edinburgh

BATES, C.J. 1891. *Border Holds*, published as *Archaeologia Aeliana*, 2nd ser., 14

BLAIR, C.H.H. 1944. 'The early castles of Northumberland', *Archaeologia Aeliana*, 4th ser., 22, 133-41

—— 1949. 'Editor's Note', *Archaeologia Aeliana*, 4th ser., 27-9

BROWN, R.A. 1953 *English Medieval Castles*, 3rd edn. (1976), London

CATHCART-KING, D.J. and ALCOCK, L. 1966. 'Ringworks of England and Wales', *Château Gaillard*, 3, 126-7.

CHARLTON, J. 1979. *Brougham Castle: Official Guide*, London

COLVIN, H.M. *et al.* 1963. *A History of the King's Works*, I, London

COULSON, C. 1982. 'Castellation in the County of Champagne', *Château Gaillard*, 9-10, 351-6

—— 1993. 'Specimens of freedom to crenellate by licence', *Fortress*, 18, 3-15

CRUDEN, S. 1963. *The Scottish Castle*, revised edn., Edinburgh

DIXON, P.W. 1972. 'Shielings and bastles: a reconsideration of some problems', *Archaeologia Aeliana*, 4th ser., 50, 249-58

—— 1975. 'Hillslap Tower, masons, and regional traditions', *Hist. Berwickshire Natur. Club*, 40, 128-41

—— 1976. *Fortified Houses on the Anglo-Scottish Border*, unpublished D.Phil. thesis, University of Oxford

—— 1979. 'Towerhouses, pelehouses, and Border Society', *Archaeol. J.*, 136, 240-52

—— 1988. *Aydon Castle*, London

—— 1990. 'The donjon of Knaresborough: the castle as theatre', *Château Gaillard*, 14, 121-40

—— 1992. 'From Hall to Tower: the change in seigneurial building on the Anglo-Scottish Border after *c.* 1250', in *Thirteenth-Century England* (ed. S. Lloyd), 4, 85-107

DIXON, P.W. and BORNE, P. 1978. 'Coparcenary

and Aydon Castle', *Archaeol. J.* 135, 234-9

DIXON, P.W. and MARSHALL, P.E. forthcoming. 'The Great Tower in the twelfth century: the case of Norham', *Archaeol. J.*

DIXON, P.W., HAYFIELD, C.C. and STARTIN, W. 1989. 'Baguley Hall, Manchester: the structural development of a Cheshire manor house', *Archaeol. J.,* 146, 384-423

FAIRCLOUGH, G. 1982. 'Edlingham Castle: the military and domestic development of a Northumbrian manor. Excavations 1978-80: interim report', *Château Gaillard,* 9-10, 373-87

FRASER, G.McD. 1971. *The Steel Bonnets,* London

HARBOTTLE, R.B. 1982. 'The castle of Newcastle upon Tyne: excavations 1973-79', *Château Gaillard,* 9-10, 407-18

HEDLEY, W.P. 1968. *Northumberland Families,* 2 vols., I, 12-14; 244-66, Newcastle

HODGSON, J., et al. 1820-58. *A History of Northumberland,* 7 vols., Newcastle upon Tyne

HOGG, R. 1954. 'The manor-house at Burgh by Sands', *Trans. Cumberland Westmorland Antiq. Archaeol. Soc,* 2nd ser., 54, 129

HONEYMAN, H.L. 1955. 'Mitford Castle', *Archaeologia Aeliana,* 4th ser., 33, 27-33

HOPE-TAYLOR, B. 1977. *Yeavering,* DoE Archaeological Report, 7, London

KAPELLE, W. 1979. *The Norman Conquest of the North of England,* London

KNOWLES, W.H. 1926. 'The castle of Newcastle upon Tyne', *Archaeologia Aeliana,* 4th ser., 2, 1-51

LESLIE, J. 1578. *De Origine Moribus et Rebus Gestis Scottorum,* Rome

LLOYD, N. 1931. *A History of the English House from Primitive Times to the Victorian Period,* London

MCCARTHY, M., SUMMERSON, H.R.T. and ANNIS, R.G. 1990. *Carlisle Castle: A Survey and Documentary History,* HBMC(E) Archaeol. Rep., 18, London

MACGIBBON D. and ROSS, T. 1887-92. *The Castellated and Domestic Architecture of Scotland,* Edinburgh

MADDICOTT, J.R. 1970. *Thomas of Lancaster,* Oxford

MAXWELL-IRVINE, A.M.T. 1970-1. 'Early firearms and their influence on the military and domestic architecture of the Borders', *Proc. Scot. Antiquarian Soc.,* 103, 192-223

MIDDLETON, A. 1910. *An Account of Belsay Castle,* Newcastle

MILLER, J.S. 1985. 'Restoration work at

Markenfield Hall, 1981-4, *Yorkshire Archaeol. J.,* 57, 101-10

MUSGROVE, F. 1990. *The North of England,* London

NCH, 1893-1940. *A History of Northumberland,* 15 vols., Newcastle upon Tyne

NIELSON, G. 1893. *Peel: Its Meaning and Derivation,* Glasgow

PARKER J.H. and TURNER, H. 1851-9. *Some Account of Domestic Architecture in England,* 3 vols., Vol. 1 (1851), *From the Conquest to the End of the 13th Century,* Oxford

RAE, T.I. 1966. *The Administration of the Scottish Frontier, 1513-1603,* Edinburgh

RAMM, H.G., MCDOWALL, R.W. and MERCER, E. 1970. *Shielings and Bastles,* London

RCAHM SCOTLAND, 1933. *An Inventory of the Historical Monuments of the Counties of Fife, Kinross and Clackmannan,* Edinburgh

RCAHM SCOTLAND, 1956. *The County of Roxburgh,* 2 vols., Edinburgh

RENN, D. 1968. *Norman Castles in Britain,* London

RYDER, P. 1986. *Blenkinsopp Castle* (Napper Collection Partnership, May 1986) [Unpublished]

SIMPSON G.G. and WEBSTER, B. 1985. 'Charter evidence and the distribution of mottes in Scotland' in *Essays on the Nobility of Medieval Scotland* (ed. K. J. Stringer), 7-11, Edinburgh

SIMPSON, W.D. 1938-9. *The Book of Dunvegan,* 2 vols., (Third Spalding Club, 1938-9), Aberdeen

——, 1940. 'Belsay Castle and the Scottish tower houses', *Archaeologia Aeliana,* 4th ser., 17, 75-84

——, 1949a. *Brough Castle: Official Guide,* London

——, 1949b. 'Further notes on Dunstanburgh Castle', *Archaeologia Aeliana,* 4th ser., 27, 1-25

SMOUT, T.C. 1969. *A History of the Scottish People*

THOMPSON, A. HAMILTON 1912. *Military Architecture in England during the Middle Ages,* Oxford

THOMSON, T. and INNES, C. (eds.) 1814-75. *The Acts of Parliaments of Scotland,* (Record Commission 1814-75).

TOUGH, D.N.L. 1927. *The Last Years of a Frontier,* Oxford

TUCK, J.A. 1971. 'Northumbrian society in the fourteenth century', *Northern History,* 6, 22-39

——, 1985. 'War and society in the medieval North', *Northern History,* 21, 33-52

WATTS, S.J. and WATTS, S. 1975. *From Border to Middle Shire,* Leicester

WINCHESTER, A. 1987. *Landscape and Society in Medieval Cumbria,* Edinburgh

WOOD, M. 1965. *English Mediaeval House,* London

Manorial Building in Timber in Central and Southern England, 1200–1550

Julian Munby

Timber framing and roof carpentry were important elements of manorial building in south-east England. Between the thirteenth and sixteenth centuries a general pattern of development in timber building can be discerned amongst the many variants that have survived, in the standardization of framing and roof types. Indeed, it may be that the degree of variety and the pace of change on this side of the Channel forms the principal difference between English and continental building practices. It is the purpose of this contribution to describe the outline of development, and the context within which it occurred. What is offered here can only be a preliminary statement, as fieldwork and publication have been uneven, and discoveries continue to be made in the context of individual and county-wide research programmes.

LOWLAND ENGLAND

In considering the buildings of one region of England it will be as well to say something of the nature of that region. A country as small as England may be regarded as a single region or province, as Russell has done in his *Medieval Regions and their Cities,* where he treats England as the region of London, undoubtedly making sense on a European scale when considering overall patterns of urbanization.[1]

Fox had introduced the idea to archaeology—following Mackinder—of a cultural division between a 'Highland' and 'Lowland' zone, by which England was divided into a lowland south-east and a highland north-west that could be traced through many aspects of material culture (including building) in the historic and prehistoric periods (fig. 1). This conforms with the marked divide evident in medieval taxation records from the thirteenth to the sixteenth century, between a prosperous south-east (one might say the London Region) and a less wealthy north and west (fig. 2).[2] Other cultural factors cut across this division; the distribution of field systems in which the 'Midland system' of two and three open fields

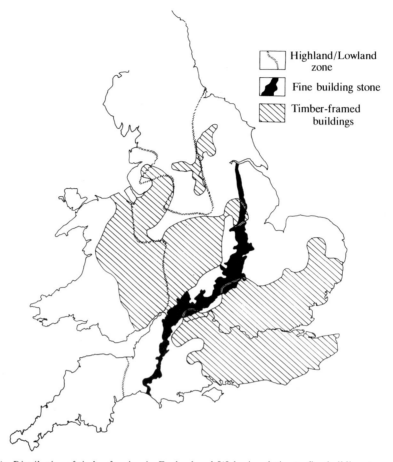

1. *Distribution of timber framing in England and Wales in relation to fine building stone and the boundary of the Highland Zone (after J. T. Smith 1966; P. Smith 1975; Darby 1976 and Fox 1947)*

occurs in a broad belt running through the centre of England into the Highland zone, but is absent from the south-east and east of the country (fig. 2).[3] One might add to this, as yet unmapped, the localization of centralized and dispersed village settlement, or the different types of manorial structure. In vernacular architecture there are identifiable regional traits in timber-framed building within the overall distribution of framed buildings (fig. 1), and the enigmatic distribution of cruck buildings which, after extensive investigation and mapping, have not been found east of a line down the centre of England (fig. 2).[4] Regional studies of building in stone (especially churches) would prove especially rewarding, but this has not yet advanced beyond a preliminary essay.[5]

It is rather to the underlying geological structure of southern England, and the physical division created by the Jurassic stone belt, which provided such good building stone along its whole length, that attention must be drawn (fig. 1). To the south and east lay the younger rocks, the chalk downland, clay vales, and the Tertiary gravels, clays and alluvium. Good

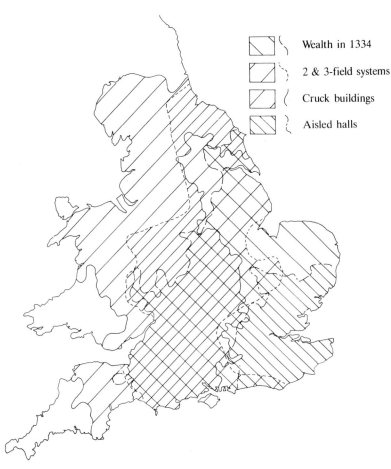

Wealth in 1334

2 & 3-field systems

Cruck buildings

Aisled halls

2. Distribution of crucks and aisled halls in England and Wales in relation to the wealthier area of England in 1334 and the extent of two- and three-field systems (after Alcock 1981; Sandall 1986; Darby 1976 and Gray 1915)

building stone, for much of this region, had to be imported—as it might easily be from across the Channel—up rivers like the Thames, or round the coast. Moreover, the distribution of woodland recorded in Domesday Book shows a heavy concentration in the south-east, and so it was that early medieval building in timber was important in this region, and has increasingly been the subject of detailed investigation and study.[6]

But this is not to say that this south-east region is homogenous or unvarying. Areas of forest, open champion country and hills divided it into a number of smaller regions with markedly different patterns of settlement and manorial organization. Extremes could be found in Oxfordshire, with its high percentage of villages with co-terminous manors and open fields, and Kent with its holdings in gavelkind (i.e. partible inheritance) and manors fragmented by their outlying wealden pastures and smallholdings.[7] Parts of Sussex and Surrey shared aspects of the Kentish pattern, but Sussex also had a rich coastal plain with open fields of the Midland type in addition to weald and downland while Essex, and parts of Hampshire, were notable for small landholders and newly-made assart lands on clay and woodland.[8] The picture of farming regions in 1600—as mapped in the *Agrarian History of England and Wales*—is complex and was probably no less so in the medieval period.[9]

In addition to spatial factors, regional patterns of building activity were cyclical, related to changes in population and available surplus wealth, as has been shown for the post-medieval 'great rebuilding'.[10] Although figures are speculative, a gradual increase in population down to the Black Death—again subject to regional variation—may have almost doubled the population between 1200 and 1350. In the great age of demesne farming, to which belong some of the finest manorial buildings, even peasants might prosper, and aspire to houses of almost manorial scale, as can be seen from the investigation of a village like Harwell (Oxfordshire).[11] After the catastrophe of the Black Death, the age of demesne farming was over and as the countryside emerged from the crisis landlords might opt for leasing their demesnes, while peasants were more likely to be paying rent in lieu of services; but recovery was not long in coming, and abandoned lands were again tenanted decades before the population at large recovered. Arguably, the landlords' crisis was postponed for twenty to thirty years, and only really came to a head in the 1370s with high labour costs and falling prices, which compounded with unpopular government and imposition of the Poll Tax led to the Peasants' Revolt of 1381.[12]

By the early fifteenth century the falling demand for land led to the desertion of villages and further reduction in demesne farming by the leasing or abandonment of arable land, though land-owning might remain very profitable for some, but disastrous for others; conversely, the free peasantry and minor gentry might prosper in an age that was difficult for the greater landholders. In all, there was a variety of circumstances and local differences that makes for no simple picture; in the long run, the south-east increased in prosperity between the recorded subsidy figures of 1334 and 1524, most markedly in the counties adjoining the capital.[13] This is reflected in the quantity of new building, often by peasant or 'yeoman' farmers rather than at manorial level.

It is in the context of this rapid overview of economic changes that the surviving buildings must be seen, although it is by no means always the case that sufficient documentation survives for a building to be located in a particular set of economic changes.

TIMBER BUILDING

There was no shortage of building timber in the south-east, whether from demesne woodland or park and hedgerow trees. Managed woodland produced timber trees alongside the cyclical cropping of underwood from coppice stands, as is well established from documentary and field studies.[14] This could supply the needs of most manorial building and—although jealously conserved by the lord—might also be called upon to meet the requirements of tenants for their *housebote,* the customary right to timber for building. Continuous demand for firewood— by villages, towns and the capital—was itself an industry of great importance, but was met from the underwood resources and did not affect the availability of building timber.[15]

Such was the general prevalence of wood and timber in the material world of the Middle Ages, for domestic, building, agricultural and engineering purposes, that most villages must have had a carpenter, though no doubt there were specialists in building construction. Carpenters went to select the trees necessary for the job in hand, and oversaw the felling and conversion of the timber, working it soon after felling. Prefabrication was the normal practice, where the frame or roof was made and part-assembled beforehand and then marked for re-erection on site. It is not known what plans or drawings were used, but the repetition of standard features implies training and memory if not the use of drawn specifications.[16]

Domestic and agricultural buildings were only a part of the wide range of the carpenter's craft. The development of building types must also be seen in the context of a rapid expansion of techniques and innovations. The appearance of the windmill in the late twelfth century is but one remarkable example, while the demands of large royal and ecclesiastical building projects led to daring experimentation in large-scale roofing in the thirteenth and fourteenth centuries. Carpenters were also pressed into military service, from which they must have gained engineering experience, being taken to Wales, Scotland, and France.[17] Even without such experience, the range of talents available in the medieval village must have considerable at a time when relatively few capable individuals could gain education and leave their home communities. But the better-quality buildings must always have been designed and built by experienced house carpenters, as conscious of new methods and forms as they were of 'vernacular' traditions. That they created buildings conforming to regional types must not obscure the fact that regional house-types were designed and planned as much as any of the mass-housing erected by twentieth-century builders, with or without an architect.

The English Mediaeval House, a fundamental text, was published prior to the revival of interest in timber framing, but it remains an incomparable introduction to the subject.[18] Studies of timber building have greatly advanced in recent years through the writings of J.T. Smith and members of the Vernacular Architecture Group.[19] In his many publications arising out of studies in Essex and elsewhere, Cecil Hewett has drawn attention to the potential, for historical studies, of details of construction (especially jointing) as a means of dating buildings, and has stimulated a revival of interest in the examination of framed buildings.[20] Critics of his preference for close dating have yet to demonstrate that Hewett's fundamental thesis is flawed. Two recently-published accounts of manorial building provide a general conspectus for the medieval period against the wider background of the agrarian scene.[21] The growth of dendrochronology as a reliable means of dating is also beginning to show results that will in course of time allow a more exact seriation of buildings that have so far only been dated stylistically.[22]

MANORIAL BUILDINGS

Manors vary greatly in size: as centres of large estates with numerous tenants to the small manors that were little more than a farm, and not dissimilar from the houses of the more prosperous peasants; ecclesiastical manors, granges and 'court lodges' with a staff but no family in occupation, and rectory farms on a discrete holding and often appropriated to a religious house, or college, and inhabited by a lay rector or tenant, rather than a priest. The range of house-size may mean that it is difficult to establish that there was a 'manorial' style of building, except at the higher level, as opposed to rural styles of building, that is buildings on unrestricted house-plots rather than on the constrained sites demanded by urban living. But features common to all down to the sixteenth century include the open hall, a public—rather than a private—space, in which rents might be collected and harvest feasts held.[23]

The larger manorial sites included a whole range of domestic and agricultural buildings, as appears from two sites in Oxfordshire: the plan of Cuxham manor, a classic example reconstructed from documentary descriptions, or the excavated site at Chalgrove.[24] Here were to be found house, kitchen, barns, granaries, cattle sheds, dovecots and other dependent buildings, most of which no longer exist except for the houses and barns. On the sites of several monastic and other manors owned by institutions it may be only the barn that survives. At Great Coxwell (Oxfordshire) the barn from the grange of the Cistercian Beaulieu Abbey alone remains, whilst on the nearby site of the lost grange at Wyke in Faringdon (Oxfordshire, formerly Berkshire), also of Beaulieu, recent aerial photography has revealed a large complex of buildings belonging to several phases.[25] The story of barns need not concern us further here, though it may perhaps be noted that they are of special interest as being traditional buildings that followed, rather than led, fashionable developments in timber architecture. Although the number of known medieval barns has greatly increased in recent years, only in Essex and Kent have they been subjected to detailed study.[26]

What is to be attempted here is a review of the development of timber-framed housing, where manorial examples form the greater part of the available evidence, though rural peasant buildings and urban houses are increasingly important towards the end of the period. It will be argued that in timber building we can see the gradual convergence of domestic functions under one roof, and that from a period of innovation and experiment with many forms emerged a standard type with a single framed-structure comprising the various plan elements under one roof.

THE DEVELOPMENT OF BUILDING TYPES

The earliest surviving timber buildings most often had aisled halls, that is they had a central area open to the roof with a central hearth, and aisle posts supporting an arcade and demarcating the aisles which were roofed by the sloping continuation of the main roof. End-blocks, containing the service and chamber end, were usually attached, although not necessarily contemporary with the hall, and formed either a rectangular block or H-plan. Although of ancient lineage, this type may in England have been a re-introduction in the late twelfth century.[27] The distribution of aisled buildings seems largely to have been restricted to the south-east (fig. 2), and was mostly a phenomenon of the twelfth to fourteenth centuries, though later examples survive, some in outlying areas.[28] As most aisled buildings have been converted at a later date, it is rarely possible to appreciate the quality of space that the aisled hall created, except in surviving barns. St Mary's Hospital in Chichester, dating from around 1290, is one of the few aisled halls still inhabited as such, though on a grand scale.[29] Examples from the thirteenth century illustrated by Hewett, from Essex, Suffolk and Hertfordshire also demonstrate the attention paid to decorative detail on the capitals of aisle posts, which, together with the bracing of the arcades, created an assemblage that was reminiscent of stone arcades in churches or major domestic buildings.[30]

Different roofing-types are to be found in aisled buildings. The earliest surviving examples have roofs that are linked to the posts and aisles, with passing braces that provided lateral support, and strengthening the roof which might have no longitudinal support other than laths for the roof covering-material.[31] A small non-manorial house, perhaps of the early thirteenth century, Songers, Boxted (Essex), has passing braces, a profusion of notch-lap joints and a plain collar-and-rafter roof.[32] By the middle of the thirteenth century passing braces continued up to the apex of the roof—to cross over as scissors—and there could be matching scissor-braces on the trusses without passing braces; examples are Great Bricett

Hall and Kersey Priory (Suffolk), Fyfield Hall and The Bury, Clavering (Essex).[33] By the end of the thirteenth century the recently-introduced crown-post roof was in general use, and continued into the fourteenth century and beyond, as at Place House, Ware (Hertfordshire), and Little Chesterford Manor (Essex).[34] But there are also fourteenth-century halls with plain collar-roofs, or with the crown-posts only in the cross-wings, as at Stantons, Black Notley and Priory Place, Little Dunmow (Essex) (fig. 3).[35]

In the innovative phase at the end of the thirteenth and beginning of the fourteenth century there appear two-centred gothic arches as a decorative and structural element in aisled-hall roofs, most notably at Nurstead Court (Kent), now dated to *c.* 1314.[36] The transition from straight to curved bracing also presented opportunities for a proliferation of arches, from the braces of the crown-posts, to the heads of the aisle posts, and within the aisles themselves. Both Place House, Ware and Little Chesterford Manor show all of these features combined. Curved braces used in wall-framing could also contribute to the 'gothic' character of timber

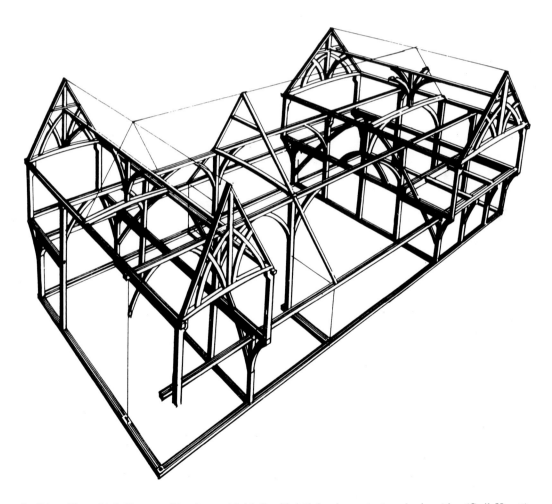

3. *Priory Place, Little Dunmow (Essex): an aisled hall with jettied ends on a rectangular base plan (Cecil Hewett)*

building, since they were left exposed and not covered by the wall-filling. An example of this is in the south wing of Middle Farm, Harwell (Oxfordshire).[37]

A further development in domestic building from around 1300 saw the removal of aisle posts by a variety of means, in order to clear the floor-space in the hall. This was of little importance in agricultural buildings, where aisled barns continued to be built for many years. One method employed was to raise the aisle construction off the floor. An institutional (though not manorial) example is Merton College, Oxford, where the Warden's Hall of 1299 has an aisled arcade lifted up on to the tie-beam, and a crown-post roof above that. Here the intended effect is purely decorative, since the span of the building hardly required aisles in the first place.[38] At Church Farm, Fressingfield (Suffolk) of *c.* 1330–40 the tie beam carries an elaborate arcade of two-centred arches with 'aisle posts' and a central crown-post, while above the tie-beam is another crown-post; all these have finely-moulded capitals, and the wall-bracing strives for an unusually decorative effect. Church Farm, Lewknor (Oxfordshire), a manorial hall of mid-fourteenth-century date that was abandoned and is now but a barn, has a raised arcade over an arch-braced tie-beam. While there is little decoration to the arcade posts, the bracing of the walls, trusses and roof shows a proliferation of decorative cusping. An example perhaps from the later fourteenth century is at Gatehouse Farm, Felsted (Essex), with a raised aisle on a long tie-beam.[39]

A second method of clearing the floor-space was the use of a single large arch across the hall, rising to collar level. These are known as base-crucks, though their relation to true crucks is not entirely clear, and their general distribution does not extend to eastern England.[40] The rectory house, today called 'The Abbey' at Sutton Courtenay (Oxfordshire), dating from the second quarter of the fourteenth century, has a fine moulded arch across the hall, with a crown-post above; this is a purely gothic form, like that at Nurstead Court described above.[41] As with so many of the features discussed here, developments in manorial buildings were copied by the more wealthy peasants in their farmhouses. Lime Tree House, Harwell (Oxfordshire), formerly thought to be the episcopal manor-house but now shown to be the house of a twenty-one-acre peasant holding, was originally built in the middle of the thirteenth century as an aisled hall. In about 1300 it was converted by inserting a base-cruck in the middle of the hall, with a crown post carrying the original roof-structure above.[42] Buildings in stone also reflected these concerns for gothic interiors, a fine example being the series of stone arches over the hall of the Archbishop of Canterbury at Mayfield Place (Sussex) *c.* 1320–30, and on a smaller scale at Ightham Moat (Kent), *c.* 1340.[43] In the vast roof at Penshurst Place (Kent), *c.* 1345, the arches no longer descend the wall (except for their decorative supports), but are in the form of arch-braces rising from the top of the wall that carry the collar and arcade plate for the upper part of the roof.[44] In a less elaborate form the arch-brace and collar roof was to become one of the standard late medieval roof-types.

The hammer-beam roof was a third way of removing the aisle posts. Its origins have now been taken back to the late thirteenth century, and it is notable that at least one early example occurs over a kitchen in the Bishop's Palace at Chichester, *c.* 1300, where the necessity to clear the floor-space for hearths was of some importance.[45] As with the other methods already described, there are instances of conversion to the new type, as at Thorley Hall (Hertfordshire) where the lower part of the aisle-post was sawn off and replaced with a hammer-beam at some date in the fourteenth century. The best known use in a domestic hall is at Tiptofts, Wimbish (Essex), probably of mid-fourteenth-century date, where the hammer beams rise from massive wall-posts to carry a crown-post roof, and the spandrels of the truss have cusped decoration. A recently discovered hammer-beam roof at Upton Court, Slough (Buckinghamshire), dated by dendrochronology to *c.* 1330, has a curious variant by which the hammer-beams seem not to have supported the roof, but were part of a more extensive arcade that incorporated dormer windows on each side of the hall. A non-manorial building that includes several types of roof is the 'Pilgrims' Hall' in the precinct of Winchester Cathedral priory, apparently dating to the first decade of the fourteenth century. It is unclear whether this was a public building, such as a guest hall, or merely a brewhouse (as it was later), but it has at one end a hammer-beam roof and at the other end a base-cruck truss, with a crown-post roof over its entire length.[46]

The Pilgrims' Hall, like many manorial buildings in the era before the Black Death, exhibits a lavish use of large and well-finished timbers, where the quantity and quality of the carpentry is as notable as the design or decoration of the roof. Characteristic features of this class of building include cambered tie-beams, moulded cornice-plates lying on the arcade-plates, and chamfered arises on the principal timbers. Examples referred to above that share some or all of these features are Place House, Ware, and Thorley Hall (Hertfordshire), Little Chesterford and Tiptofts (Essex), Nurstead Court (Kent), Lewknor and Sutton Courtenay (Oxfordshire). Some of these, and other buildings of the early fourteenth century, make use of cusped decoration on bracing, while the use of cusped wind-braces became increasingly common, especially in central and western England.[47] This can be seen as the high point of conspicuous consumption in the use of timber at a manorial level, when cost was no object in achieving aesthetic ends. The final expression of these concerns was in the royal hall of Westminster Palace, *c.* 1395, where the duplication and decoration of timber members reached its apogee.[48] Thereafter, in line with the more simple forms of the Perpendicular style in stone architecture, the amount of decoration tends to decrease, though when desired the use of profligate quantities of timber remained an option, especially in wall-framing. In the south-east the crown-post roof was to remain the standard domestic type, eventually to be superseded by the side-purlin roof which had already become widespread in central southern and western England.[49]

In all the attention paid to the development of carpentry details and roof-type the matter of plan forms has been somewhat neglected. Since the all-in-one hall building can at one level be regarded as a single type, the structural aspects of its variant forms have been given less attention.[50] Yet in the buildings considered above can be seen the germ of the later medieval and post-medieval compact house-plan, where the principal rooms were brought together under one roof, and structural complexity was reduced to a more simple formula. Although this process is as yet imperfectly understood, it may rank as one of the most significant developments of the medieval carpenter. Most of the houses mentioned above have or had service and chamber blocks at either end of the hall. Both were not necessarily part of the original plan, and even if contemporary with the hall have often been rebuilt in subsequent periods. However, from those examples where there is clear evidence of elements linking the hall and end blocks we can derive some indications of progress.

The development of flooring and the jetty is closely related to the plan arrangement, and this is a matter to which Hewett has paid close attention.[51] As he observes, the earliest floors are 'lodged', that is the joists are simply laid on the horizontal beams in the side walls (rather than being tenoned into them); this is likely to have suggested the possibility of extending the joists outside the walls to create an overhanging jetty. It must be remembered that this is not solely an English phenomenon, as the jetty was used across northern Europe, but Hewett's examples include some experimental forms, as in the service wing of Tiptofts and Priory Place, Little Dunmow (Essex) probably of the early fourteenth century, where large brackets support the jetties (fig. 3).[52] A more assured type is found at Baythorne Hall, Birdbrook (Essex), perhaps of the mid-fourteenth century, where joists forming the jetties are tenoned (as was the standard later practice), though they are supported on posts independent of the storey-post for the wing.[53] The jetty may have originated in urban building, and was to find its ultimate expression there in multi-storey buildings; it allowed the designers of framed rural housing a series of variations on plan and form whereby the plan of hall and projecting cross-wing might be based on a simple rectangular plan at ground level, projecting only at first-floor level.

The development of the unified plan of a single block can be discerned in the larger houses under consideration, but may always have been present in smaller houses, and may have a long tradition in the 'long-house' type with accommodation for men and beasts under one roof. In the small aisled house at Boxted (Essex) the arcade-plate of the hall continues through into the cross-wing thus forming a continuous roof over the whole (though the wing is wider than the hall); a manorial example is The Bury, Clavering (Essex), perhaps of the mid-thirteenth century, where the aisled profile is continuous for hall and service end, and the end wing is only distinguished by the lodged first floor.[54] The use of a single profile throughout may have been more common in service ends, as in the early fourteenth-century examples at Southchurch Hall and Stanton's Farm, Black Notley (Essex), where either the arcade-plate or the collar-purlin support a continuous roof-structure, and the cross-wings do not project.[55] The late thirteenth-century hall at Place House, Ware (Hertfordshire) had a jettied service wing on a unified rectangular ground plan, but with separate framing.[56] A complete example of the H-plan on a rectangular base can be seen at Priory Place, Little Dunmow (Essex) probably of the early fourteenth century (fig. 3). Here the wall- and arcade-plates are continuous throughout hall and cross-wings, and the storey-posts in the cross-wings are in line with the aisle-posts in the hall; but the roofs of the wings are at right-angles to the hall, and together with the jetties emphasize the H-plan effect.[57] Elsewhere, even with a rectangular ground-plan the cross-wings may be separately framed, as at Gatehouse Farm, Felsted (Essex), though the discontinuity here may be an indication of its being a later addition.[58] Similarly, the true H-plan of the early fourteenth-century Little Chesterford Manor (Essex) is probably due to the subsequent addition of the service wing.[59] Baythorne Hall, Birdbrook (Essex), perhaps of the mid-fourteenth century, has a hall and contemporary jettied cross-wings on a rectangular plan. Although the framing of the cross-wings supports the aisle system of the hall, this does not correspond with the bay divisions of the wings, though the central trusses of the right-angled roofs of the cross-wings are aligned and partially linked with the crown-posts of the hall roof.[60] Independent framing and roof of the service-wing is also seen in St Clere's Hall, St Osyth's (Essex), probably of late fourteenth-century date, where the wall-plate of the cross-wing is higher than the arcade-plates of the hall.[61]

The abandonment of the aisled hall would result in halls of narrower breadth, but although this might be expected to produce houses of the true H-plan at ground level, there are instances which show that this was not necessarily so. The farm on the large freeholding of Kennington's, Aveley (Essex), was rebuilt in the late fourteenth century on a smaller rectangular plan, with a continuous crown-post roof over the hall and ends. A non-manorial building on a moated site, Wynter's Armourie, Magdalen Laver (Essex), was originally built on a rectangular plan with a jettied wing but was rebuilt with a narrower hall thus creating the H-plan at ground level. Another peasant house of the late fourteenth century, Hill Farm, Fyfield (Essex), was built on a rectangular base, with the jettied ends forming the H-plan at first floor. The hall had an arch-braced roof and there are crown-posts in the wings, the one element of structural unity being the beam below the jetties of the wings that continues as a high middle rail in the walls of the hall.[62] Equivalent developments are apparent from urban examples, and again it must be stressed that there is no certainty that rural house-types were leading the field in structural innovation, and urban carpenters (especially in London) may have been producing exemplars that were copied elsewhere. Two instances, significantly both of them likely to have been inns, are recorded by Hewett, the Old Sun Inn, Saffron Walden and Jacobe's Hall, Brightlingsea (Essex). The former is of the second half of the fourteenth century, on a rectangular base plan but with jettied ends having independent framing; the latter is of the second half of the fifteenth century; and is of interest for having a service-wing longer than the breadth of the hall.[63]

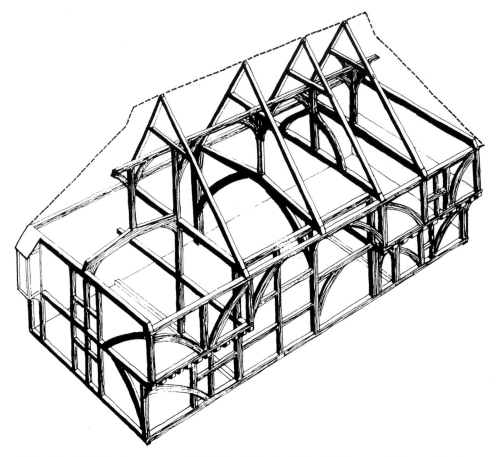

4. *Bayleaf, a Wealden House now at the Weald and Downland Open Air Museum, Singleton, West Sussex (John Warren 1990)*

The final step in the sequence was the rotation of the roofs in the cross-wings to be in line with the hall roof. We have already noted one house (Kennington's) where this was done in the process of conversion of an aisled building. The resultant combination of H-plan on a rectangular base and a continuous roof over a recessed hall was exemplified in the very widespread type known as the Wealden house, which can be seen as the culmination of the medieval carpenter's efforts at hall-house design (fig. 4). The distribution of the type is well established, and is not dissimilar from that of aisled halls (fig. 2), with a south-eastern (and particularly Kent/East Sussex) predominance, and the outliers often being found in towns. Its origins are less well understood, though the current research programme in Kent will no doubt elucidate this; the tree-ring dates from Wealden houses published so far range from 1379 to 1497.[64] Wealden houses are not uniform in size, and they occur as manor-houses, often as the houses of prosperous smaller landholders, and also in towns, where smaller variants of terraced 'half-Wealdens' have been identified.[65] The relative simplicity of Wealden house construction in the unified framing of the cross-wings under one roof (nearly always a crown post, and often with hipped ends) must have made them more economical to build, while the end-jetties and recessed hall gave them a handsome appearance. While the fifteenth century saw less of the magnificence in timber decorative details than earlier ages, in line with the greater simplicity of Perpendicular forms in masonry buildings, there was no falling off in quality of workmanship, and the frequent use of close studding allowed an ostentatious display of timber.

Possibly slightly later than the Wealden house was the continuous jetty house, suitable for a storeyed layout that did not include a hall, but also found with open halls and a narrow gallery on the hall jetty. The well known example of Paycocke's House, Coggeshall (Essex) is of c. 1500, and the dates given so far for Kentish examples are all in the sixteenth century, but fifteenth-century examples are known from elsewhere, and one in Winchester dates to the late fourteenth century.[66] Certainly it was generally of later occurrence as a common house-type, and led the way to the standard timber-framed houses of the post-medieval period, with which we are not concerned here.[67] This was not, of course, the whole story, since large framed houses of less regular plan continued to be built in the post-medieval period, until replaced by the fashion for building in brick and stone.

While it may be over-simplistic to attempt to find a single course of development in the later medieval framed house, it will not be unreasonable to seek precursors for the very common fifteenth- and sixteenth-century types. But what must be apparent is the extent to which the medieval carpenter, as a designer/builder, was at the forefront of innovation in domestic architecture, and played as important a part as the mason in the development of manorial architecture, and in laying the foundation for later house-types.

ABSTRACT

MANORIAL BUILDING IN TIMBER IN CENTRAL AND SOUTHERN ENGLAND, 1200–1550

The development of building in timber between the thirteenth and sixteenth centuries is discussed in manorial and related contexts. Regional variations in building-types in England are considered in relation to the highland/lowland zones, wealth and agricultural practices, and the availability of timber and stone. Status and range of carpentry are briefly discussed together with its place in surviving manorial buildings. The aisled hall and its derivatives are described, from the varieties of roof-structures and decorative elements, to the means by which aisle-posts were replaced with new types of construction. The development of plan-types is considered including the relationship of jetties to the H-plan and the gradual evolution of a unified three-part plan on a rectilinear base, culminating in the plan of the late medieval Wealden house.

RÉSUMÉ

LA CONSTRUCTION SEIGNEURIALE EN BOIS DANS LE CENTRE ET LE SUD DE L'ANGLETERRE, 1200–1550

L'évolution de l'architecture en bois entre le XIIIe et le XVIe siècle est étudiée dans son contexte seigneurial et ses ramifications. Les différences régionales entre les types de construction sont examinées en fonction des zones de hautes et basses terres, de la prospérité et des pratiques agricoles ainsi que de l'approvisionnement en bois et en pierre. La place et la variété de la construction en bois sont brièvement présentées ainsi que son usage dans les bâtiments seigneuriaux qui subsistent. Le *hall* à bas-côtés et ses dérivés sont décrits, de la diversité des formes de toitures et des éléments décoratifs jusqu'aux modes de remplacement des poteaux des bas-côtés par de nouvelles techniques de construction. L'évolution des plans-types est abordée, notamment la relation de l'encorbellement avec le plan en H, ainsi que la transformation progressive du plan tripartite qui aboutit à la fin du Moyen-âge au plan-type connu sous le nom de *Wealden house*.

NOTES

[1] Russell 1972, 121-30.
[2] Fox 1947; Darby 1976, 78-9, 137-43, 195-6.
[3] Gray 1915; Darby 1976, 82.
[4] Smith 1965; Alcock, 1981.
[5] Atkinson 1947.
[6] Parsons 1991; Rackham 1986, 75-85.
[7] Hallam 1988, 662; Witney 1976; Everitt 1986.
[8] Palmer 1990; Blair 1991; Brandon 1974; Hallam 1988, 162-9, 209-11.
[9] Thirsk 1967, 4; Darby 1976, 265.
[10] Machin 1977.
[11] Currie 1987; (Harwell was formerly in Berkshire).
[12] Bolton 1980, 209-17.
[13] Bolton 1980, 218-45.
[14] Rackham 1980; 1986; Munby 1991.
[15] Rackham 1972 for the timber requirements of one house; Rackham 1980, 142-3; Munby 1991, 399.
[16] Munby 1991, 382-4.
[17] Munby 1991, 389-96.
[18] Wood 1965.
[19] Smith, in a series of publications, 1955-74; Mercer 1975; Brunskill 1985.
[20] Hewett 1969; 1980.
[21] Hurst 1988; Le Patourel 1991.
[22] Annual lists of tree-ring dates now appear in *Vernacular Architecture*.
[23] Wood 1965, 49-66; Hurst 1988; Le Patourel 1991.
[24] Harvey 1965; Hurst 1988, 860 [Cuxham]; Le Patourel 1991, 837 [Chalgrove].
[25] Horn and Born 1965; information Mr Grahame Soffe of RCHME. For a plan of the cropmarks see 'Wyke grange' in Royal Commission on the Historical Monuments of England, *Newsletter*, number 6 (Spring 1992), p. 7 [but unpaginated].
[26] Hewett 1969; Rigold 1963.
[27] Wood 1965, 35-48 for stone and timber examples; see Blair, above, p. 13.
[28] Sandall 1986.
[29] Munby 1985; 1987.
[30] Hewett 1976, 47-54; this conveniently brings together material from his earlier study (Hewett 1969) which is partly repeated but with further

additions in his later summary (Hewett 1980).
31 Smith 1974.
32 Hewett 1980, 85-7.
33 Hewett 1976, 46-50; Hewett 1980, 53-5, 108-9.
34 Munby *et al.* 1983; Hewett 1976, 50-1, 63-4; Hewett 1980, 122-3, 132-3.
35 Hewett 1976, 53-5, 62-3; Hewett 1980, 129-30, 135-6.
36 Cherry 1989.
37 Fletcher 1966; in this, as in several other matters, I am indebted to ideas of Christopher Currie in an unpublished lecture on 'The Age of Carpentry', of which he has kindly allowed me to see a copy.
38 Hewett 1980, 124.
39 Hewett 1976, 66; Hewett 1980, 164-5 [Fressingfield]; Morrey and Smith 1973; Fletcher 1975 [Lewknor]; Hewett 1976, 75-6; Hewett 1980, 131 [Felsted].
40 Alcock and Barley 1972; 1981.
41 Wood 1965, pl. 23; Fletcher 1990, 58-60.
42 Fletcher 1979; Currie 1986.
43 Wood 1965, pl. 24, pl. xlvi A.
44 Wood 1965, pl. xl A; Binney 1973; Lloyd 1931, 360.
45 Courtenay 1984; 1985; Munby 1985.
46 Hewett 1976, 60-1 [Thorley]; Wood 1965, 315-16 [Wimbish]; Thornes and Fradgley 1988 [Slough]; Crook 1991 [Winchester].

47 Wood 1965, 310-11.
48 Courtenay 1987; 1990.
49 Mercer 1975, 82-95; Gray 1990, 54.
50 Wood 1965, 189-207, 216-19.
51 Hewett 1976, 91-4; Hewett 1980, 171-2, 286-7, 293-5, 317.
52 Quenedey 1926, 183-200 [*l'encorbellement*]; Binding *et al.* 1975; Hewett 1976, 57-8, 62-3; 1980, 126-30.
53 Hewett 1976, 70-1; 1980, 140-1, 172.
54 Hewett 1980, 86-7, 108-9.
55 Hewett 1976, 53-5, 64-5; 1980, 134-5.
56 Hewett 1976, 50-1; 1980, 122-3.
57 Hewett 1976, 62-3; 1980, 129-30.
58 Hewett 1976, 75-6; 1980, 131.
59 Hewett 1976, 63-4; 1980, 132-3.
60 Hewett 1976, 70-1; 1980, 140-1.
61 Hewett 1976, 72-4; 1980, 173-5.
62 Hewett 1980, 159-60 [Aveley]; Walker 1987 [Laver]; Hewett 1976, 79-80 [Fyfield].
63 Hewett 1976, 72; 1980, 177 [Saffron Walden]; Hewett 1976, 81-2; 1980, 206-7 [Brightlingsea].
64 Coutin 1990; Rigold 1963; Pearson *et al.* 1988-91.
65 Coutin 1990, 80-1.
66 Hewett 1980, 211; Pearson *et al.* 1988-91; Lewis *et al.* 1988, nos. 13 and 16.
67 Gray 1990, 50-2; Hewett 1973.

BIBLIOGRAPHY

ALCOCK, N.W. 1981. *Cruck Construction. An Introduction and Catalogue,* C.B.A. Res. Rep., 42, London

ALCOCK, N.W., and BARLEY, M.W. 1972. 'Medieval roofs with base-crucks and short principals', *Antiq. J.,* 52, 132-68

——, 1981. 'Medieval roofs with base-crucks and short principals: additional evidence', *Antiq. J.,* 61, 322-8

ATKINSON, T.D. 1947. *Local Style in English Architecture: An Enquiry into its Origin and Development,* London

BINDING, G., MAINZER, U. and WIEDENAU, A. 1975. *Kleine Kunstgeschichte des Deutschen Fachwerkbaus,* Darmstadt

BINNEY, M. 1973. *The Architectural Development of Penshurst Place,* Dunstable

BLAIR, W.J. 1991. *Early Medieval Surrey: Landholding, Church and Settlement before 1300,* Guildford

BLAIR, J., and RAMSEY, N. (eds.) 1991. *English Medieval Industries,* London

BOLTON, J.L. 1980. *The Medieval English Economy 1150-1500,* London

BRANDON, P. 1974. *The Sussex Landscape,* London

BRUNSKILL, R.W. 1985. *Timber Building in Britain,* London

COUTIN, K. 1990. 'The Wealden House', in Warren 1990, 73-86

CHERRY, M. 1989. 'Nurstead Court, Kent: a reappraisal', *Archaeol. J.,* 146, 451-64

COURTENAY, L.T. 1984. 'The Westminster Hall roof and its 14th-century sources', *J. Soc. Architect. Hist.,* 43, 295-309

——, 1985. 'Where roof meets wall: structural innovations and hammer-beam antecedents, 1150-1250', *Annals of the New York Academy of Sciences,* 441, 89-124

——, 1987. 'Westminster Hall roof: a historiographic and structural study', *J. Soc. Architect. Hist.,* 46, 374-93

——, 1990. 'The Westminster Hall roof: a new archaeological source', *J. Brit. Archaeol. Assoc.,* 143, 95-111

CROOK, J. 1991. 'The Pilgrims' Hall, Winchester:

hammerbeams, base-crucks and aisle-derivative roof structures', *Archaeologia,* 109, 129-59

CURRIE, C.R.J. 1987. 'Harwell houses to the 18th century: an interim gazetteer' in *Vernacular Architecture Group Spring Conference 1987 Oxfordshire Programme* (eds. J. Ashdown and J. Munby)

——, 1986. 'Bishops's Manor and Cateway's Farm, Harwell', *Vernacular Architecture,* 17, 51

DARBY, H.C. (ed.) 1976. *A New Historical Geography of England before 1600,* Cambridge

EVERITT, A. 1986. *Continuity and Colonization: the Evolution of Kentish Settlement,* Leicester

FLETCHER, J. M. 1966. 'Three medieval farmhouses in Harwell', *Berkshire Archaeol. J.,* 62, 45-69

——, 1975. 'The medieval hall at Lewknor', *Oxoniensia,* 40, 247-53

——, 1979. 'The Bishop of Winchester's medieval manor house at Harwell, Berkshire, and its relevance in the evolution of timber-framed aisled halls', *Archaeol. J.,* 136, 173-92

——, 1990. *Sutton Courtenay. The History of a Thames-side Village,* Sutton Courtenay

FOX, SIR C. 1947. *The Personality of Britain its Influence on Inhabitant and Invader in Prehistoric and Early Historic Times* (4th edn.), Cardiff

GRAY, H.L. 1915. *English Field Systems,* Cambridge Mass.

GRAY, P. 1990. 'Dating Wealden buildings', in Warren 1990, 47-60

HALLAM, H.E. (ed.) 1988. *The Agrarian History of England and Wales II: 1042-1350,* Cambridge

HARVEY, P.D.A. 1965. *A Medieval Oxfordshire Village: Cuxham 1240 to 1400,* Oxford

HEWETT, C.A. 1969. *The Development of Carpentry 1200-1700: An Essex Study,* Newton Abbot

——, 1973. 'The development of the post-medieval house', *Post-Medieval Archaeol.,* 7, 60-78.

——, 1976. 'Aisled timber halls and related buildings, chiefly in Essex', *Trans. Ancient Monuments Soc.,* 21, 45-99

——, 1980. *English Historic Carpentry,* Chichester

HORN, W. and BORN, E. 1965. *The Barns of the Abbey of Beaulieu at it Granges of Great Coxwell and Beaulieu St Leonards,* Berkeley, California

HURST, J.G. 1988. 'Rural building in England and Wales: England' in Hallam 1988, 854-930

LE PATOUREL, H. E. J. 1991. 'Rural building in England and Wales: England' in Miller 1991, 820-89

LEWIS, E., ROBERTS, E. and ROBERTS, K. 1988. *Medieval Hall Houses of the Winchester Area,* Winchester

LLOYD, N. 1931. *History of the English House* (repr. 1975), London

MACHIN, R. 1977. 'The great rebuilding: a reassessment', *Past and Present,* 77, 33-56

MERCER, E. 1975. *English Vernacular Houses,* London

MILLER, E. (ed.) 1991. *The Agrarian History of England and Wales III: 1348-1500,* Cambridge

MORREY, M.C.J., and SMITH, J.T. 1973. 'The Great Barn' Lewknor: the architectural evidence', *Oxoniensia,* 38, 339-45

MUNBY, J.T. 1985. 'Thirteenth-century carpentry in Chichester', *Archaeol. J.,* 142, 13-17

——, 1987. *St Mary's Hospital Chichester: A Short History and Guide,* Chichester

——, 1991. 'Wood' in Blair and Ramsay (eds.) 1991, 379-405

MUNBY, J.T., SPARKS, M., and TATTON-BROWN, · T. 1983. 'Crown-post and king-strut roofs in south-east England', *Medieval Archaeol.,* 27, 123-35

PALMER, A. 1990. 'Land tenure and medieval housing in the western Weald' in Warren 1990, 61-71

PARSONS, D. 1991. 'Stone' in Blair and Ramsay (eds.) 1991, 1-27

PEARSON, S. *et al.* 1988-91. 'Nottingham University tree-ring dating laboratory results: Kent', *Vernacular Architecture,* 19-22, lists 28, 30, 34 and 40

QUENEDEY, R. 1926. *L'Habitation Rouennaise,* repr. Monfort, Saint-Pierre-de-Salerne

RACKHAM, O. 1972. 'Grundle House: the quantities of timber in certain East Anglian buildings in relation to local supplies', *Vernacular Architecture,* 3, 3-7

——, 1980. *Ancient Woodland: Its History, Vegetation and Uses in England,* London

——, 1986. *The History of the Countryside,* London

RIGOLD, S.E. 1963. 'The distribution of Wealden Houses' in *Culture and Environment: Essays in Honour of Sir Cyril Fox,* (eds. I. Ll. Foster and L. Alcock), 351-4, London

RUSSELL, J.C. 1972. *Medieval Regions and their Cities,* Newton Abbot

SANDALL K. 1986. 'Aisled halls in England and Wales', *Vernacular Architecture,* 17, 21-35

SMITH, J.T. 1955. 'Medieval aisled halls and their derivatives', *Archaeol. J.,* 112, 76-94

——, 1958. 'Medieval roofs: a classification', *Archaeol. J.,* 115, 111-49

——, 1966. 'Timber-framed building in England: its development and regional differences', *Archaeol. J.,* 122, 133-58

——, 1970. 'The reliability of typological dating of medieval English roofs' in *Scientific Methods in Medieval Archaeology* (ed. R. Berger), 239-69, Berkeley, California

——, 1974. 'The early development of timber

buildings: the passing-brace and reversed assembly', *Archaeol. J.*, 131, 238-63

SMITH, P. 1975. *Houses of the Welsh Countryside,* London

THIRSK, J. (ed.) 1967. *The Agrarian History of England and Wales IV: 1500-1640,* Cambridge

THORNES, R. and FRADGLEY, N. 1988. 'Upton Court, Slough: an early fourteenth-century open hall', *Archaeol. J.*, 145, 211-21

WALKER, J. 1987. 'Wynter's Armourie: a base-cruck hall in Essex and its significance', *Vernacular Architecture*, 18, 25-33

WARREN, J. (ed.) 1990. *Wealden Buildings: Studies in the Timber-Framed Tradition of Building in Kent, Sussex and Surrey,* Wealden Buildings Study Group, Horsham

WITNEY, K.P. 1976. *The Jutish Forest: A Study of the Weald of Kent from 450 to 1380 AD,* London

WOOD, M. 1965. *The English Mediaeval House,* London

De la Motte au Château de Pierre dans le Nord-Ouest de la France

Joseph Decaëns

Ce sujet est d'abord à limiter dans le temps. Je me bornerai à cette période, le XIe et le XIIe siècles, où l'on a vu, comme on disait autrefois, 'la France se hérisser de châteaux',[1] la période par excellence de l'innovation, de l'invention et du développement extraordinaire en matière de constructions castrales.

Le titre donné à cet exposé pourrait aussi être trompeur. Il ne faut pas donner l'impression que l'on va décrire une évolution qui conduirait progressivement, pendant ces deux siècles, du château de terre et de charpente au château de pierre. S'il y a parfois continuité sur le même site, il n'y a pas de filiation de l'une à l'autre forme de château. Dès le début du XIe siècle, il y a co-existence de la construction en terre et de la construction en pierre pour l'édification des châteaux. On peut seulement dire qu'au XIe siècle, il y a certainement prédominance des châteaux de terre et de bois, qu'au XIIIe siècle, à l'inverse, la pierre paraît l'avoir emporté et qu'au XIIe siècle, on peut observer une transition au cours de laquelle les proportions premières vont s'inverser.

Il faut dire encore que ce titre est trop ambitieux vu l'état de la recherche dans ce domaine, recherche encore trop ponctuelle: la recherche historique portant sur les textes avait paru s'épuiser sur des exemples peu nombreux et surtout souvent peu explicites (description de la motte de Merkhem,[2] du donjon en bois d'Ardres,[3] de la motte d'Annebec,[4] etc.), mais elle a trouvé, semble-t-il, un nouveau souffle grâce à la linguistique, à l'étude du vocabulaire des auteurs de chroniques, étude rendue plus efficace grâce à l'ordinateur, grâce à une nouvelle approche des textes et en tenant compte des découvertes de l'archéologie; la recherche archéologique dont les résultats seront exposés plus loin, n'est pas parvenue encore à donner un nombre d'exemples suffisants pour être significatifs. Les fouilles de châteaux longues et coûteuses (au minimum trois ou quatre années pour explorer un château à motte de taille moyenne) sont finalement trop peu nombreuses dans le nord-ouest de la France pour qu'une synthèse puisse être valablement tentée. On essaiera donc seulement de faire le point de la question.

Il y a seulement une trentaine d'années en France, la thèse 'légaliste' triomphait.[5] La plupart des historiens, à la suite des historiens des institutions, ne voyaient que très peu de châteaux au XIe siècle, quelques châteaux dépendant tous de la puissance publique, rois ou comtes, ou construits avec l'autorisation de la puissance publique. C'est ainsi que le professeur Yver enseignait à Caen, en 1955, qu'il y avait au XIe siècle, seulement une dizaine de châteaux en Normandie, tous d'origine publique.[6] A peu près au même moment Georges Duby décrivait ainsi la vie de la petite aristocratie rurale: 'A Germolles, la maison qu'habite Guigonnet, l'un des membres de la famille noble, n'est pas une 'tour', car le simple chevalier du XIIe siècle n'a pas de château, ni même de maison-forte; [sa maison] est un centre de travail agricole, peuplé de serviteurs et de servantes, garni du bétail nécessaire au labour et qui abrite le vin et le blé récoltés dans l'année'.[7] Dix ans plus tard, G. Duby complète le tableau, la maison de ces seigneurs de seconde zone, 'ce n'était pas une forteresse, mais un centre d'exploitation agricole, plein de valets et de bestiaux'.[8]

Aujourd'hui, grâce à l'archéologie médiévale, le tableau a bien changé: à la suite des recherches entreprises dans plusieurs régions, notamment en Normandie, sous l'impulsion de Michel de Bɔüard, mais aussi en Flandre, en Champagne, en Lorraine, en Ile-de-France, en Anjou, en Bretagne, des inventaires sont dressés qui font apparaître un nombre de châteaux beaucoup plus important qu'on ne le soupçonnait, en tenant compte, naturellement, des mottes et des enceintes. Il faudrait cependant pouvoir dater tous ces châteaux, afin de situer leur construction dans un cadre historique correct: peu à peu, les fouilles permettent de le faire. Plusieurs périodes apparaissent suivant les régions: la première moitié du XIe siècle, la fin du XIe siècle et le début du XIIe siècle. Les historiens prennent en compte ces recherches. Le plus illustre d'entre eux, Georges Duby, fait ainsi, en 1988, l'éloge de l'archéologie médiévale et revient sur son opinion antérieure concernant les châteaux: 'Ses progrès [ceux de l'archéologie médiévale] depuis une vingtaine d'années sont fulgurants. Ce qu'elle met au jour complète heureusement l'enseignement des textes. Souvent aussi ces documents irrécusables que sont les objets de fouille contredisent ce que la recherche historique croyait fermement établi sur le témoignage des sources écrites. Ainsi, par exemple, à propos de l'aristocratie militaire qui établit sa domination sur le peuple aux environs de l'An Mil: l'archéologie d'une part découvre un semis de points fortifiés beaucoup plus serré qu'on ne croyait; elle montre d'autre part en très étroite cohabitation ces deux groupes sociaux, celui des hommes de guerre, celui des hommes de peine, que les idéologues de ce temps désignent comme nettement séparés.'[9]

Ce changement concernant la recherche historique sur les châteaux: nous le devons, en France, à l'effort continu de Michel de Boüard. A partir des années 1955–60, tirant la leçon des résultats obtenus en Angleterre (fouilles de B. Hope-Taylor à Abinger)[10] et en Allemagne (fouille d'A. Herrnbrodt au Husterknupp),[11] M. de Boüard lance la recherche archéologique francaise dans cette double direction: les ouvrages de terre et de charpente et les châteaux de pierre (fouilles du Hague-Dike en 1951–3[12] et début des fouilles du château de Caen en 1955[13]).

En 1962, pour bien illustrer les buts qu'il entend poursuivre, il organise aux Andelys (Eure), au pied de la célèbre forteresse de Richard Coeur de Lion, un colloque international sur les châteaux qui devient le premier colloque du Château-Gaillard.[14] Depuis, tous les deux ans, dans un pays européen, les spécialistes de la castellologie se retrouvent toujours avec le même succès comme au mois d'Août 1990, en Allemagne, à Schwäbisch Hall.

En France, c'est donc à Michel de Boüard que nous devons le renouveau de nos études sur les châteaux. Les recherches dont je vais rendre compte sont le résultat direct de son oeuvre ou de son influence.

Concernant les ouvrages de terre, il faut distinguer les enceintes et les mottes. L'enceinte, caractérisée par son rempart de plan circulaire ou ovalaire est une forme de fortification qui remonte au moins à la protohistoire où elle est connue comme habitat ou comme refuge pour des tribus ou de petits groupes humains. On utilisa, ou réutilisa, pendant le haut Moyen Age, des grandes enceintes de ce type, ceinturées de hauts remparts de terre, complétés par des palissades de bois. Parfois la forteresse épousait une forme naturelle facile à défendre et à fortifier comme une colline en forme d'éperon que l'on isolait par un fossé et un rempart. Parfois, c'est l'eau ou le marécage qui procurait une défense efficace. Les derniers rois carolingiens, contraints à la défensive par le danger des incursions vikings ou hongroises ont construit de telles forteresses le long des fleuves et des grands axes de communication (Pîtres, Pontoise, Etrun), le long de la mer du Nord, en Flandre (*Castella recens facta*) où le long des frontières.[15]

L'enceinte de Fécamp (Seine-Maritime), au temps des premiers ducs de Normandie, Guillaume Longue Epée, Richard I, Richard II (Xe siècle) qui en avaient fait une de leur résidence favorite, était encore de ce type. Annie Renoux nous la montre couvrant onze hectares et cernée d'un rempart de terre: à l'intérieur, on trouvait une résidence de campagne avec un bâtiment en silex et une cuisine dont les murs étaient en charpente de bois.[16] Pourrait aussi être classé dans cette catégorie, bien qu'il n'ait pas comporté de structures en terre, le château de Caen (5ha), voulu par Guillaume le Bâtard, au milieu du XIe siècle, est un immense éperon séparé du plateau par un fossé large et profond (fig. 1).

1. *Château de Caen (Calvados): vue aérienne*

Ce sont surtout les enceintes de petites ou de moyennes dimensions qui m'intéressent ici. Au premier abord, elles peuvent paraître comme des ouvrages en réduction par rapport aux grandes enceintes. Mais leurs dimensions plus réduites montrent à l'évidence que leur destination est différente. L'aspect individuel l'emporte ici visiblement sur l'aspect collectif.

Notre équipe de recherche (le Centre de Recherches archéologiques médiévales [C.R.A.M.] de Caen) a étudié et fouillé une dizaine de ces enceintes. Leur diamètre est compris entre 50m et 100m, les remparts élevés (entre 5m et 10m), les fossés profonds. Presque toutes sont munies de grandes basses-cours comportant des bâtiments résidentiels ou agricoles, souvent une chapelle. Ces enceintes sont des châteaux au même titre que les mottes. On peut même dire qu'il s'agit très probablement de l'ancêtre ou de l'archétype du château à motte. Cette thèse défendue par Brian K. Davison[17] et reprise par Jacques Le Maho[18] peut être admise, au moins comme une bonne hypothèse de travail. Plusieurs de ces enceintes fúrent, dans les premières décennies du XIe siècle, les centres de grandes seigneuries ou d'honneurs, comme on disait en Normandie. Par exemple, le château primitif des Talbot (importante famille de l'époque ducale en Normandie) à Sainte-Croix-sur-Buchy (Seine-Maritime) est une enceinte de terre; elle a été fouillée, il y a plus de vingt-cinq ans, par l'archéologue suédois Holger Arbman et datée par lui de la première moitié du XIe siècle.[19]

A Fécamp, le nouveau château de Richard II (début XIe siècle) est encore une enceinte dont la surface a été réduite (2ha). Son rempart est renforcé par un mur en pierre dont la base à arcades est noyée dans la masse de terre. Une tour carrée (8m de côté) est liée à ce mur et appartient au dispositif de défense. Contre ce rempart, un véritable palais a été construit comprenant une immense *aula*. Ce palais, centre politique, économique et religieux, est nettement séparé d'une vaste basse-cour.[20]

Le Plessis-Grimoult (Calvados), situé à environ 40km au sud-ouest de Caen, a été fouillé par Elisabeth Zadora-Rio. L'enceinte de terre a été plusieurs fois remaniée, au cours de la première moitié du XIe siècle. Elle fut abandonnée par son seigneur, Grimoult, en 1047, date à laquelle il fut battu sur le champ de bataille du Val-ès-Dunes par le jeune Guillaume le Bâtard qui le fit prisonnier et l'enferma dans une prison à Rouen où il mourut. L'enceinte qui comportait dans son dernier état, peu avant 1047, un mur de pierre planté au sommet du rempart de terre ne fut jamais réoccupée.[21]

A Notre-Dame-de-Gravenchon (Seine-Maritime), l'habitat seigneurial des comtes d'Evreux à La Fontaine-Saint-Denis comporte, au XIe siècle, des édifices en bois. La fouille de Jacques Le Maho a montré qu'il avait été transformé au XIIe siècle après un incendie et probablement fortifié par une enceinte de terre à la même époque.[22]

Enfin à Saint-Vaast-sur-Seulles (Calvados), j'ai fouillé au début des années 1980 une enceinte édifiée par les Taisson au XIIe siècle. L'ouvrage principal comprenait un habitat seigneurial construit en pierre, la vaste basse-cour contenait une chapelle, une grande salle des chevaliers et des bâtiments domestiques. Comme au Plessis-Grimoult, les remparts de terre étaient probablement surmontés d'une muraille en pierre (figs. 2 et 3).[23]

Cependant la fortification de terre la plus répandue et la plus originale au XIe et au XIIe siècles dans la France du nord-ouest est, sans conteste, la motte ou plutôt comme on disait déjà au Moyen Age le château à motte ('châtel sor motte', Roman de Renart XIIe siècle). Des centaines d'exemplaires, peut-être des milliers d'exemplaires ont été dénombrés, des inventaires régionaux ont été réalisés dans le Nord (Flandre), en Champagne, en Normandie, en Bretagne. On a même commencé à s'intéresser aux mottes construites par les Normands en Italie du sud (San Marco Argentano, XIe siècle).

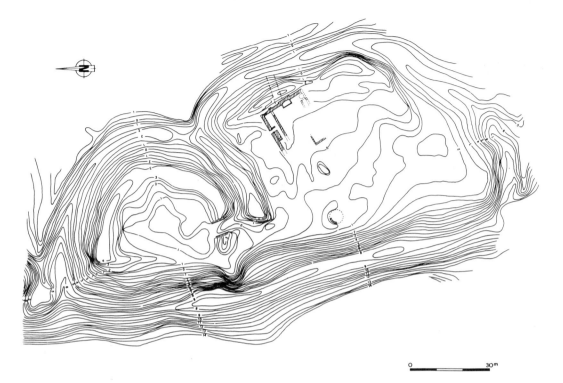

2. *Saint-Vaast-sur-Seulles (Calvados): plan de l'enceinte et de sa basse-cour*

3. *Saint-Vaast-sur-Seulles (Calvados): le rempart de l'enceinte vu du fossé de la basse-cour*

On discute toujours des origines de la motte, de sa forme caractéristique, celle d'un tronc de cône fait de terre artificiellement accumulée. L'hypothèse la plus simple et sans doute la plus exacte est celle qui fait sortir la motte de l'enceinte circulaire. Celle-ci est, on le sait, un rempart de terre annulaire fait à partir du creusement d'un fossé. Pour construire une motte, il suffit de combler la dépression centrale d'une enceinte circulaire. L'idée inventive pourrait être venue, soit d'une volonté consciente d'édifier un tertre élevé, bien fait pour observer un vaste territoire et plus facile à défendre, soit, par hasard en surhaussant, de façon exagérée, les remparts d'une enceinte de faible diamètre, la surface intérieure de l'enceinte se trouvant ainsi trop encombrée, il n'y avait plus qu'à compléter le comblement pour obtenir la motte. Cela n'est d'ailleurs pas une pure hypothèse, nous avons observé plusieurs mottes qui ont connu un stade préalable sous la forme d'une enceinte.

Beaucoup de mottes ne sont pas entièrement artificielles. On a souvent utilisé d'abord une butte naturelle ou une émergence rocheuse. La construction artificielle, dans ce cas, ne concerne que le sommet de la motte. Les mottes sont régulièrement flanquées d'une ou plusieurs basses-cours. On retrouve là la disposition binaire si caractéristique de ces types d'habitat qui ont été le siège d'une autorité: motte et basse-cour, *motte and bailey*.

Les fouilles récentes ont bien montré le caractère à la fois militaire et résidentiel du château à motte (on vient de voir qu'il en est de même pour l'enceinte castrale). Une tour de bois s'élevait sur la motte: elle pouvait être résidence seigneuriale ou simple poste de guet. La basse-cour abritait des bâtiments à usage domestique, agricole ou artisanal. La plupart du temps, on trouvait aussi dans la basse-cour une salle *(aula)*, une chapelle *(capella)* et des appartements et services privés *(camera)*, c'est-à-dire les trois éléments essentiels qui étaient déjà ceux des palais antérieurs ou contemporains. Le château à motte est bien un château de plein exercice, le centre politique, social et économique d'une seigneurie qu'on appellera justement châtelaine, selon la terminologie proposée par Georges Duby.

En France, l'existence des mottes est solidement attestée par les textes dès les années 1020–40 dans la région de la Loire moyenne, vers 1050 en Normandie, ensuite les mentions de mottes deviennent très fréquentes pour tout le nord-ouest de la France, entre la Loire et le Rhin. L'un des apports essentiels de l'archéologie récente est d'avoir montré que de nombreuses mottes ont été utilisées avant le milieu du XIe siècle, par exemple la motte de Grimbosq (Calvados).

La motte d'Olivet à Grimbosq est perchée sur un éperon formé par la convergence de deux petites vallées étroites et profondes où coulent des ruisseaux affluents de l'Orne. La motte occupe une position centrale, elle est encadrée par deux basses-cours, l'une, au nord de la motte, à l'extrémité de l'éperon, l'autre au sud, du côté du plateau d'où sort cet éperon. Les fouilles archéologiques ont été effectuées de 1974 à 1978 et publiées en 1981 (figs. 4 et 5). [24]

Dans la basse-cour nord, on a découvert un grand bâtiment d'habitation, probablement à deux niveaux, la salle *(aula)* étant à l'étage, l'ensemble divisé en trois nefs par deux rangées de poteaux, une chapelle, une cuisine isolée sans doute par crainte du feu. Tous ces éléments étaient en charpente de bois reposant sur des solins de pierres sèches; ils étaient tous couverts en chaume. Un petit bâtiment rectangulaire donnait accès à une passerelle permettant de rejoindre le sommet de la motte où se trouvait une tour de bois, simple poste d'observation ou de guet rappelant la reconstitution de B. Hope-Taylor à Abinger. La basse-cour sud était un enclos à chevaux où ont été mis au jour quantité de fers à cheval, des pièces de harnais en fer ou en bronze, des éperons: il y avait là une écurie et une petite forge. La présence du cheval et de certains objets comme des pièces de jeux (pions de tric-trac) et

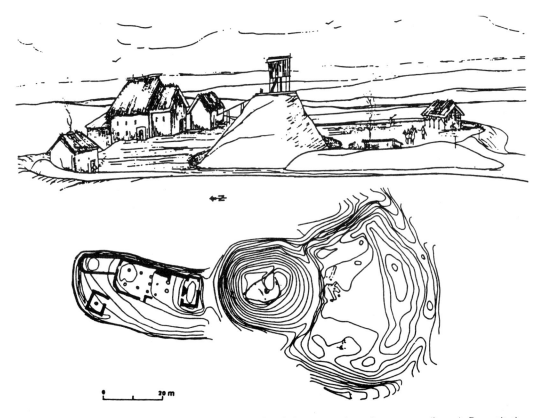

4. *Grimbosq (Calvados): la Motte d'Olivet:* (upper) *Plan de la motte et de ses basses-cours;* (lower) *Reconstitution des bâtiments*

5. *Grimbosq (Calvados): la Motte d'Olivet*

des bijoux (pendentif) renforcent l'impression de résidence aristocratique. Les découvertes archéologiques permettent d'évoquer la vie de ce château, le va-et-vient des cavaliers qui ont laissé tant de traces de leur passage, ces *milites castri* dont la rudesse guerrière va bien avec ce château aux installations très primitives. L'analyse des pollens conservés dans les couches archéologiques a montré que l'implantation de ce château d'Olivet dans la forêt de Grimbosq s'est accompagné d'une tentative de défrichement. L'existence très courte de ce château (1030–50) est à placer dans le contexte des rivalités familiales entre les branches aînée et cadette de la famille Taisson.

A Douai (Nord), au lieu-dit La Neuve-Tour, malgré les difficultés d'une fouille urbaine, Pierre Demolon a réussi à nous faire suivre le développement de la résidence des comtes de Flandre (X[e] au XIIIe siècle).[25] Sur un site habité depuis l'époque mérovingienne s'urbanisant peu à peu à l'époque carolingienne en s'entourant notamment d'un rempart de terre et de bois, le comte Arnoul I construit, vers 945, une résidence en bois non fortifiée. Sur cet emplacement, vers 965, le roi Lothaire qui s'est emparé de Douai, construit un vaste bâtiment en bois (entre 13m et 14m x 4.50m) qui est emmotté sur trois côtés, le tout entouré de fossés. Pendant ce temps, le rempart de ville est reconstruit en pierre. Vers 987, Douai est revenue au comte de Flandre: le bâtiment de Lothaire sert de soubassement à un petit donjon de bois (4m à 5m de côté). La motte est rehaussée. A la fin du XIIe siècle, la pierre remplace enfin le bois. La motte est encore rehaussée et cernée d'un mur-chemise. Sur la plate-forme de la motte s'élève un donjon quadrangulaire (entre 18m et 19m de côté) murs en grès épais de quatre mètres.

A Hordain (Nord), Etienne Louis suppose que la motte devait porter une tour de résidence en bois détruite par un donjon circulaire en pierre du XIIIe siècle car il n'a trouvé dans la basse-cour que des bâtiments en bois très rustiques qui se sont succédé pendant trois siècles (XIIe au XVe siècle). Au XIIe siècle, le bâtiment en bois semble une maison paysanne mixte divisée en deux parties: d'un côté, l'habitation, de l'autre, l'étable, et accompagnée de petites constructions annexes, des greniers, poulaillers, etc.[26]

Le château des comtes de Champagne, Montfélix, à Chavot (Marne) comporte un éperon puissamment défendu par un rempart de barrage en terre et une motte. Mais les bâtiments résidentiels du XIe (avec une cheminée) et du XIIe siècles mis au jour par Annie Renoux sont en pierre.[27]

A la Chapelle du Pin, près de Grosley-sur-Risle (Eure), Pierre Lemaître a mis au jour un ensemble composé d'une résidence seigneuriale des XIe et XIIe siècles, abandonnée au XIIIe siècle et d'un village qui n'a été déserté qu'au XVIe siècle. Les seigneurs du Pin, dépendants de la grande famille normande des Beaumont, ont fait construire, sur le rebord du plateau qui domine la vallée de la Risle, une motte ou une enceinte étroite surmontée d'un *shell-keep* en pierre de plan polygonal. La basse-cour présente un tracé trapézoïdal qui est un mur maçonné (épaisseur environ 2m) fait de silex et de pierres calcaires (fig. 6).[28]

A Rivray (Orne), le château qui fait l'objet de mes recherches actuelles est une motte construite au XIe siècle par un seigneur qui est dans l'orbite des seigneurs de Nogent, futurs comtes du Perche. Au XIIe siècle la motte a reçu un donjon de pierre de plan carré. C'était un bâtiment résidentiel comme l'ont montré les nombreux objets mis au jour (tessons de poterie, clés, monnaies, pièces de jeu) et les déchets de cuisine. A la même époque dans la basse-cour, au pied de la motte, une grande et belle chapelle était élevée dont il reste un choeur surélevé sur une crypte (fig. 7).[29]

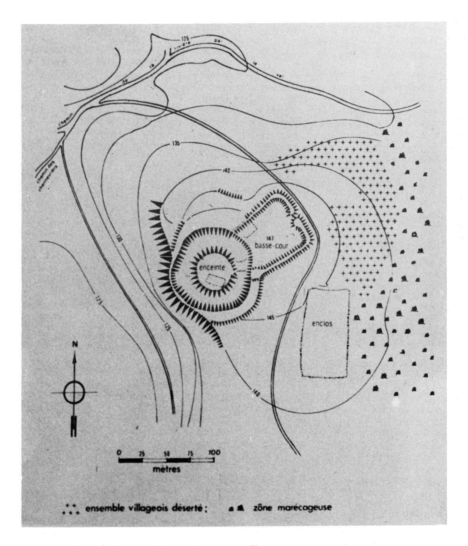

6. *Grosley (Eure). Plan:* shell-keep, *basse-cour, village*

A Mirville (Seine-Maritime), une fouille très complexe conduite par Jacques Le Maho·
a montré les états successifs d'un habitat seigneurial appartenant à un petit lignage dépendant
des seigneurs de Tancarville. On passe, au cours du XIe siècle, d'un simple enclos palissadé
à une petite enceinte de terre et de bois entourée d'un fossé. La motte qui recouvrira
l'ensemble ne sera construite qu'à l'extrême fin du XIe siècle. L'habitation seigneuriale
sera reconstruite à chaque étape. Il n'y a pas de construction en pierre avant le manoir
du XVIe siècle. [30]

On l'a dit en commençant, dès le début de la période qui nous retient ici, dès le XIe
siècle, la pierre est présente dans la construction militaire. C'est, il est vrai, surtout le cas
des palais fortifiés: à Rouen, à Ivry s'élèvent des grosses tours de pierre *(domus lapidea)*,

7. *Condé-sur-Huisne (Orne): la Motte de Rivray*

à Fécamp, à Caen, ce sont les remparts qui sont en pierre. Dans ces palais existent aussi des grandes salles d'apparat, des chapelles, et même des bâtiments annexes qui sont en maçonnerie. A partir des premières années du XIIᵉ siècle, la pierre tend à remplacer le bois. Des donjons carrés s'élèvent sur les mottes, nous l'avons noté, des remparts de pierre remplacent parfois les palissades au sommet des talus de terre. Cependant le bois se maintient vigoureusement dans certains sites sans qu'on sache vraiment pourquoi, ces régions n'étant pas particulièrement riches en forêts. Le donjon en bois d'Ardres, si merveilleusement décrit par Lambert est fait à l'imitation des donjons de pierre, jusque dans les détails.[31] Il semble curieusement décrire le double donjon en pierre de Falaise (XIIᵉ siècle).

Entre les châteaux de terre et de charpente et les forteresses de pierre, il n'y a pas de différence de fonction. Le rôle des uns et des autres est tout à fait comparable. La plupart du temps, il y a seulement une différence de niveau social entre les constructeurs. Un prince ou un grand seigneur dispose de ressources notamment monétaires qui lui permettent de construire en pierre, alors qu'un seigneur de village doit réquisitionner les paysans de son district pour élever sa motte et construire sa tour de bois, il lui est impossible de payer en numéraire les maçons-itinérants qui n'acceptent que ce mode de rémunération.

Sans qu'on puisse parler de filiation entre les châteaux de terre et de bois et les châteaux de terre, il y a au moins parallélisme des formes et de la destination. Dans l'étude des châteaux de pierre, on distingue au moins au XIᵉ siècle les enceintes maçonnées sans donjon et les châteaux à donjon. Ne retrouve-t-on pas ici une distinction qui rappelle celle des ouvrages de terre: enceintes, d'un côté, et château à motte, de l'autre.

Les fouilles du château de Caen dirigées pendant dix ans par M. de Boüard fournissent un bon exemple d'enceinte sans donjon (XIe siècle). On a une immense enceinte (environ 5ha) couvrant un vaste éperon séparé du plateau par un fossé profond. L'aspect militaire tient à ce fossé, aux bords abrupts de la colline, à la muraille en pierre élevée dès la fin du règne de Guillaume-le-Conquérant et surtout à la porte fortifiée qui, au nord, commande l'accès. L'aspect résidentiel, c'est le palais composé d'une *aula,* d'une *capella,* d'une *camera.* A part les dimensions et le matériau, ce sont les dispositions du petit château seigneurial de Grimbosq. A Caen, un village avec son église paroissiale complète cet habitat. Au XIIe siècle, Henri I Beauclerc construit un donjon et une nouvelle *aula* plus vaste (salle dite de l'Echiquier). En 1204 Philippe Auguste entourera le donjon d'une chemise cantonnée de quatre tours rondes. L'accès au nord sera alors remplacé par la Porte des Champs située au nord-est de l'enceinte (fig. 8).[32]

Cependant la découverte archéologique la plus extraordinaire qu'il nous a été donné de faire, toujours sous la direction de M. de Boüard, est certainement celle du grand bâtiment de Doué-la-Fontaine (Maine-et-Loire) en Anjou.[33] Ce bâtiment (23.50m x 16.50m) en pierre était enfoui dans une motte. Tout laissait penser qu'il s'agissait d'une résidence ouverte n'ayant pas de caractère militaire: elle ne comportait qu'un rez-de-chaussée où l'on pénétrait par deux portes, des fenêtres s'ouvraient dans les murs pignons, les murs étaient peu épais (1.70m). Un mur de refend divisait l'intérieur en deux parties: l'une, plus petite, était une cuisine avec une cheminée adossée au mur de refend, l'autre, plus vaste, était une *aula* dont la fonction résidentielle ne faisait pas de doute: céramique, verrerie, silos-greniers, déchets alimentaires dont une arête d'esturgeon. Ce bâtiment, construit à la fin du IXe siècle appartenait à un palais dont l'origine remontait aux rois d'Aquitaine, héritiers de la couronne carolingienne. Ce bâtiment fut incendié au milieu du Xe siècle (datation par mesure du magnétisme thermorémanent). Michel de Boüard a placé cet incendie dans le cardre des luttes guerrières qui opposèrent longtemps, au Xe siècle, dans cette partie de la vallée de la Loire, les comtes d'Anjou et ceux de Blois. La preuve du caractère belliqueux de cette destruction par le feu est démontrée par l'obturation immédiate des portes et des fenêtres et par la surélévation des murs. Bref le bâtiment devient un donjon fermé au rez-de-chaussée; deux nouvelles portes seront ménagées à cinq mètres de hauteur. L'accès se fera désormais par une passerelle de bois (figs. 9 et 10).

Cette transformation de l'*aula* en donjon est peut-être à l'origine de l'invention du donjon rectangulaire. On a démontré récemment que le donjon de Langeais qui passe pour le plus ancien de France (994) a subi une évolution comparable.[34]

L'*aula*-donjon de Doué-la-Fontaine, enfoui dans une motte au début du XIe siècle, devient le château d'un petit seigneur local. Peut-être utilisait-il le haut des murs émergeant de la motte comme une palissade en pierre?

CONCLUSION

Mottes et enceintes construites en terre et en bois ou forteresses de pierre sont des châteaux, c'est-à-dire à la fois, des ouvrages militaires, des résidences aristocratiques, le centre économique et politique des seigneuries, le symbole de l'autorité seigneuriale. Il est possible cependant de distinguer dans cet ensemble si important en nombre de sites variés, deux sortes de châteaux ou plutôt trois sortes car la seconde catégorie doit elle-même se diviser en deux.

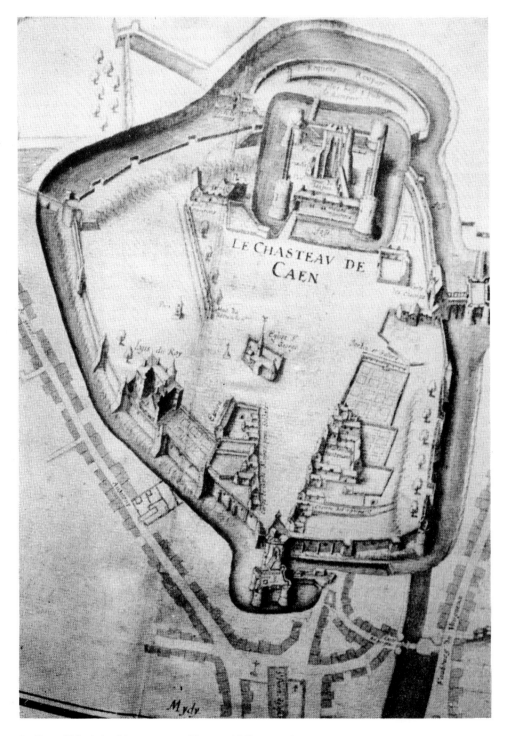

8. *Caen (Calvados): château, vue cavalière vers 1640*

9. *Doué-la-Fontaine (Maine-et-Loire): sommet de la motte*

10. *Doué-la-Fontaine (Maine-et-Loire): mur ouest du bâtiment vu de l'intérieur*

Il y a des châteaux dont l'aspect militaire paraît l'emporter sur toute autre considération. Il s'agit surtout de mottes ou d'enceintes, isolées par rapport à l'habitat, implantées sur des sites de hauteur d'où la vue est très étendue, au-dessus de larges vallées ou de vastes plaines. La destination stratégique de ces sites est évidente. On a cherché, à partir de là, la protection des voies de passage ou d'accès ou la protection de frontières. Certains de ces châteaux trouvent leur origine dans une guerre de conquête où ils marquaient la prise de possession progressive du terrain.

D'autres châteaux ont une fonction politique, économique et sociale primordiale et l'aspect militaire n'est là que pour imposer le but essentiel recherché. Ils sont aujourd'hui encore au centre d'un village ou au coeur d'une petite ville. La construction de ces châteaux au XIe siècle (première moitié) paraît liée au développement économique et notamment à la croissance agricole dont les premiers germes sont apparus au cours du Xe siècle et dont les manifestations les plus visibles sont la naissance des marchés locaux et les grands défrichements. A partir de l'An Mil, on peut repérer, en différentes régions, une évolution du peuplement dans le sens de la concentration, renforcement des villages et renaissance des villes. Les aristocrates, maîtres du sol, ont voulu diriger à leur profit un tel mouvement démographique et une telle conjoncture économique favorable. La fondation de châtellenies rurales et la création de 'bourgs' ruraux, monastiques ou castraux répondent à cette intention. L'apparition de la seigneurie châtelaine a parfois modifié l'ordonnance des villages. Mais ce regroupement des maisons paysannes ou artisanales régulièrement disposées en rues ou en places (autour du marché) ne prouve pas que le village soit né au XIe siècle, comme on l'a dit récemment. Souvent il existait auparavant, sous une autre forme. D'ailleurs le château n'entraîne pas partout cette concentration ou celle-ci se produit à quelque distance du château comme si ce dernier avait joué plutôt un rôle de repoussoir. Combien de châteaux sans village groupé! Quant aux bourgs castraux, ce sont des habitats nouveaux à vocation urbaine qui, eux aussi, se développent à partir de noyaux plus anciens. La présence du château peut là aussi jouer en sens contraires: elle peut assurer une meilleure sécurité, mais elle peut aussi faire sentir la contrainte. On y a sans doute attiré les 'bourgeois' par la promesse de tenures fiscalement moins lourdes. Quand ils n'existent pas déjà, des marchés y sont créés à l'initiative seigneuriale. Bref le seigneur châtelain fait tout pour entraîner le processus de formation urbaine et la plupart du temps, il y réussit. Les bourgs castraux sont à l'origine du développement de la plupart des petites villes ou des villes moyennes dans le nord-ouest de la France : beaucoup de nos chefs-lieux de canton ou même de chefs-lieux de département: Caen, Alençon, Laval sont des bourgs castraux. Il est probable que des noyaux préurbains existaient avant l'implantation des châteaux (dédicaces des églises à saint Martin, saint Germain ou autres dédicaces remontant au haut Moyen Age, présence de cimetière mérovingien attestent occupation ancienne) de même que certains marchés ou même certains bourgs : le marché et le bourg de Caen sont signalés dans des actes de 1024 et 1025 alors que l'archéologie a montré que le château n'apparaît qu'après la crise de 1047 vers 1050-60. Les châteaux et la fondation d'églises (prieurés ou collégiales) ont seulement donné un coup de fouet à un mouvement de développement déjà bien amorcé. L'imitation de ce qui réussit aura entraîné la multiplication des bourgs castraux. Ainsi les seigneurs ont-ils vu assez rapidement, au cours du XIe siècle, tout le parti qu'ils pouvaient tirer de la croissance agricole et du développement urbain. Ils ont donc cherché à se les approprier, à faire main basse sur cette économie renaissante. Le château fut l'instrument de cet établissement de l'ordre seigneurial.

RÉSUMÉ

DE LA MOTTE AU CHÂTEAU DE PIERRE DANS LE NORD-OUEST DE LA FRANCE

Les mottes et les enceintes construites en terre et en bois ou les châteaux de pierre sont à la fois des constructions militaires et des résidences aristocratiques aussi bien que les centres économiques et politiques de la seigneurie, symboles de l'autorité châtelaine. L'examen d'un grand nombre de sites permet de distinguer plusieurs types: certaines places-fortes ont avant tout une fonction militaire et leur importance stratégique est claire; d'autres ont d'abord une fonction politique, économique et sociale, à laquelle l'aspect militaire est subordonné; enfin, la troisième catégorie est celle des châteaux associés à une ville et au développement d'un marché et du commerce.

A partir du début du XIe siècle, terre et pierre sont toutes deux utilisées pour la construction de châteaux mais les ouvrages en terre sont les plus nombreux à cette date précoce. Le XIIe siècle vit la transition progressive qui aboutit à la prépondérance des châteaux en pierre au XIIIe siècle, même si les fortifications en terre continuèrent d'exister. Entre ces deux groupes, il n'existe pas de différence de fonction mais dans la plupart des cas ils expriment la différence de rang social de leurs constructeurs.

Les textes attestent avec certitude l'existence de mottes dans la vallée de la Loire moyenne aux alentours de 1020–40 et en Normandie autour de 1050. Ensuite, leur mention devient très fréquente dans l'ensemble de la France du nord, de la Loire jusqu'au Rhin. On a récemment montré que de nombreuses mottes étaient en utilisation au milieu du XIe siècle.

Les mottes existent en grand nombre comme les enceintes, les premières probablement édifiées à l'origine par le remplissage d'enceintes plus petites. Beaucoup de mottes exploitent partiellement une éminence naturelle ou un affleurement rocheux. Une ou plusieurs basses-cours sont chose commune. Des fouilles récentes ont montré le caractère résidentiel et militaire du château à motte et basse-cour. Une tour en bois, qui pouvait être une résidence seigneuriale ou bien une simple tour de guet, se dressait sur la motte. La basse-cour accueillait les bâtiments domestiques et agricoles et les autres dépendances. Dans la plupart des cas, la salle (angl. *hall*), la chapelle et les appartements privés—les trois éléments essentiel des résidences aristocratiques de cette époque—sont aussi situés dans la basse-cour.

ABSTRACT

FROM THE MOTTE TO THE STONE-BUILT CASTLE IN NORTH-WEST FRANCE

Mottes and ringworks built of earth and wood, or castles constructed of stone, are at the same time military works and aristocratic residences as well as being the economic and political centres of a lordship, symbols of seigneurial authority. Examination of a very large number of sites permits a subdivision according to type: some strongholds have a military function above all other and their strategic importance is clear; others have primarily a political, economic and social function, to which the military aspect is subordinate; in a third category are those castles associated with a town and the development of a market and commerce.

From the beginning of the eleventh century earth and stone are both used as building materials for castles, but earth defences were in the majority at this early date. The twelfth century saw a gradual transition so that by the thirteenth century stone building were preponderant even though earth fortifications continued to exist. Between earth and stone castles there is no difference of function; in most cases they express only a difference in the social level of their builders.

Texts firmly attest the presence of mottes in the middle Loire valley by 1020–40 and in Normandy by *c.* 1050. Thereafter mention becomes very frequent in the whole of northern France from the Loire to the Rhine. It has recently been shown that many mottes were in use by the middle of the eleventh century.

Mottes are found in large numbers, so too are ringworks; the former probably originating by the infilling of smaller ringworks. Many mottes make partial use of a natural eminence or rocky outcrop. One or more baileys are usual. Recent excavations have shown the residential and military character of the motte-and-bailey castle. A wooden tower, which might be either a seigneurial residence or merely a simple look-out post, stood on the motte. The bailey housed the domestic, agricultural and other dependent buildings. In most cases a hall, chapel and the private apartments—the three essential elements of contemporary aristocratic houses—are located in the bailey.

NOTES

[1] Fliche 1930, 169.
[2] Gautier de Thérouanne, *Acta Sanctorum,* t. 3, 414-15; *Monumenta Germaniae Historica,* t. XV-2, 1146-7.
[3] Lambert d'Ardres, t. XXIV, 609-40.
[4] *Inventio et Miracula sancti Vulfranni,* 77, 67.
[5] Aubenas 1938, 561, 573 note 1, 578.
[6] Yver 1957, 28-115 et 604-9.
[7] Duby 1953, 425.
[8] Duby 1962, t. II, 400.
[9] Duby 1988, 15.
[10] Hope-Taylor 1950.
[11] Herrnbrodt 1958.
[12] De Boüard 1956.
[13] De Boüard 1979.
[14] *Château-Gaillard,* 1 (1964).
[15] Decaëns 1981a.
[16] Renoux 1991.

[17] Davison 1969.
[18] Le Maho 1976.
[19] Arbman 1966-8.
[20] Renoux 1991.
[21] Zadora-Rio 1973-4.
[22] Le Maho 1986; 1990b, 173-6 et 194-5.
[23] Burnouf et Decaëns 1985.
[24] Decaëns 1981b.
[25] Demolon et Louis 1982.
[26] Louis 1989.
[27] Renoux 1990.
[28] Lemaître 1990.
[29] Decaëns 1990a; 1990b.
[30] Le Maho 1984, 48; 1990a.
[31] Lambert d'Ardres, t. xxiv, 609-40.
[32] De Boüard 1979.
[33] De Boüard 1973-4.
[34] Deyres 1970; 1974.

BIBLIOGRAPHIE

ARBMAN, H. 1966-8. 'Fortifications autour de Buchy', *Meddelanden fran Lunds Universitets Historika Museum,* Lund

AUBENAS, R. 1938. 'Les châteaux forts des Xe et XIe siècles', *Revue historique de Droit français et étranger,* 62, 548-86

BOUARD, M. de. 1956. 'Le Hague-Dike', *Cahiers archéologiques,* 8, 117-45

——. 1973-4. 'De l'aula au donjon, les fouilles de la motte de la Chapelle à Doué-la-Fontaine (X^c-XIe siècles)', *Archéologie Médiévale,* 3-4, 5-110

——. 1979. *Le château de Caen,* Caen.

BURNOUF, J. et DECAENS, J. 1985. 'La fin du château de Saint-Vaast-sur-Seulles (Calvados)', *Château-Gaillard,* 12, 23-37

CHÂTEAU-GAILLARD, I, Etudes de castellologie européenne. 1964. Colloque des Andelys (1962), Caen

DAVISON, B. K. 1969. 'Early earthwork castles: a new model', *Château-Gaillard*, 3, London, 37-47

DECAENS, J. 1981a. 'Les enceintes circulaires médiévales', Colloque de Caen 1980, Les fortifications de terre en Europe occidentale du Xe au XIIe siècle, Thème II, *Archéologie Médiévale*, 11, 39-71

——. 1981b. 'La motte d'Olivet à Grimbosq (Calvados), Résidence seigneuriale du XIe siècle', *Archéologie Médiévale*, 11, 167-201

——. 1990a. 'La fouille de la motte de Rivray à Condé-sur-Huisne (Orne)', *Les Cahiers Percherons*, 3-20

——. 1990b. 'Fortifications et châteaux d'origine médiévale dans le département de l'Orne. Inventaire', *Empreintes, l'Orne archéologique*, 79-85, Alençon

DEMOLON, P., et LOUIS, E. 1982. *Douai, une ville face à son passé*, Douai

DEYRES, M. 1970. 'Le donjon de Langeais', *Bulletin Monumental*, 128, 179-93

——. 1974. 'Les châteaux de Foulques Nerra', *Bulletin Monumental*, 132, 7-28

DUBY, G. 1953. *La société aux XIe et XIIe siècles dans la région mâconnaise*, Paris

——. 1962. *L'économie rurale et la vie des campagnes dans l'Occident médiéval*, II, Paris

——. 1987. 'Le Moyen Age, 987-1460', *Histoire de France*, Paris

——. 1988. 'Préface' au Catalogue de l'Exposition: *Un village au temps de Charlemagne*, Paris

——. 1991. *L'Histoire continue*, Paris

FLICHE, A. 1930. 'L'Europe Occidentale de 888 à 1125', Collection Glotz, *Histoire Générale, Histoire du Moyen Age*, II, Paris

GAUTIER DE THEROUANNE, 'Vie de Jean, évêque de Thérouanne', *Acta Sanctorum*, janvier, III, Anvers-Bruxelles, 414-15; *Monumenta Germaniae Historica, Scriptores*. 1843-1940. XV-2, 1146-7, Munich

HERRNBRODT, A. 1958. *Der Husterknupp*, Köln-Graz

HOPE-TAYLOR, B. 1950. 'The excavation of a motte at Abinger in Surrey', *Archaeol. J.*, 107, 15-43 .

INVENTIO ET MIRACULA SANCTI VULFRANNI, ed. J. Laporte, Rouen, 1938

LAMBERT D'ARDRES 'Histoire des comtes de Guines et des seigneurs d'Ardres', *Monumenta Germaniae Historica, Scriptores*, 24, 609-40

LE MAHO, J. 1976. 'L'apparition des seigneuries châtelaines dans le Grand Caux à l'époque ducale', *Archéologie Médiévale*, 6, 5-148

——. 1984. *La motte seigneuriale de Mirville (XIe-XIIe siècles)*, Rouen

——. 1986. *Un domaine normand du Xe au XIIe siècle. Gravenchon, fief des comtes d'Evreux*, Rouen

——. 1990a. 'Mirville (Seine-Maritime)', *De la Gaule à la Normandie, 2000 ans d'histoire, 30 ans d'archéologie*, 169-72, Rouen

——. 1990b. 'Notre-Dame-de-Gravenchon (Seine-Maritime), La Fontaine-Saint-Denis. Enceinte fortifiée (XIIe-XIIIe s.)', *De la Gaule à la Normandie, 2000 ans d'histoire, 30 ans d'archéologie*, Rouen, 173-6 et 194-5

LEMAITRE, P. 1990. 'Grosley-sur-Risle (Eure), résidence seigneuriale fortifiée (XIe-XIIIe siècle)', *De la Gaule à la Normandie, 2000 ans d'histoire, 30 ans d'archéologie*, 134-7, Rouen

LOUIS, E. 1989. *Recherches sur le château à motte de Hordain (Nord)*, Archaeologia Duacensis, 2, Douai

RENOUX, A. 1990. 'Le château des comtes de Champagne à Montfélix (Xe-XIIIe siècle). Bilan d'une expérience en cours', *La Vie en Champagne*, 408, 3-9, Reims

——. 1991. *Fécamp: du palais ducal au Palais de Dieu*, Paris

YVER, J. 1957. 'Les châteaux forts en Normandie jusqu'au milieu du XIIe siècle', *Bull. Soc. Antiq. de Normandie*, 53, 28-115; 504-9

ZADORA-RIO, E. 1973-4. 'L'enceinte fortifiée du Plessis-Grimoult (Calvados). Contribution à l'étude historique et archéologique de l'habitat seigneurial au XIe siècle', *Archéologie Médiévale*, 3-4, 111-243

Seigneurial Domestic Architecture in Normandy, 1050–1350

Edward Impey

Normandy is rich in surviving examples of the late medieval *manoir*. In these houses all essential accommodation was contained in a single building of two or more storeys, an arrangement which differs markedly from the 'hall-and-chambers' pattern which prevailed in England throughout the Middle Ages; it is therefore unlikely to have been typical of Norman building during the eleventh and twelfth centuries. It is in fact evident, from a limited number of surviving buildings in Normandy, that the development of seigneurial domestic architecture in the two regions ran a virtually parallel course until *c.* 1225, when the storeyed house, antecedent of the *manoir,* first emerges (fig. 1). Neither of these points, however, has been widely recognized, nor has any general survey of Norman domestic architecture during the Middle Ages yet been attempted: the aim of this paper is to outline, through the presentation of examples, what appear to be the major phases of development during the period 1050–1350. The first section presents the evidence for the community of tradition between England and Normandy in the twelfth century, and the second outlines the characteristics of the new storeyed house, developed in the thirteenth. The final section discusses the evidence for the continuity of the communal-hall tradition well beyond 1200, as an archaic alternative to the storeyed house, and ultimately the possible origin of the 'storeyed' form itself.

THE LATE ELEVENTH AND TWELFTH CENTURIES

The characteristics and development of manorial buildings in England during the twelfth and early thirteenth centuries have been the subject of several general studies, notably those of Wood and Faulkner;[1] both are further discussed and much clarified by Blair, above. Discouraged by the apparent rarity of examples and a tacit assumption that the late medieval format was employed throughout the period, attention to the same subject in Normandy has been severely limited. However, several buildings do exist which show that the ensemble

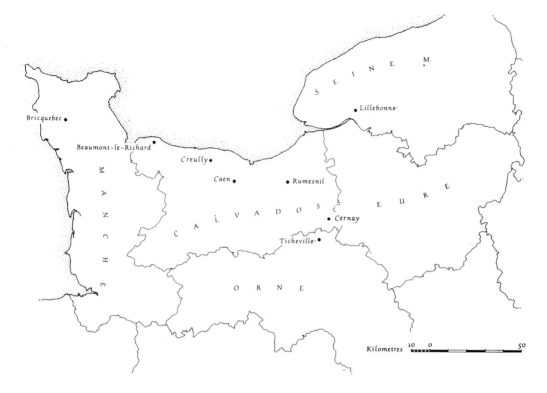

1. *Location map of sites mentioned in the text*

of ground-floor hall and detached seigneurial chambers or 'chamber-block', typical of Romanesque domestic architecture in England, was also employed in Normandy. The main characteristics of these buildings are described below, prefaced by an interpretation of the destroyed 'Great Hall' at Lillebonne.

Lillebonne; the 'Great Hall'

Included in Cotman and Turner's *Architectural Antiquities of Normandy* is an oblique view of the 'Great Hall' at Lillebonne, a massive late eleventh-century[2] building which then survived, as a roofless shell, in the castle bailey (fig. 2).[3] The side elevation had arched openings at two levels (the lower ones carried down to the ground), and a series of seven identical windows above. No details are given of the interior, but the raised doorway in the gable and the design of the windows—of a type which can be expected to have had window seats on the inside—indicate that it had a first floor. This suggests that it was not a hall but a chamber-block, akin in scale although probably larger than the near-contemporary English example at Richmond Castle[4] and the Norman example at Bricquebec (figs. 14, 16, 17); what appears to be blind arcading in the gable is also reminiscent of that on the smaller mid-twelfth-century chamber-block at Beaumont-le-Richard (fig. 7). The function of the ground-floor openings, however, is puzzling:[5] they are unlikely to have been separate

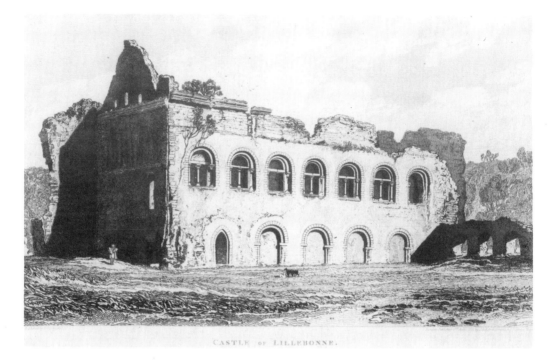

CASTLE of LILLEBONNE.

2. *View of the 'Great Hall', formerly standing in the castle at Lillebonne, published by Cotman and Turner in 1822 (Architectural Antiquities, II, plate 69, opp. p. 75). It probably contained a chamber, raised over storage rooms and an open-fronted 'loggia'*

entrances to a compartmentalized interior and are too widely spaced to have formed an aisle arcade. The most plausible interpretation is that they opened into a 'loggia'; a similar arrangement is to be found in the mid-thirteenth-century bishop's palace at Laon, where the area behind a similarly placed arcade is partitioned off from the rest of the ground floor by a spine wall.[6] It seems likely that although unusual in being raised over a partly open-sided ground floor, of exceptional size and as much as fifty years earlier than the other dateable Norman example, the Lillebonne building can be identified as a chamber-block.[7]

The château at Caen: the 'Échiquier' and associated buildings

Studied by de Boüard in the 1960s and 1970s,[8] the 'Échiquier', the adjacent 'Palais de Guillaume' (known only from excavation)[9] and the palatine chapel form the only Norman complex which has so far been interpreted with clear reference to the English evidence. Although badly damaged in 1944, the early twelfth-century fabric of the Échiquier, consisting of a stone shell measuring 30.70m by 11.02m on the inside, survives substantially intact (fig. 3).[10] This has an original entrance at ground-floor level at its south end and is lit by six single-light windows in the upper half of each side-wall and another in the south gable; the windows are flanked by pilaster-buttresses, both external and internal sills standing on string-courses. The top of the wall is finished with a corbel-table. There seems no reason

3. *The 'Échiquier' in the château at Caen, an unaisled ground-floor hall dating from the reign of Henry I*

to doubt that this was built as a ground-floor hall of the high-walled and unaisled[11] early twelfth-century type represented in England, for example, at Monks Horton,[12] Dover priory,[13] and Minster Court;[14] the elevations are also similar to that of Westminster Hall in its original form.[15] Monsieur de Boüard, while identifying the building as the *aula* mentioned in the twelfth century,[16] assumed it to have been of two floors, misled above all by the current misinterpretation of English chamber-blocks as 'first-floor halls'.[17] The complex to the east of the Échiquier (fig. 4), known largely from excavation and referred to by de Boüard[18] as the 'Palais de Guillaume', incorporated the footings of a building measuring approximately 16m by 8m, quite substantial enough to have supported an upper floor, and which can thus be readily interpreted as a chamber-block;[19] as this probably dates from the late eleventh century, it was presumably accompanied by a more modest hall which the Échiquier replaced. The palace buildings, as they stood in the time of Henry I, can therefore be identified as an ensemble of the 'hall and chamber-block' type.

Beaumont-le-Richard

The outstanding importance of Beaumont-le-Richard lies in the survival of a virtually complete twelfth-century chamber-block in conjunction with the remnants of a contemporary, or near-contemporary, ground-floor hall. The castle stands on a steep-sided limestone outcrop in the former parish of Beaumont in the extreme north-west of Calvados.[20] Although held from the mid-twelfth to the late thirteenth century by the prominent Du Hommet family,[21] the defences may never have consisted of more than a towered curtain-wall, and the domestic buildings, although of the highest quality in terms of construction and decoration, are similarly modest in scale.

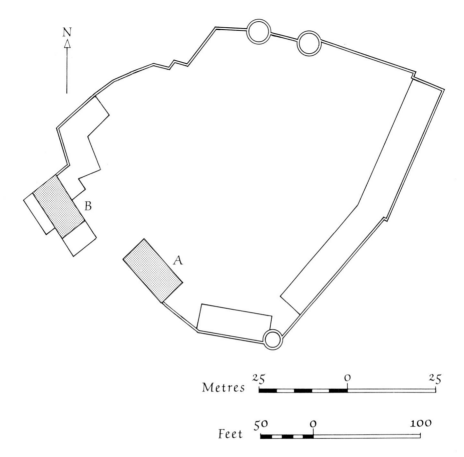

4. *Caen: the chamber-block (A) and existing remnants of the hall (B) in relation to the* enceinte *and other buildings as shown (much enlarged, with corresponding inaccuracies) on a map of 1769 (Archives Départementales du Calvados, Série G, Chapitre de Bayeux, MS 314). Currently surviving stretches of a late medieval curtain wall are shown in black; the earlier circuit, probably including the towers (now destroyed), almost certainly extended further south, encompassing the domestic buildings*

THE CHAMBER-BLOCK. The chamber-block is a free-standing two-storey building measuring approximately 18m by 8m, aligned north-west–south-east;[22] although converted into a chapel *c.* 1630, and still known as *la chapelle,* there can be little doubt that its purpose was originally domestic (figs. 5-9). At ground-floor level the exterior has been almost entirely refaced, notably on the west side where subsidence has required its repeated reinforcement; apart from a partly-concealed pilaster-buttress at the north-east corner, the only original features are the buttresses and windows at the south end. Much of the external masonry at first-floor level is also refacing, but enough of the original surface remains to show that the eastern third of the building was decorated with blind arcading, four bays at the end and five bays along each side; each recess is flanked by two receding orders, lined with colonnettes with cushion caps and moulded bases, standing on a cable-moulded string-course (fig. 7).

The ground floor, entered through an original doorway at the north end, is spanned by a barrel-vault, reinforced by three plain, flat, ribs. The stonework of the two southern bays and that of the ribs suggests that they are contemporary with seventeenth-century alterations to the floor above; the northern bays were rebuilt in 1921, following a collapse in the previous year.[23] However, as the base and springing of the northern rib on the east side are of *in situ* Romanesque stonework, it would appear that the vault reproduces an original construction of similar form, weakened by the subsidence of the west wall. No traces of original openings survive on either of the side-walls, but the southern end retains two double-splayed single-light windows, one of which (reopened in the 1980s) was superseded by a doorway shortly after its construction.

The entrance to the first floor, directly above the ground-floor doorway, is reached by an exterior stair, probably of seventeenth-century date, but perhaps incorporating medieval remnants.[24] Here the interior is divided by a transverse wall carrying the seventeenth-century reredos of the chapel, the northern and southern sections respectively measuring 8.50m by 5.60m in length.[25] The side-walls of the larger northern section each incorporate four bays of elaborate blind arcading (figs. 5, 6, 8) and the north wall a single bay on each side of the doorway. The arches spring from volute capitals and are embellished, on the eastern

5. *Beaumont-le-Richard: general view of the domestic buildings from the south-east. In the foreground is 'La Chapelle', a mid-twelfth-century chamber-block, converted into a chapel c. 1630. To the right are the ruins of the* manoir, *incorporating remnants of the single-aisled hall*

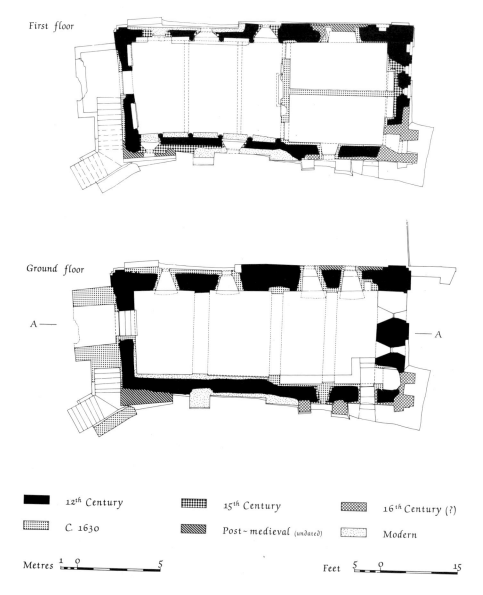

First floor

Ground floor

A —

— A

■ 12th Century   ▦ 15th Century   ▨ 16th Century (?)

C. 1630   ▧ Post-medieval (undated)   Modern

Metres 1 0   5   Feet 5 0   15

6. *Beaumont-le-Richard: ground- and first-floor plans of the chamber-block (surveyed E.A.I and M.A.I., 1991)*

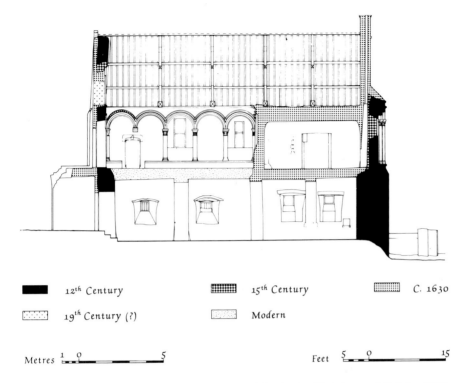

| | 12ᵗʰ Century | | 15ᵗʰ Century | | C. 1630 |
| | 19ᵗʰ Century (?) | | Modern | | |

Metres 1 0 5   Feet 5 0 15

7. *Beaumont-le-Richard: section (A-A; see fig. 6) of the chamber-block (surveyed E.A.I., 1991)*

8. *Beaumont-le-Richard: the chamber-block from the south-east, showing exterior blind arcading at the south end; this originally extended for 6.40m along the side walls*

9. *Beaumont-le-Richard: the chamber-block, showing decorative arcading in the larger of the two first-floor compartments (east side). The cross-wall, visible to the right, dates from* c. *1630, but replaces an original partition in the same position*

and western sides respectively, with orders of moulding and an incised star motif; on the west side the engaged columns (damaged and partly concealed) descend to floor level, those to the north and east standing on a stone bench running along the base of the walls.

The construction of the southernmost arcading suggests that the seventeenth-century cross-wall replaces an original partition in the same position; the arches here spring from quarter-round colonnettes engaged in flat pilaster-like abutments (as do those flanking the northern doorway), demonstrating that the arcading terminated at this point.

The main room has two east-facing windows, both late medieval insertions and probably contemporary with the external doorway (now blocked) towards the north end. The two windows in the west wall, of the same period, were blocked when the wall was thickened up on the inside.[26] Some of these must replace Romanesque openings, as the only openings of that date to survive are two loops recessed into the blind arcading at the south end. There are no traces of an original fireplace; the existing chimney in the south gable, obscuring the original windows, is clearly an insertion.

THE HALL. Unlike the chamber-block, the twelfth-century hall survives only in part, as it was shortened and floored over in the fifteenth century and subsequently twice remodelled;[27] this and the adjoining buildings to the north and east, in recent times known

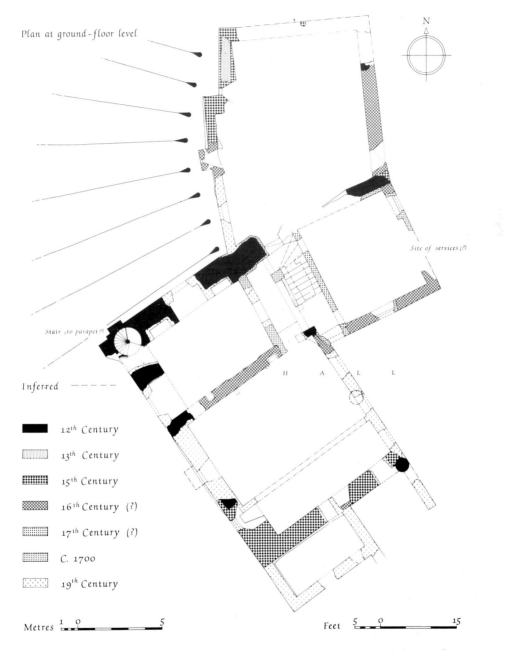

Plan at ground-floor level

N

Site of services (?)

Stair (to parapet?)

H   A   L   L

Inferred   - - - - -

■ 12th Century

▨ 13th Century

▨ 15th Century

▨ 16th Century (?)

▨ 17th Century (?)

▨ C. 1700

▨ 19th Century

Metres 1 0   5

Feet 5 0   15

10. *Beaumont-le-Richard: ground-floor plan of the* manoir, *incorporating remnants of the twelfth-century hall and other medieval fragments (surveyed E.A.I., M.A.I., J.-P.C., 1991). The building has been in ruins since at least 1944*

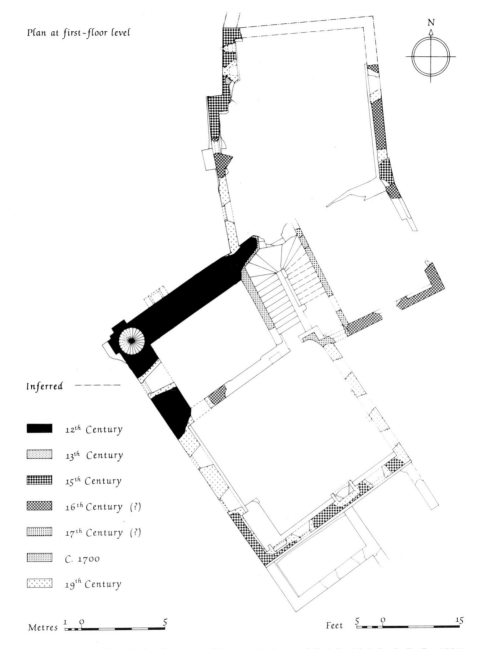

Plan at first-floor level

N

Inferred — — — —

■ 12th Century

▨ 13th Century

▨ 15th Century

▨ 16th Century (?)

▨ 17th Century (?)

▨ C. 1700

▨ 19th Century

Metres 1 0 5

Feet 5 0 15

11. *Beaumont-le-Richard: first-floor plan of the* manoir (*surveyed E.A.I., M.A.I., J.-P. C., 1991*)

collectively known as the *manoir,* have been in ruins since bombardment in 1944 (figs. 10–12).[28]

The most prominent fragment of the Romanesque hall is a round column, 3.02m high— including capital and base—and 0.80m in diameter, incorporated in the south-east corner of the building in its truncated form.[29] This was evidently an arcade pier, for 8.75m to the north, incorporated in the same post-medieval side-wall, is a second pier, badly damaged but clearly of the same design (fig. 11); above this pier the springing of a moulded arch protrudes from the later wall. The spacing of the piers and the curvature of the arch show that there must have been a third pier between them; the survival of the original end wall (although not the respond itself)—at the appropriate interval to the north—indicates the former presence of a third arch. As the southernmost pier was clearly freestanding, there must have been at least one further bay at the other end, but the extent of the hall in this direction is otherwise unknown (the existing end wall, incorporating the pier, dates from the fifteenth century). Analogy with Bricquebec, below, and with the halls at Oakham Castle and Hereford suggests that the fourth bay was the last. The width of the aisle can only be estimated, but that of the 'nave', at 8.15m, is clear from the partial survival of its western wall; this is both too high and too close to the arcade for there to have been a second aisle on this side.

The Romanesque facing of the west wall, visible on the outside below the lower windows, extends southwards for *c.* 12m from the north-west corner, beyond which the masonry is

12. *Beaumont-le-Richard: the hall; the western of the two surviving aisle piers and the springing of the arcade incorporated in the wall above*

integral with that of the fifteenth-century gable end; above this level the central portion of the wall was rebuilt, on the same line but much thinner, in the nineteenth century (figs. 9, 10). At the north end, however, a 7m stretch of original masonry survives up to eaves height, incorporating the remnants of a contemporary window. On the inside this is marked by a 2.45m wide square-sided embrasure, flanked by quarter colonnettes with carved capitals, both formerly recessed by 0.23m from the main splays; a recent fall of masonry has exposed the main rere-arch, hidden from below by an inserted lintel. On the outside, the bases and parts of the colonnettes which framed the opening remain *in situ*. Further elements, at present concealed, may also survive.[30] The placing of the window, equidistant between the west-facing pilaster buttress at the north end and that of which traces survive 8m further south, suggest that there was one more window beyond but no more.[31] The size of the embrasure in the north wall suggests that it contained a contemporary window of similar design.[32] The north-west corner, reinforced by original pilaster buttresses on both sides, houses a spiral staircase within the thickness of the wall. This was modified to give access to a garderobe in the fifteenth century, but as it continues to the summit of the wall, may originally have led to a parapeted wall-walk.

Analogy with Bricquebec and contemporary English buildings indicates that the hall would have been accompanied by a service-block. Unlikely to have intervened between the hall and the detached chamber-block, it presumably communicated with the north end of the hall, but cannot in this case have been axial to it, as the ground falls away sharply to the north and west; it may therefore have been attached to the east side of the aisle at its northern end, incorporating the detached spur of Romanesque wall which survives in this area.

OTHER BUILDINGS. Although the suggested site of the services is occupied by the shell of a post-medieval building, the ruins of those immediately to the north contain fabric of the twelfth, thirteenth and fifteenth centuries. The structural history of these is complex and not fully resolved, although work of eight phases can be distinguished (figs. 10, 11). However, two surviving features, one still visible above ground level and the other known only from a photograph of 1919[33] deserve a brief mention. The first consists of a series of *in situ* quoins with zig-zag decoration and finished with a roll moulding, situated at the north-east corner of the ruins as they stand (fig. 10); these apparently formed the jamb of a doorway, originally opening into a building to the east, but later adapted to open inwards to the west.[34] The second feature consisted of an arched opening about 1.30m wide and of roughly equal height in the north side of the detached Romanesque wall mentioned above; although located on site, this was largely destroyed by the collapse of the wall between *c.* 1964 and 1986.[35] Identified in 1919[36] and 1922[37] as a window, its proportions and probable proximity to floor level suggest that it was a fireplace, perhaps served by the chimney which the wall is known to have contained at the time of its collapse.[38].

The identification of the buildings of which these two features formed a part can be no more than guesswork. Nevertheless, it might be suggested that the first feature was the west entrance of a chapel, and that, less tentatively, the fireplace belonged to a subsidiary ground-floor chamber.

Bricquebec

The relevant domestic buildings which survive in the bailey of the château at Bricquebec consist of a large single-aisled hall with an end-bay chamber, dating from about 1190, and the basement of a detached chamber-block, probably contemporary, but remodelled *c.* 1350–1400 (figs. 13–18).[39] The scale of the domestic buildings and of the castle as a whole reflect its status as the *caput* of the influential noble family of the Bertrands.[40] The hall and integral chamber at its west end stand parallel to the curtain-wall on the south side of the bailey, separated from it by a gap of about 7m; additional chambers were probably included in the large building of twelfth- or early thirteenth-century date which formerly adjoined its south-west corner.[41] The undercroft of the free-standing chamber-block lies to the east, at right-angles to the hall, adjoining it only at its south-west corner (fig. 14).

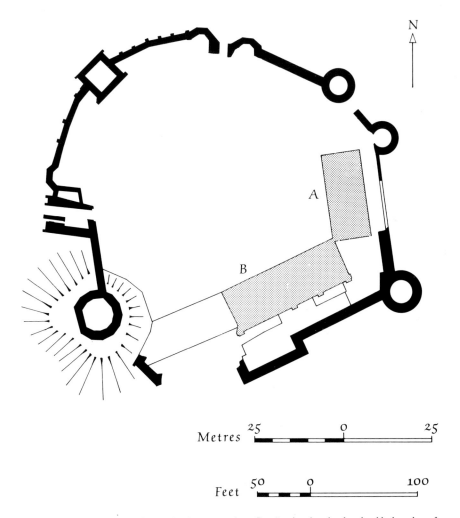

13. *Bricquebec: plan of the château (to the same scale as fig. 4), showing the chamber-block undercroft (A) and hall (B) in relation to each other and to the surviving medieval defences (adapted from Traverse 1979, after Scuvée 1979). Post-medieval buildings to the east of the hall, extending over the chamber-block undercroft, were demolished in 1979–80*

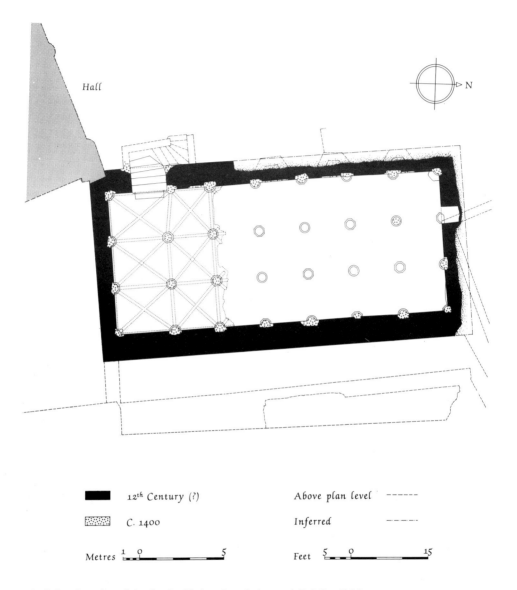

14. Bricquebec: plan of the chamber-block undercroft (surveyed E.A.I., 1991)

THE FREE-STANDING CHAMBER-BLOCK. The vaulted basement on the eastern side of the bailey (fig. 14), adjacent to the hall, is interpreted here as the undercroft of a detached chamber-block. The upper part of the building has been entirely destroyed, and only the southern two bays of the triple-aisled vault which carried the 'first floor' (a little over 1m above original ground level) remain intact. The vault itself, carried on diagonally alternating round and hexagonal piers, dates from the second half of the fourteenth or early fifteenth century, but is clearly later than the walls; the floor which it replaced was presumably of wood, carried by a row of piers down the centre. The exceptional size of the building (19.80m by 8.20m) suggests that it may have had more than one habitable floor. The undercroft was lit by windows just above ground level in the western wall, with steeply-sloping inner sills; the jambs themselves are missing, but parts of the splays are original. At the south end of the west wall is a doorway, respected by the vault, but adapted to fit the profile of the wall-ribs. If the existing stair reproduces the medieval arrangement, it would have led down from the bailey, but if that shown on a plan of 1843[42] was original it must have opened out of the hall; in either case the hall is likely to have communicated directly with the 'first-floor' chamber.

THE HALL AND END-BAY CHAMBER. In spite of the demolition of the aisle, the walling-up of the arcade, the insertion of a first floor in the fifteenth century, and extensive post-medieval alterations, the basic fabric of the hall survives largely intact.[43] This had an internal length of 24m, and a width, across the 'nave', of 9.40m; the missing aisle would have provided at least 5.50m in addition, and as such it is among the larger of the known twelfth- or early thirteenth-century halls.[44] The arcade-piers are round, resting on moulded bases and have elaborate water-leaf capitals, some embellished with other decorative details; the arches themselves are lined on both sides (the apexes of the inner sides are visible in the roof-space) with roll-mouldings. The scars of the western and eastern end walls of the aisle are clearly visible adjacent to the responds at each end of the arcade.

The main lighting of the hall was provided by three large windows on the south side, facing the curtain-wall; the side-wall is divided into three bays by pilaster buttresses, and thus does not mirror the four-bay articulation of the arcade. The original external arches and rere-arches of the windows survive intact, along with the bases of the two orders of colonnettes which originally lined the embrasures, but the existing tracery is a replacement, probably of the late thirteenth century. Additional lighting was provided by pairs of windows high up in each gable, with round roll-moulded rere-arches.[45]

The main entrance to the hall from the bailey was destroyed, along with the aisle, in the fifteenth century, but the western end-wall of the hall is pierced by an original doorway at its northern end. The mid-nineteenth-century plan suggests that the wide doorway in the southern section of the wall was also original, but there is now no evidence for this.[46] The site of the main exterior doorway is unknown, because it was destroyed with the aisle; there was almost certainly no entrance on the south side, as its only possible site, close to the western cross-wall, would have been obscured by the stair to the first-floor chamber.

In the area to the west of the service-doorway the only twelfth-century features visible at ground-floor level are two double-splayed loop windows in its western wall. Access to the end-bay chamber above was provided by an elaborate doorway at the southern end of the cross-wall (figs. 16, 18), reached by a stair ascending directly from the hall. Nothing of this survives, but the thickening of the adjacent side-wall below first-floor level and the position of the nearest window suggest that it was built against the cross-wall; the existence of the masonry abutment also suggests that it was of stone. Inside the chamber, immediately to the left of the entrance, is a small round-arched doorway opening at the base of a spiral stair. This gives access to a barrel-vaulted gallery, at the same level, extending westwards in the thickness of the wall, and formerly led to a second gallery immediately above (now collapsed); above these it continues to the summit of the wall, suggesting that it opened on to a parapet overlooking the curtain. Modern plaster and partitions conceal all other

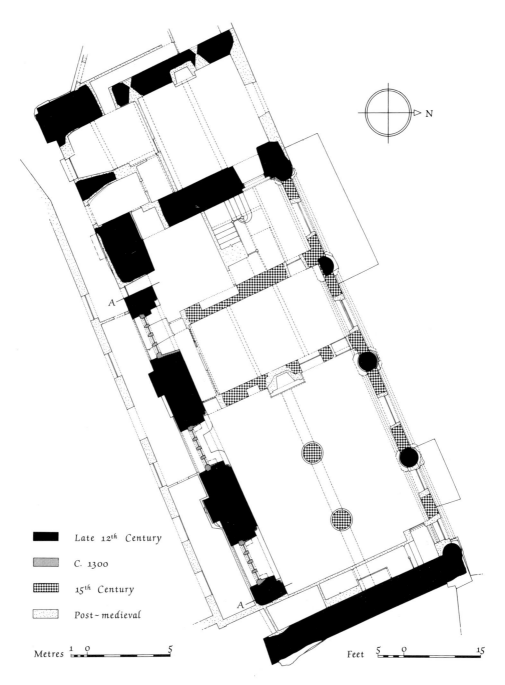

15. *Bricquebec: ground-floor plan of the hall (surveyed E.A.I., 1991). The high sills of the windows require much of the south wall (A-A) to be shown at a higher plan level than the remainder*

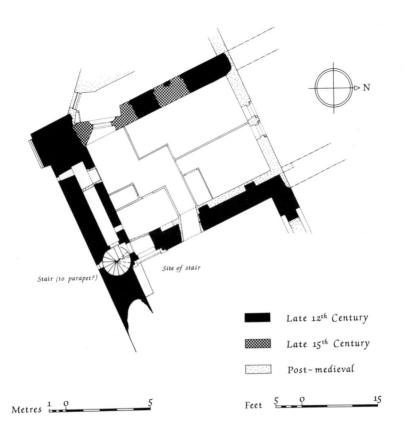

N

■ Late 12ᵗʰ Century

▨ Late 15ᵗʰ Century

▢ Post~medieval

Stair (to parapet?)

Site of stair

Metres 1 0   5   Feet 5 0   15

16. Bricquebec: plan of the first-floor 'end-bay' chamber (surveyed E.A.I., 1991). The doorway in the south-east corner (fig. 17) opened on to a stair leading down into the hall; the adjacent spiral staircase led upwards, probably to a wall-walk, but also to a pair of barrel-vaulted galleries, one above the other, in the thickness of the wall. The interruption of the internal arcading (visible above the inserted ceiling) shows that the chamber originally extended further north

original detail below the inserted ceiling, but the remains of windows and blind arcading are visible in the attic above. Roughly in the centre of the west wall are the upper parts of two adjacent arches, each lined with roll-mouldings; these evidently belonged to windows, as their outer heads appear in the loft of the adjoining building. On the opposite wall, the upper parts of two arches can be seen extending northwards from beside the doorway, each lined with a roll moulding, beyond which a third arch is interrupted by the post-medieval northern wall. This shows that in its original form the chamber extended by at least a further half-bay to the north, but perhaps far enough for alignment with the outer wall of the aisle. The two-light window in the existing wall is a modern creation in Romanesque style. An offset on the east wall of the chamber about 0.50m above the top of the arcading indicates that the chamber roof was aligned at right-angles to the hall, in the manner of a cross-wing.

17. *Bricquebec: the hall and chamber-block undercroft from the north-east*

18. *Bricquebec: the doorway of the end-bay chamber, formerly overlooking the hall*

Creully

The château at Creully,[47] ten kilometres due east of Bayeux, stands on the lip of a steep slope at the western edge of the village, overlooking the valley of the Seulles. In 1108 the barony passed to Robert of Gloucester by his marriage to Mabel, heiress of Robert Fitz Hamon.[48] Architectural detail suggests that the surviving structure could have been his work, but that it was more probably that of his son Richard.[49]

The medieval domestic buildings are built up against the scarp on the western side of the bailey, which is itself enclosed by a dry moat and sections of post-medieval curtain-wall. They consist essentially of two parallel and contiguous blocks, the longer axis orientated north-south. Major transformations took place in the fourteenth, fifteenth and seventeenth centuries, but the detailed analysis of these and numerous other phases is not yet complete.[50] The form of the building as it existed in the second half of the twelfth century, however, is fairly clear: the western section was a single-aisled ground-floor hall, while the longer and narrower eastern building—once, it seems, of two floors but now consisting only of a vaulted basement—can be seen as an equivalent to the chamber-blocks at Beaumont-le-Richard and Bricquebec.

19. *Creully: 'Le château' from the south-east, showing the much altered twelfth-century hall. Part of the original gable can be seen to the left, incorporated in the fifteenth-century staircase tower; the façade to the right incorporates the wall of the single aisle, heightened when the hall was floored over and fortified in the fourteenth century*

THE HALL. The present form of building derives largely from its flooring-over and transformation into a fortress in the fourteenth century—largely effected by the digging of a moat up against its western and southern sides.[51] In the fifteenth century a staircase turret was built inside the south-west corner of the hall, and in the late sixteenth or seventeenth century the main body of the building was vaulted at both levels. The striking skyline seen today owes much to the loss of the medieval roof, which has left the staircase turret towering above the flat terrace which replaced it (fig. 19).

The northern and southern walls of the hall survive substantially intact, although pierced by numerous later openings. The full-height western wall, shared by the adjoining building, is also largely original; a series of south-facing lights visible on the outside suggest that it incorporated a vice at its junction with the south wall, blocked up and replaced in the fifteenth century. Internally the 'nave' of the hall measured just over 17m in length and 8.25m across, the aisle adding 5.25m to its overall width.

The aisle piers were virtually destroyed at ground level by the insertion of the vault, but the upper parts of the northern respond and of two shafts and their capitals have recently been revealed on the floor above. Their spacing indicates that the arcade was of four bays, slightly irregular in width, although damage and their partial concealment in the blocking wall makes it difficult to be certain. The detail shows considerable variety: the capitals of the respond and the third pier from the north (the second is missing) have primitive water-leaf decoration, suggesting a date in the second half of the twelfth century; the capital opposite the respond (fig. 20), however, has scalloped decoration of a kind more typical of the pre-1150

20. *Creully: the capital and springing of the northernmost freestanding arcade pier, showing the side formerly facing the hall. The detailing, both here and elsewhere, suggests a date between 1150 and 1170 (Dr Lindy Grant, pers. comm.)*

period. The arches themselves were also of varied design; the springing which survives above the respond capital shows that the northern arch had an embattled fret moulding facing the hall, while the adjoining one has a chevron decoration. Taken together, however, these details suggest that the hall was probably built in the period between 1150 and 1170.

As part of the fourteenth-century alterations the external wall of the aisle, instead of being demolished, was thickened, heightened and provided with loop-holes. This unusual procedure has meant that an original east-facing doorway, although much modified, can still be identified. Recent plaster-stripping on the inside has uncovered the roll-moulded rere-arches of two original windows. As the main roof was retained, the wall above the arcade also survives, in part, to its original height; this carries clear traces of two clerestory windows and is capped by two stretches of the external corbel-table. A further window at the same level has been preserved, along with part of the original gable (elsewhere destroyed), where the fifteenth-century stair turret was built up against its inner face. A single west-facing window in the return wall has survived by the same means (see below).

In addition to the modified but original entrance opening out of the aisle, only one other medieval doorway, communicating with the adjoining basement, survives intact. This may be original, but is more probably an insertion of *c.* 1200. The lower part of the southern gable wall, however, incorporates slight but convincing traces of two original openings, probably doorways, in its western half.

THE WESTERN BUILDING. The western building now consists of a vaulted basement, 32m long and 6m across, with an open-air terrace above. Its southern wall, adjoined by a series of later medieval structures,[52] is in line with that of the hall, but it extends beyond the hall for a further 13.25m to the north. Until the 1950s it was divided by a cross-wall, pierced by a small doorway, in line with the end wall of the hall.[53] Differences in the height and detailing of the vaulting suggest that this partition was original. The basement is lit by a series of seven windows set in deep recesses in the west wall, each consisting of two arched lights. The vault, consisting of five quadripartite bays to the south of the destroyed cross-wall and four to the north, has plain chamfered ribs springing from clusters of capitals; the engaged shafts beneath have been cut back and only the upper sections survive. The capitals themselves show a great variety, but are predominantly of plain cushion form, scalloped, or have simple volutes. Their design suggests that the undercroft is contemporary with the hall, although the detailing is in general cruder and in places archaic.

The existence of an upper floor over the basement would have been structurally logical, as appropriate external walls existed in any case; the western wall of the basement must have been crowned at least by a defensive parapet, and this was mirrored by the side-wall of the hall; in fact, its existence is more or less confirmed by two pieces of more specific structural evidence. The first consists of the original hall window, mentioned above, embedded in the massive masonry of the fifteenth-century tower. As this is at the same level as the east-facing clerestory windows, it suggests that the western building, against which the hall was built, already had an upper floor; had it not, advantage would surely have been taken—as at Beaumont-le-Richard and Bricquebec—of the full-height outer wall as a site for much larger windows. The second feature which suggests this is that the wall in question clearly extended further north at first-floor level. The exposed stretch of its western face contains five recesses, spanned by segmental arches supported on square abutments; four of them are complete, but the fifth, at the north end, has been truncated and the recess blocked up. Details suggest that the recesses date from *c.* 1200 at the earliest, so that the upper floor could perhaps have been a later improvement. The existence of the upper window, however, militates against such an interpretation.

DISCUSSION OF THE LATE ELEVENTH- AND TWELFTH-CENTURY EVIDENCE

The buildings described show that the essential elements of the typical twelfth-century manorial ensemble in England were also employed in Normandy. Moreover, various features of these buildings suggest that the twelfth-century developments identifiable in English seigneurial architecture, as outlined by John Blair, above, are also represented. The Échiquier is a ground-floor hall of familiar type, but one which pre-dates standardization of the positioning of doorways—and the development of the cross-passage—which occurred in the last quarter of the twelfth century; the original entrance (if not the only one, almost certainly the main exterior entrance) is not in the side of the building, but in the gable-end. Beaumont-le-Richard, however, not only represents the use of this pattern at a site of marginally lower status, but at a more advanced stage in its development. The hall, although identifiable as such, survives only in part, but the well preserved chamber-block belongs to a recognized type employed in England between the mid-twelfth and early thirteenth century; this is evident from the similarity in its general form, in the raising of the first floor over a vaulted basement, but also in detail, notably in the division of the upper floor into two unequal parts, as at Boothby Pagnell, and Christchurch and Richmond castles.[54] In addition, the larger section is finished with internal blind arcading, arranged in a way strikingly similar to that at Strood Temple in Kent.[55]

The relative siting of the chamber-block and hall at Beaumont, as independent freestanding elements, is precisely what would be expected at English sites of the same date had both buildings in any single case survived;[56] the attachment of the services to the side rather than the end of the hall, postulated above, can be attributed to the peculiarity of its situation on the edge of an escarpment.

As at Beaumont, the domestic buildings at Bricquebec complement the English evidence in retaining the remnants of both hall and chamber-block at the same site. In this case, however, the two buildings are adjoined, presumably allowing communication between them without the aid of an intervening *tresaunce* or covered way; this suggests that by the 1190s the developments which were to lead thirteenth-century English builders to place the 'chamber-block' across the end of the hall were also represented in Normandy. Parallel development is also suggested by what can be deduced with regard to the plan of the hall, as it had at least one doorway in its western wall which can be assumed to have communicated with services beyond. This is an arrangement known in near-contemporary English examples such as Oakham Castle,[57] and likewise predates the introduction, in the early thirteenth century,[58] of the central doorway and passage leading directly to the kitchen (but cf. Blair, above, p. 14). The position of the main lateral entrance is, unfortunately, unknown; it would be interesting to know whether the logic of the service-doors arrangement had already led it to be placed against the lower end of the hall, as became standard practice in the thirteenth century, or whether, as in earlier English examples such as Hereford and Old Sarum,[59] it was placed midway along one side. In the manner anticipated at Wolvesey[60] and Hereford, the hall at Bricquebec was accompanied by an end-bay chamber, which, as also at Oakham, was raised over the services and reached by a staircase descending into the body of the hall.

Although earlier than Bricquebec, Creully may in some ways be the most advanced building of its period; the layout of the hall itself, coupled with its relationship to the western building display some features unknown in England before the last decades of the twelfth century. In this case the hall had a main external doorway at the extreme end of the aisle, as originally at Oakham. This immediately suggests that it was likewise associated with an early form of the cross-passage and service doorway arrangement: the traces of two openings, almost certainly doorways, in the adjacent gable wall would tend to confirm this interpretation.

Assuming that the western building had an upper floor, it can be plausibly interpreted as a chamber-block; it would have conformed to the 'standard' format in having a vaulted basement, while the provision of a massive cross-wall at ground-floor level suggests that the upper part may also have been divided into two unequal parts. Unlike at Beaumont-le-Richard, or Bricquebec, however, chamber-block and hall are built side by side, sharing a common wall; in this the closest parallel may be Stamford Castle, Lincolnshire, where the late twelfth-century chamber-block was attached axially to the gable end of an aisled hall;[61] both could be said to represent an experimental stage, characterized by a readiness to consider the two elements as a single structural unit, but which pre-dates the practice of placing the chamber across the upper end of the hall.

THE THIRTEENTH CENTURY

During the first half of the thirteenth century a form of domestic building was developed which differed radically from that represented by the Échiquier, Beaumont, Bricquebec and Creully; although for at least half a century it seems that more immediate derivatives of twelfth-century format continued to be built, the new pattern was ultimately to supersede it, and thereafter to dominate Norman seigneurial building for the remainder of the Middle Ages.

Surviving examples of these buildings are not numerous, but they are certainly better represented than those of the twelfth century;[62] it is not therefore proposed to discuss examples individually, but to describe the basic characteristics of the type. In essence they consisted of two-storeyed blocks in which both floors were occupied by a single room, or one at least not usually divided by permanent partitions; in some cases the central block is accompanied by further attached buildings such as a chapel as at Cernay (fig. 21),[63] or subsidiary chambers, as at the priory houses at Ticheville (fig. 25) and Surcy,[64] but the basic pattern remains the same.

Although in the one case where the original entrances to both floors are preserved there are significant differences in their arrangement, the lower room is essentially a duplication of the one above; the most obvious distinction is that the upper room had the benefits of greater privacy, better lighting, and of a high, open roof rather than a ceiling. In cases where a comparison is possible, the decoration and fittings of the upper room were also of a higher quality; at Ticheville, for example, the first-floor windows, and in particular the fireplace, are much more elaborate than those below. There can be no doubt that these buildings formed complete, self-contained houses, and were not accompanied by other residential buildings of any importance (they were not, in particular, chamber-blocks formerly accompanied by ground-floor halls); this is most clearly apparent from the fact that it was undoubtedly true of their structural descendants, the fifteenth- and sixteenth-century storeyed

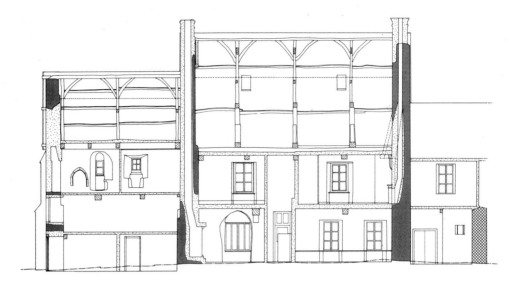

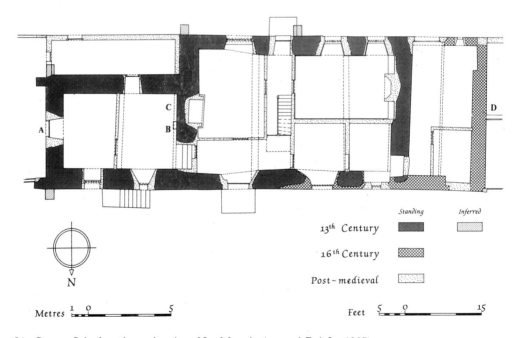

Standing   Inferred

13th Century

16th Century

Post–medieval

N

Metres   1 0   5

Feet   5   0   15

21. *Cernay, Calvados: plan and section of* Le Manoir *(surveyed E.A.I., 1987)*

manoirs of the type found all over Normandy and most of modern France.

The absence above all of the structurally and functionally distinct halls and chambers typical of medieval domestic architecture in England and twelfth-century Normandy, raises the question of how such buildings functioned. As mentioned above, the internal arrangement of the buildings gives a strong impression of 'duplication', in that the upper and lower rooms are essentially similar. That this 'duplication' applied not only to the layout and form, but also to the function of these rooms is implied by the thirteenth-century use of the word *aula* to describe both floors, qualified by *inferior* and *superior;*[65] the same is true of the later medieval application of the vernacular *salle,* qualified in this case by the suffix of *basse* or *haute,* although in the late Middle Ages the lower room could be referred to specifically as the *tinel.*[66] An explanation for this arrangement has recently been suggested with reference to the structurally akin, although generally later and more elaborate manor-houses and small châteaux of Brittany;[67] this lies in the requirement for a segregation of the household according to rank, a consideration which is suggested architecturally and well served by the superimposition of one apartment over the other; it is also suggested by the differences in quality of decoration. This interpretation was subscribed to, in more general terms, by Viollet-le-Duc; the ground-floor *salle,* he explains, was reserved for the use of 'les gens, les familiers; la salle haute, (au premier étage), pour le mâitre et ses siens'.[68]

An arrangement of this sort presupposes that the distinction between communal hall and private seigneurial chambers had been abandoned, and that each floor was intended to serve the dual function of dining hall and sleeping quarters for different sections of the household. This development must have been brought about by, or made possible by, changes in social custom governing the organization of the household, as formerly reflected in their use of a communal dining hall. The same process was of course at work in England; the communal role of the hall was in decline from at least the early to mid-fourteenth century onwards, a process recognized by contemporaries and regretted, for example, in *Piers Plowman;*[69] the architectural response, however, was quite different, for although chambers became increasingly elaborate and important, halls continued to be built, according to the traditional plan, even in late and post-medieval houses in which they were no longer open to the roof.[70] As will be seen, however, the processes by which the integrated, storeyed post-medieval houses of Normandy and England developed from the 'hall and chambers' ensemble was markedly different.

THE PERSISTENCE OF THE OPEN HALL. The survival of a group of *logis* dating from the first half of the thirteenth century, and the identification, so far, of no more than one post-twelfth-century example of the 'hall-and-chamber' type, gives the impression of an abrupt abandonment of the old pattern. This is, however, inherently unlikely, and the 'sudden' preponderance of the new type surely owes much to differences in the rate of survival: as the earliest representatives of the type later universally adopted, and as such more acceptable and adaptable to later medieval requirements,[71] *logis* were more likely to be retained than ensembles of the earlier type.[72]

There is therefore no reason to suppose that the 'hall and chambers' format was no longer, on occasion, employed by Norman seigneurial builders during the thirteenth century; that the open hall did in fact persist well beyond *c.* 1225 is suggested by its survival in Brittany into the mid-fourteenth century.[73] The most important evidence, however, not simply of the persistence of the communal hall, but that its development continued during this period, is provided by the surviving mid-thirteenth-century building at Rumesnil in Calvados.

RUMESNIL: THE 'GRANGE AUX DIMES'. The so-called 'Grange aux Dîmes'[74] consists of a stone 'shell', measuring 27.5m by 12m, within which virtually all internal constructions were originally, as now, of timber (figs. 22–4). This contained a single-aisled hall and 'end-bay' chamber, occupying roughly equal portions of the building; unless there was also a free-standing chamber-block, this represents the complete medieval house. The hall, occupying the southern half, had at least three exterior doorways, one at the extreme west end of the south gable and another, much larger, at the north end of its western side; the third doorway was directly opposite the main entrance (where the wall has since been rebuilt) as is shown in a drawing of 1874.[75] The full-height east wall contained two or possibly three windows and there was a fireplace against the south wall, furnished with a hood which rose to about 8m above ground level. The timber aisle arcade (fig. 23) was originally of two bays, of which one survives entirely intact, although shifted slightly from its original position;[76] this consists of the massive central upright and more slender post against the gable, linked by an arcade plate and formerly, by means of a 'normal-assembly', to tie-beams spanning the body of the hall. The uprights are linked to the plate by braces forming a semi-circular arch and by subsidiary struts in the spandrels; the construction therefore differs from that of contemporary aisled barns by little more than the arch and the decorative chamfering and capitals below. The arcade-plate and braces in the adjoining bay have been removed, but the third aisle-post, originally built into the partition at the north end of the hall has survived, now incorporated in the framing of the inserted first floor; corresponding mortices in this and the central upright show that the construction of the two arches was similar but not identical.

To the north of the hall, the building was always of two storeys, containing what may be interpreted as service-rooms on the ground floor and a substantial chamber, provided with its own fireplace, above.

Thus far the building demonstrates that a version of the 'hall-and-chamber' pattern could still be considered suitable for a newly-built seigneurial residence in the second half of the thirteenth century. More significantly, however, the remains incorporate evidence that this was not simply a late employment of an archaic form, but belonged to a tradition which had continued to evolve since the end of the twelfth century. Projecting westwards from the masonry immediately to the right of the main entrance to the hall, is the jamb and springing of an arched doorway. This shows beyond any doubt that the south end of the hall was originally closed off, at ground level, by a stone wall; the upper part was timber-framed, as is shown by the close-set mortices in the soffit of the *in situ* tie-beam overhead and the absence of a wall-scar on the inner face of the east wall. The placing of the doorway at the extreme east end of the cross-wall, in the corner of the room, suggests that there may also have been others, in the manner of service-doors, linking the hall to the room beyond; together with the corresponding external doorway on the west this would have completed a fully developed cross-passage and service-door arrangement of the familiar type.

If such a layout did exist, it would indicate that in spite of the emergence of the *logis,* the 'hall-and-chamber' formula had continued to develop in the first half of the thirteenth century: although service-doors and the inclusion of a chamber over them were employed at Bricquebec, at Rumesnil the hall and end-bay chamber occupy approximately equal halves of the building, and are both included within a single structure under an axial roof; the

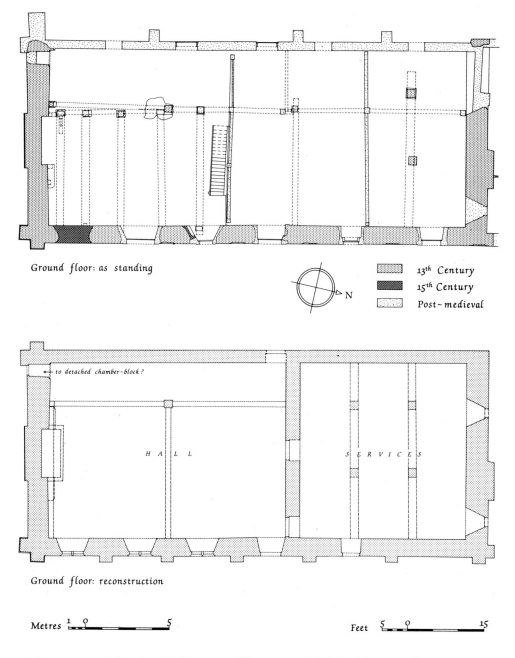

Ground floor: as standing

13th Century
15th Century
Post-medieval

N

Ground floor: reconstruction

to detached chamber-block?

H A L L

S E R V I C E S

Metres 1 0   5

Feet 5 0   15

22. *Rumesnil: ground-floor plan of the* Grange aux Dîmes *(surveyed E.A.I., 1987), as standing, with conjectural reconstruction below*

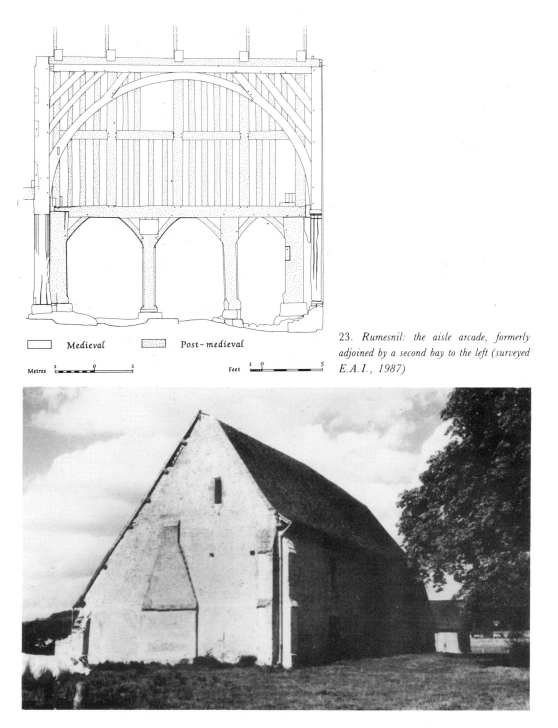

☐ Medieval   ⬚ Post~medieval

Metres |1 0 1| Feet |1 0 5|

23. *Rumesnil: the aisle arcade, formerly adjoined by a second bay to the left (surveyed E.A.I., 1987)*

24. *Rumesnil: the* Grange aux Dîmes *from the south-east. The asymmetric gable conforms to the profile of the single-aisle hall*

juxtaposition of the main entrance and cross-wall, even if it was not part of a fully developed screens and cross-passage arrangement, at least demonstrates some evolution in this respect.

In spite of the persistence and apparent development of the communal hall pattern in the thirteenth century which this suggests, the universal employment of the 'storeyed' form in the fifteenth century shows that it was ultimately supplanted. [77] It can probably be assumed that in the half century after 1200 an increasing proportion of new and replacement houses were built according to the new pattern: glimpses of the process are given, for example, by several entries in the *Regestrum Visitationem* of Eudes Rigaud, archbishop of Rouen from 1249 to 1269, which refer to the rebuilding of the logis of minor monastic houses; when he inspected the priory at Sainteny in Manche in 1266, for example, he found that the monks were burdened by the cost of the *domus lapidee quam de novo faciebant construi et fundari iuxta aulam veterem*. [78] The implication is that the *aula* was of the obsolete communal ground-floor type, and that the new *domus* was a *logis*.

THE ORIGINS OF THE LOGIS

Three explanations for the origins of the *logis* are possible: first, that it was an innovation introduced from elsewhere, without structural antecedents in Normandy; second, that it had had a much longer history as an alternative to the 'hall and chamber-block' ensemble; third, that it represented an adaptation of this pattern, either of one element alone, or of the ensemble in its entirety.

On the face of it, the possibility that the design was introduced, in particular from the Ile-de-France, is not unlikely; the earliest examples are contemporary with the influx of French styles and structural techniques, and it is conceivable that these could have been accompanied by a new fashion in domestic architecture. However, there is no evidence that the *logis* appears any earlier in France than it does in Normandy; there are examples of the type (for example, at Crépy-en-Valois near Compiègne); [79] but these date from no earlier the first quarter of the thirteenth century.

The second possibility is suggested by the fact that the 'hall and chamber-block' format, although clearly the most common, was not the basis of all English domestic architecture in the eleventh and twelfth centuries: [80] the 'country house' at Castle Acre, in particular, consisting of two equal-sized and adjoining rooms raised over a basement, would appear to represent a quite different approach; [81] the origin of the *logis* could perhaps lie in the development of buildings of this or some other 'unorthodox' type, otherwise unknown. However, it is significant that the habitable part of the 'country house' was confined to the first floor, whereas the *logis,* its form dictated by the functional differentiation between *salle haute* and *salle basse,* was by definition inhabited at both levels. Moreover, the likelihood that by the thirteenth century the storeyed house had already had a long history is much reduced by the evidence that it was a thirteenth-century innovation: this is suggested by the existence, as mentioned above, of a group of near-contemporary examples; had buildings of the same basic type also existed in the twelfth century, one would expect at least some examples, equally adaptable to late medieval requirements, to have survived. Furthermore, the internal arrangement of the storeyed house reflects a quite different social attitude from that indicated by twelfth-century buildings, again suggesting that the two types co-existed for no more than the two or three generations in which they are known to have overlapped in the thirteenth century.

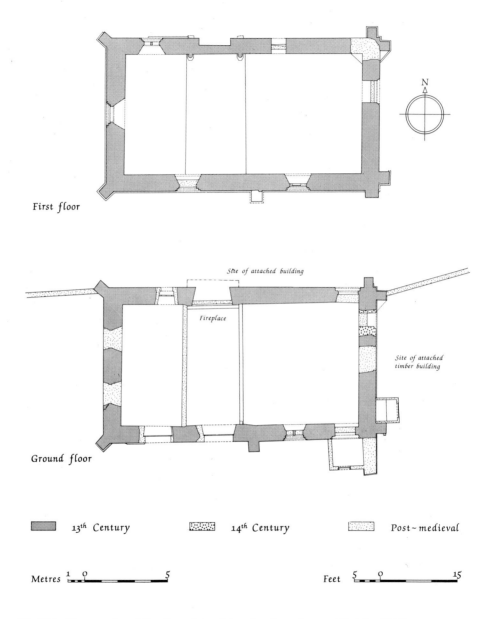

First floor

Site of attached building

Fireplace

Site of attached
timber building

Ground floor

13th Century   14th Century   Post-medieval

Metres 1 0   5   Feet 5 0   15

25. *Ticheville: ground- and first-floor plans of the priory house (surveyed E.A.I., 1987)*

The *logis* could also have developed, perhaps in the mid-twelfth century, out of one or other element of the hall and chamber-block ensemble, of which the likeliest candidate, as a two-storeyed building, is the chamber-block; a process can be envisaged whereby the increasingly exclusive use of the chambers by the upper household led to a decline in the importance of the communal hall—so far familiar enough from what happened in England—but which in this case led to the abandonment of the hall proper, the conversion of chamber-block undercrofts into *salles basses*, and the subsequent construction of new houses designed along these lines. However, few chamber-blocks could have been converted in this way and provided adequate accommodation for the whole household, and there is no direct evidence, structural or otherwise, for such a process.

The most convincing hypothesis, namely that the origin of the *logis* does in fact lie in an adaptation of the integrated 'hall-and-chamber' ensemble, relies for the moment largely on the evidence of no more than two crucial buildings; one of these is Rumesnil, described above, and the other the *logis* at Ticheville. Among the surviving storeyed houses, Ticheville is virtually unique in that the original ground-floor openings, the most vulnerable to post-medieval alterations, remain intact (fig. 25). The most significant feature is the layout of the doorways at its east end, consisting of two facing east and two others opposite each other in the immediately adjacent sections of the side-walls, and thus conforming to the familiar service-door and cross-passage format; there is even some evidence that the remainder of the hall was partitioned off from the extreme east end by some sort of screen.

It might be suggested, therefore, that the ground-floor room at Ticheville represents the layout of the communal hall on the eve of its abandonment; the traditional arrangement of service-doors remains, no doubt still serving as such, but its role as a room in which the seigneurial household and the *familia* would congregate for formal meals had been much reduced, if not surrendered. Bearing in mind that it was the lower apartment of the segregated house which was, in late medieval parlance called the *tinel*, a word which in its original sense probably referred to halls of traditional type,[82] it seems highly likely that this is what became of the 'communal' hall. The presence of this traditional hall-like layout in the *logis* might be explained simply as an element of conservatism in an otherwise completely innovative design. However, there may in fact be a direct developmental and typological relationship between the communal hall and the *logis* in so far as the latest, integrated versions of the old 'hall-and-chamber' design may have suggested the structural answer to the new requirements; had the end-bay chamber at Rumesnil been extended over the body of the hall, it would have resulted in a building essentially like Ticheville, in which the ground floor, at this transitional stage, retained its hall-like ground-plan.

CONCLUSION

The scarce remnants of twelfth-century examples in Normandy suggest that orthodox seigneurial domestic architecture adhered, as in England, to the 'hall and chamber-block' pattern. While the use of this formula appears to have persisted well into the thirteenth century, by about 1225 it was being supplanted by a radically different design, in which all essential accommodation was contained in a single two-storeyed building: the former distinction between communal hall and private seigneurial chambers had been abandoned, and the upper and lower floors of the new buildings served the combined functions of hall and chamber for each section of the household, differentiated by social status; although considerably refined, this design remained typical of seigneurial domestic architecture throughout the remainder of the Middle Ages. The structural origins of the storeyed house are not entirely clear, but the evidence of the 'transitional' buildings at Ticheville and Rumesnil suggests that the new design was arrived at by an adaptation of the traditional format, namely by an extension of the integrated end-bay chamber over the body of the hall.

ACKNOWLEDGEMENTS

The author is very grateful to Monsieur and Madame Hubert Hardy of Bricquebec, Monsieur Henri Clairon and Monsieur and Madame Jacques Riffi of Creully, and Monsieur Jean-Philippe Schnell, owner of Beaumont-le-Richard, for their help and hospitality; many thanks are due to Monsieur and Madame Marcel Lebeurier, Monsieur Jean-Marie Lebeurier, Monsieur Serge Brard and Monsieur Xavier de Pallières for permission to survey the medieval buildings at Rumesnil, Cernay and Ticheville; to Matthew Impey for help in surveying; to Roger Ainslie for the repeated loan of his theodolite; to Colonel Pierre Garrigou Grandchamp for bringing Beaumont to the author's attention; to Yves and Elisabeth Lescroart for pointing out Bricquebec and other buildings listed above and to Dr John Blair, Monsieur Jean-Paul Corbasson, Dr Elisabeth Lorans and Professor Gwyn Meirion-Jones for much help and information.

ABSTRACT

SEIGNEURIAL DOMESTIC ARCHITECTURE IN NORMANDY 1050–1350

Based on the study of a small but significant group of standing buildings, this paper summarizes the basic design of medieval seigneurial dwellings in Normandy as it developed during the period 1050–1350.

An interpretation of the palatine buildings in the castle at Caen and studies of Beaumont-le-Richard (Calvados), Bricquebec (Manche) and Creully (Calvados) indicate that twelfth-century seigneurial builders shared a common tradition with those of England. All four ensembles included ground-floor halls (at Caen, the *Échiquier*), while Beaumont and Bricquebec also retain detached storeyed buildings of the so-called 'first-floor hall' type and Creully an attached building of similar form; the survival of these elements in conjunction substantiates the reinterpretation of the latter (here referred to as 'chamber-blocks') as adjuncts to ground-floor halls, and that their upper floors contained private seigneurial chambers. Beaumont and Bricquebec (surveyed by the author in 1991) are presented and discussed in some detail. At the time of writing the investigation of Creully remains to be completed.

The thirteenth century, however, saw the replacement of the 'hall and chamber-block ensemble' by self-contained structures (referred to below as *logis*) in which upper and lower floors served the combined functions of hall and chamber for socially differentiated sections of the household. As this was the direct antecedent of the typical late medieval *manoir,* early examples were still acceptable to later medieval occupants and have survived in substantial numbers; the comparative rarity of hall and chamber-block ensembles can be attributed to their unsuitability for conversion to *logis.* The origins of the new design are far from clear: possibly it was introduced from elsewhere, or was an innovation without structural antecedents in Normandy; it might also have been a development of the hall or chamber block alone. However, the evidence of two buildings (Rumesnil, Calvados and Ticheville, Orne, surveyed by the author in 1987) which may be interpreted as 'transitional', suggests that the emergence of the *logis* was preceded by an integration of the hall and chamber within a single axial block, and that the *logis* was a development.

RÉSUMÉ

L'ARCHITECTURE SEIGNEURIALE DOMESTIQUE EN NORMANDIE, 1050–1350

Fondé sur l'étude d'un nombre réduit mais significatif de bâtiments en élévation, cet article présente l'organisation de l'habitat seigneurial normand et son évolution de 1050 à 1350.

Une interprétation des éléments résidentiels du château de Caen et l'analyse des sites de Beaumont-le-Richard (Calvados), Bricquebec (Manche) et Creully (Calvados) révèlent que la construction seigneuriale du XIIᵉ siècle y a partagé une tradition commune avec celle de l'Angleterre. Ces quatre ensembles incluent un *hall* de plain-pied (à Caen, la salle de l'Échiquier), tandis que Beaumont et Bricquebec présentent en outre des bâtiments distincts à étage, du type *first-floor hall* ou salle haute; à Creully il y a un bâtiment annexe d'une forme comparable. L'association de ces deux éléments autorise l'interprétation du second type (ici qualifié de *chamber-block*) comme une adjonction au *hall* et suggère que l'étage réunissait les chambres ou appartements privés. Beaumont et Bricquebec (relevés par l'auteur en 1991) font l'objet d'une discussion détaillée. Au moment de la rédaction de cet article le travail sur le terrain à Creully n'était pas encore terminé.

Le XIIIᵉ siècle vit le remplacement de l'ensemble associant *hall* et *chamber-block* par un édifice unique (désigné comme le 'logis'), dans lequel les deux niveaux remplissaient chacun les fonctions combinées de *hall* et de chambre pour des groupes socialement distincts de la maisonnée. Comme cette forme architecturale fut l'antécédent immédiat du manoir du bas Moyen Age, des exemples précoces restèrent longtemps en usage et il en subsiste un grand nombre. En revanche, la difficulté de convertir en logis les ensembles du premier type peut expliquer leur relative rareté, comparé au second type.

Les origines de cette nouvelle organisation sont loin d'être claires : il peut s'agir d'un modèle importé ou d'une innovation dépourvue d'antécédent en Normandie. Cela pourrait aussi représenter le développement du *hall* ou du *chamber-block* isolément. Cependant, l'analyse de deux autres édifices présentant un type transitoire (Rumesnil, dans le Calvados et Ticheville, dans l'Orne, tous deux étudiés par l'auteur en 1987) suggère que l'émergence du logis fut précédée par l'intégration du *hall* et de la chambre dans une seule construction, à axe unique, dont le logis fut le développement.

NOTES

[1] Wood 1935, 1965; Faulkner 1958.

[2] Turner's attribution of the building to William I seems acceptable, although the various details could admit of any date between *c.* 1070 and 1120. The walls were finished with an elaborate cornice, probably reused from a nearby Roman building.

[3] Demolished by *c.* 1850. No dimensions are given in Turner's description, but the view suggests that it was as much as 30m long, 9m across and about 8m high (excluding the gable which survives at one end). The description of the building as the 'Great Hall' is that used by Turner.

4 The building in question has been known as *Scolland's hall* since at least *c.* 1350 (Peers 1953, 11) and served as such, in the conventional way, at least after the insertion of the existing service-door through the west wall (formerly free-standing and occupied by a window), probably in the thirteenth or fourteenth century. However, its similarity to other supposed 'first-floor halls' (notably in that the habitable floor is raised over a basement and divided into two unequal parts) suggests that it too was actually built as a 'chamber-block', formerly accompanied by a hall standing nearby.

5 The arcade is shown as blind, but presumably the intervening walls are a later blocking.

6 See Verdier and Cattois 1857, plate opposite p. 198. The ground- and first-floor plans of Bishop Jocelyn's *camera* at Wells (Wood 1965, 84-5) suggests a similar arrangement, although in this case the area corresponding to the 'loggia' is walled in.

7 No record appears to exist of the site or the design of the hall by which the 'Great Hall', if it is a chamber-block, would have been accompanied; it is tempting to interpret the three ragged openings in the ruinous wall to the right of the building as its service-doors, but difficult to see how a building in this position could have related to the chamber-block.

8 De Boüard 1979, 63-97.

9 This is de Boüard's name for the building, not one known to have been applied to it when still standing. The site, however, including the accretion of medieval and later buildings destroyed in 1944, had long been known as the *vieux palais (ibid.,* 63).

10 For an early view, see Cotman and Turner, 1822, I, plate facing p. 48.

11 The building is too narrow to have been double-aisled, while the position of the doorway in the centre of the end wall suggests that the roof was not supported by a single row of piers down the centre. It must therefore have been covered by a single span, the largest of any known twelfth-century domestic building.

12 See Baily 1876, 81, 83.

13 See Turner 1851, 43-5, and Haines 1930, 168-70 and plate vii.

14 See Kipps 1929, 213-23.

15 See *RCHM London,* II, 122 (reconstructed elevation) and 120 (plan).

16 An *Aula Domini Regis* at Caen is mentioned in 1176 (de Boüard 1979, 67) and an *aula* in 1180 (*ibid.,* 68).

17 According to de Boüard 'Il n'est pas douteux . . . que l'édifice ait comporté, à l'origine, deux étages' (1979, 70); the floor was then removed in the late Middle Ages (*ibid.*), put back in the nineteenth century (*ibid.*), and then not replaced after 1944. Nevertheless, the evidence for an original first floor is far from conclusive. As summarized by de Boüard (*ibid.*) this consists of: (1) The absence of any traces of twelfth-century paving; (2) the inadequacy of the windows (owing to their size and position high up in the walls), to light a building open throughout its entire height; (3) the fact that in their original form the inner sills of the windows were stepped, not sloped. These features, however, are surely not incompatible with its identification as a ground-floor hall; neither the absence of paving, the positioning of the windows nor the stepping of their inner sills implies the original presence of an upper floor, nor distinguishes it significantly from known English examples. Its interpretation as a ground-floor hall solves some of the questions raised by de Boüard himself, including the absence of ground-floor windows (*ibid.,* 72), the height of the doorway in relation to the supposed floor (which requires him to suppose that it has been re-set) (*ibid.,* 79) and of traces of posts by which it could have been supported (*ibid.,* 72).

18 *Ibid.,* 63-7.

19 In this case the chamber may have been at ground-floor level, particularly if the hearth against the north wall (de Boüard 1979, 65) was original. Chamber-blocks accompanying ground-floor halls were not always two-storeyed, especially in the eleventh century (Blair, above).

20 In the commune of Englesqueville-la-Percée; the author is grateful to Colonel Pierre Garrigou Grandchamp for bringing this site to his attention.

21 Du Hommet 1922; Hubert 1977.

22 For the sake of simplicity in describing the building the north-west is hereafter referred to as 'north'.

23 Létienne and Mons 1922, 10.

24 This is shortly to be rebuilt under the supervision of the Conservation des Monuments Historiques. It is to be hoped that any surviving medieval fabric may be identified during the process.

25 These measurements are taken along the line of the section A-A (fig. 7). When the reredos was constructed, the compartment to the south was divided by a longitudinal wall and the

subdivisions vaulted. A fireplace built into the gable end in the late Middle Ages (blocking two twelfth-century windows) was split in two and adapted to provide each cell with a hearth.

[26] This was done in 1955 (Le Balch 1976, 17) to prevent the walls collapsing inwards. No traces of blocked Romanesque windows in the intervening bays show in either of the photographs taken for the Conservation des Monuments Historiques (Bibliothèque et Archives du Patrimoine. 12, rue du Parc-Royal, 75003 Paris) before this was carried out.

[27] The twelfth-century fabric has been exposed by the decay of the building following its bombardment and abandonment in 1944.

[28] Local tradition asserts that the site was shelled after the *débarquement* but, as no claim for compensation was lodged with the Mairie at Grandcamps, the buildings may already have been semi-ruinous well before 1944 (pers. comm., Monsieur J.-P. Corbasson); some outbuildings had already collapsed by 1922 (Létienne and Mons 1922).

[29] The badly damaged base of the pier, *c.* 0.40m below present ground level, was uncovered by the Abbé Langlois (pers. comm., Monsieur Lucien Musset and Monsieur J.-P. Corbasson) in the 1950s and remains exposed.

[30] A full examination of this feature must await the consolidation of the wall and complete removal of its ivy covering; partial removal at this stage could endanger the structure.

[31] If so, as at Bricquebec, the articulation of the west front did not correspond to that of the arcade.

[32] Particularly as its western splay is finished with what may be a quarter-colonnette, the surface of which is at present concealed by plaster.

[33] Preserved in the Bibliothèque et Archives du Patrimoine. I am grateful to Colonel Pierre Garrigou Grandchamp for bringing these to my attention. The photographs were taken following the *classification* of the *chapelle* and elements of the *manoir* on the recommendation of Monsieur J. Ruprich-Robert in 1919. The correspondence is contained in the dossiers of the Direction du Patrimoine, Section Documentation Immeubles, 3 Rue de Valois, 75042 Paris-Cedex 01.

[34] Another photograph of 1919 (Bibliothèque et Archives du Patrimoine) shows fragments of a Romanesque arcaded cornice above the remodelled doorway on the outside, but this was almost certainly not *in situ*. These were described and *classé* as 'une partie de corniche romane et des arcatures situées en dessous'.

[35] The wall is shown still standing in a photograph taken by the present owner *c.* 1965; it had long collapsed when he purchased the castle in 1986.

[36] Described as *une ancienne fenêtre à bâtons brisés* by J. Ruprich-Robert in a letter dated 24 July 1919, and *classé* as such on 16 September of the same year (Direction du Patrimoine).

[37] Létienne and Mons 1922, 11.

[38] The most unusual feature of this is the flat and effectively 'four-centred' profile of the arch, quite clearly original. Twelfth-century fireplaces with segmental arches are known in England (one survives at Nottingham Castle; pers. comm., Dr John Blair), but this 'four-centred' example is perhaps unique.

[39] I am grateful to Monsieur Yves Lescroart for bringing this building to my attention.

[40] For the history of Bricquebec see Moncel 1843, 13-20 (with plan), and Desquesnes 1978.

[41] An engraving of this was published by Cotman and Turner (1822, II, facing p. 77).

[42] Moncel 1843.

[43] The present form of the building owes to the removal of the aisle and the insertion of an upper floor in the fifteenth century. In the process the eastern half of the ground floor was retained as a 'hall', conforming to the standard plan in so far as the inserted cross-wall contains an adjacent pair of openings perhaps intended as service doorways (although one may have been a service-hatch). The two massive pillars in the centre of the room were built to carry the inserted floor, supported in the western half of the building by a second cross-wall. The re-dressing of the original arcade-piers on the inside shows that the demolition of the aisle was carried out at the same time.

[44] The floor area of the hall at Bricquebec (depending on the width of the aisle) was approximately 380m². It was thus larger than the Échiquier (338m²), and only marginally smaller than the largest twelfth-century English example at Clarendon (393m²). Nevertheless, it is dwarfed by the eleventh-century Westminster Hall and the thirteenth-century archbishop's hall at Canterbury, measuring 1501m² and 725m² respectively.

[45] The *charpente* was replaced after a fire in the 1950s (pers. comm., Madame H. Hardy); whether the preceding structure contained any medieval elements is not recorded.

[46] The 1843 plan may show the surviving first-floor doorway rather than a doorway at ground-floor level.

[47] The château has been the property of the *commune* since 1946. The author is extremely grateful to the Maire, Monsieur Henri Clairon and the administrators, Monsieur and Madame Jacques Riffi, for their assistance and hospitality during the process of surveying the building.

[48] For a brief account of the Barons of Creully see Vigoureux 1972.

[49] The author is grateful to Dr Lindy Grant for advice on this point and on others concerning the dating of the building.

[50] Plans of all floors and a longitudinal section were made by the author in September 1992. A clearer understanding of the building will be possible after a transverse section has been made in March 1993.

[51] This was possible because the foundations were laid directly on bedrock. The reason for this transformation may lie in the events of the 1350s: in 1358 the Baron of Creully, having dismantled the defences and retreated before the English advance in the previous year, retook the castle and began its refortification (for a summary of these events see Vigoureux, 1972, 20-1); the improvised conversion of the hall into a *maison forte* may have been the first stage in the process, achieved before the main defences could be fully reconstructed.

[52] Including a tall, machicolated, tower used by the BBC during the Battle of Normandy.

[53] As is shown on a pre-war architect's plan, kindly supplied by Monsieur Marcigny of Creully.

[54] For Boothby Pagnell see Wood 1935, 198-200, and Faulkner 1958, 151 (description), 153, fig. 1; for Christchurch Castle (the 'Constable's house') see Wood 1935, 186 and Faulkner 1958, 151 (description) and 153, fig. 4.

[55] Rigold 1962a and 1962b.

[56] With the possible exception of Leicester Castle, where an undercroft—which may have been that of a chamber-block—exists to the south of the twelfth-century hall; the vault dates from *c.* 1400 but the walls are probably earlier. For a rough plan see Toy (1953, 157) and for its English context see Blair, above.

[57] For a plan see Wood 1935, 201-3.

[58] Blair 1987, 67.

[59] See Blair 1987 and above p. 13.

[60] Biddle 1986.

[61] Mahany 1977, 231, 239.

[62] Identified examples include those at Ailly (Eure), Betteville (Seine-Maritime), Boos (Seine-Maritime), Cernay (Calvados), Mesnil-sous-Jumièges (Seine-Maritime), Ouézy

(Calvados), Sept-Vents (Calvados), Surcy (Eure) and Ticheville (Orne).

[63] Also at Betteville and Mesnil-sous-Jumièges.

[64] For plans, descriptions and photographs of the *logis* at Ticheville and Surcy see Impey 1991, III, 122-35, 135-45.

[65] For example, in March 1264 the archbishop of Rouen held court at Andelys *in aula nostra superiori in manerio nostro (Regestrum Visitationem,* 511); in May 1267 he found that the Prior at La Lande Patry *non iacebat cum eis, sed in quadam aula inferiori (ibid.,* 577).

[66] According to Godefroy (1892, VII, 721), the *tinel* was 'proprement salle basse ou mangeaient les officiers des rois, des princes et des grands seigneurs'.

[67] Jones *et al.* 1989, 84-7.

[68] Viollet-le-Duc 1858-68, VIII, 71.

[69] As referred to by Wood (1965, 91); the relevant passage is

Elenge is the halle, ech day in the wike
Ther the lord ne the lady liketh noght to sitte
Now hath ech riche a rule-to eten by hymselve
In a pryvee parlour for povere mennes sake
Or in a chambre with a chymenee
and leve the chief halle
That was made for meles, men to eten inne. . . .

(A. V. Schmidt, *A Critical Edition of the B. Text,* 103).

[70] A possible English example of the superimposition of halls with an implied social differentiation, however, exists in Acton Burnell Castle in Shropshire, built between 1284 and *c.* 1300 (West 1981; Hartshorne 1845, 338). Consisting of a massive two-storeyed block, this contains a hall of more or less standard plan, complete with service-hatches, at first-floor level. This is not in itself unusual in the thirteenth century, but it is interesting that in this case a large part of the ground floor, more usually used for storage, is partitioned off to form what could be interpreted as a second 'hall'; if so, this is a rare employment of the continental pattern in England.

[71] In particular by the addition of new windows, enclosed staircase-turrets and second floors (lit by *lucarnes);* such adaptations probably disguise as late medieval a large number of *manoirs* which are essentially of thirteenth- or fourteenth-century date.

[72] This also explains the rarity of twelfth-century ensembles compared to their relative abundance in England. It is significant that of the examples which have survived, all later converted into

storeyed buildings, one was unaisled and the other two single-aisled; a double-aisled hall would have been more difficult to adapt, and thus less likely to be preserved.

[73] Notably Le Carpont (Trédarzec, Côtes-d'Armor) and Le Téhel (Saint-Symphorien, Ille-et-Vilaine); Jones *et al.* 1989, 93-4.

[74] The building was erected when Rumesnil was held by the Brucourt family, although given to the Cistercians at Val Richer, six kilometres to the south-east, in 1364 (*Gallia Christiana*, XI, 448); it may have served as a tithe barn towards the end of the Ancien Régime.

[75] The drawing of 1874 is the property of Monsieur and Madame Marcel Lebeurier, Rumesnil. The author is grateful to Monsieur Jean-Marie Lebeurier for bringing this drawing to his attention.

[76] Although the masonry 'shell' can be firmly dated to the thirteenth century, the decorative detailing of the arcade piers suggests a date in the first half of the twelfth century (the author is grateful to Dr Lindy Grant for advice on this point), so that the arcade may have been reused from an earlier building. Nevertheless this dating is not conclusive, as there are no known Norman examples of twelfth-century decorative timberwork to which it can be compared; furthermore, various structural features, in particular the jowling and 'normal assembly' at the head of both piers are, at least in England, typical of the period after *c.* 1200 but not before.

[77] A passage in Joinville's *Histoire et Chronique du Très Chrétien Roi St. Louis* (Michel (ed.) 1858) suggests that in France, at least at a high social level, the communal ground-floor hall had become a rarity by the 1260s. The king, we are told *tint cele feste es hales de Saumur; et disoit l'un que le grant Roy Henri d'Angleterre les avoit faites pour ses grans festes tenir.* The fact that it accommodated diners of all social strata (at least from Louis to his knights) and that *Au chef du cloistre . . . estoient les cuisines, les bouteilleries, les paneteries et les despenses,* coupled with the kind of structure Henry II might be expected to have built, suggests that this was a 'communal' hall

of traditional type. To Joinville, however, it was evidently puzzling: in the first sentence he describes the building not in loose terms as a *salle* or *tinel,* as might be expected, but as the *hales,* a word which at least in later centuries was applied to market-halls, usually in the plural as *les halles.* The implication is that to Joinville the hall more closely resembled one of these than any familiar type of domestic building; the fact that such a structure was outside the chronicler's experience indicates that it was a rare survival at that date.

In the fifteenth century witnesses in a Breton lawsuit described a lately-destroyed building as *une vielle salle fondée sur postz de boays ou maniere de cohue;* like Joinville, they resorted to the market-hall as the best analogy for a type of structure no longer found in a domestic context, in this case presumably a timber-built aisled hall (Jones *et al.* 1989, 82).

[78] Bonnin 1852, 556.

[79] Mesqui 1988, 161-70.

[80] Nor of all domestic building dating from the twelfth century and earlier in Normandy, as is suggested by the remains of the tenth-century ducal palace at Fécamp (Renoux 1979). Other 'unorthodox' structures, in France but outside Normandy, include Doué-la-Fontaine (de Boüard 1973-4) and the 'Résidence des Comtes d'Anjou' at Tours (Galinié 1977).

[81] Coad and Streeten 1982, fig. 7, 154 and fig. 13, 197.

[82] As well as referring to the *salle basse, tinel* could also refer to the retinue of a prince or prelate, or, more significantly, to what amounts to 'court' in both the social and the judicial sense of the word (Godefroy, 1892, VII, 721 for examples); presumably if it can refer to both the 'servants hall' and the court of a nobleman, then it is likely that in its original sense it referred to a single apartment which served both these functions, in other words the communal seigneurial hall. It continued to be applied to buildings of this form which remained in use in the later Middle Ages, such as the Échiquier itself (de Boüard 1979, 68, note 16).

BIBLIOGRAPHY

BAILY, C. 1876. 'Monks Horton priory', *Archaeologia Cantiana*, 10, 81-9

BIDDLE, M. 1986. *The Old Bishop's Palace, Winchester, Hants,* London

BLAIR, J. 1987. 'The twelfth-century bishop's palace at Hereford', *Medieval Archaeol.,* 31, 59-72

BONNIN, Th. (ed.) 1852. *Regestrum Visitationum Archiepiscopi Rothomagensis; Journal des Visites*

Pastorales d'Eudes Rigaud, Archévêque de Rouen 1248-1269, Rouen

BOÜARD, M. de. 1973-4. 'De l'aula au donjon: les fouilles de la motte de la chapelle à Doué-la-Fontaine (X^e-XIe siècle)', *Archéologie Médiévale,* 3-4, 6-110

——, 1979. *Le Château de Caen,* Centre de Recherches Archéologiques Médiévales, Caen

COAD, J. and STREETEN, A. 1982. 'Excavations at Castle Acre Castle, Norfolk, 1972-7: country house and castle of the Norman earls of Surrey', *Archaeol. J.,* 139, 138-301

COTMAN, J.S. and TURNER, T.H. 1822. *Architectural Antiquities of Normandy,* 2 vols., London

DESQUESNES, R. 1978. 'La baronnie de Bricquebec et ses seigneurs', *Vikland: Revue du Cotentin,* 11, 37-40

FAULKNER, P.A. 1958. 'Domestic planning from the twelfth to the fourteenth centuries', *Archaeol. J.,* 115, 150-84

GALINIÉ, H. 1977. 'La résidence des comtes d'Anjou à Tours', *Archéologie Médiévale,* 7, 95-107

GODEFROY, F. 1892. *Dictionnaire de l'ancienne langue française et de tous les dialectes du XIe au XVe siècle,* 10 vols., Paris

HAINES, C.R. 1930. *Dover Priory: A History of the Priory of St Mary the Virgin and St Martin of the New Work,* Cambridge

HARTSHORNE, C.H. 1845. 'On the ancient parliament and castle of Acton Burnell', *Archaeol. J.,* 3, 323-8

HOMMET, Baron Th. du. 1922. 'Les Du Hommets: barons de Beaumont-le-Richard, connétables de Normandie 1150-1271', *Société Historique de Trévières,* 2, 14-32.

HUBERT, M. 1977. 'Le château de Beaumont'. [Unpublished paper read before the Société des Antiquaires de Normandie]

IMPEY, E.A. 1991. 'The origins and development of non-conventual monastic dependencies in England and Normandy, 1000-1350', unpublished D.Phil thesis, Oxford: Bodleian Library

JONES, M., MEIRION-JONES, G.I., GUIBAL, F., PILCHER, J.R. 1989. 'The seigneurial domestic buildings of Brittany: a provisional assessment', *Antiq. J.,* 69, 73-110

KIPPS, P.K. 1929. 'Minster Court, Thanet', *Archaeol. J.,* 86, 213-23

LE BALCH, C. 1976. 'L'architecture romane du Bessin côtier occidental', unpublished dissertation *(maîtrise),* Caen: Université de Caen

LÉTIENNE, A. and MONS, L. de. 1922. 'Le Château de Beaumont-le-Richard', *Société Historique de Trévières,* 2, 1-14

MAHANY, C. 1977. 'Excavations at Stamford Castle, 1971-6', *Château Gaillard,* 8, 223-45

MESQUI, J. 1988. *Ile de France gothique. 2: les Demeures seigneuriales,* Paris

MICHEL, F. (ed). 1858. *Histoire et Chronique du Très Chrétien Roi Saint-Louis,* Paris

MONCEL, Th. du. 1843. 'Le château de Bricquebec; aperçu général sur le château', *Revue archéologique de la Manche,* 1 [only issue], 1-37

PEERS, C. 1953. *Richmond Castle,* London

RCHM London, II, 1925, London

RENOUX, A. 1979. 'Le château des ducs de Normandie à Fécamp (X^e-XIIe siècles)', *Archéologie Médiévale,* 9, 5-35

RIGOLD, S. 1962a. 'Two *camerae* of the Military Orders', *Archaeol. J.,* 122, 86-122

——, 1962b. *Temple Manor, Strood,* London

SCUVÉE, F. 1979. 'Le château de Bricquebec', *Vikland: Revue du Cotentin,* 13, 3-33

TOY, S. 1953. *The Castles of Great Britain,* London

TURNER, T. H. 1851. *Some Account of Domestic Architecture in England from the Conquest to the End of the Thirteenth Century,* Oxford

VERDIER, A. and CATTOIS. F. 1855-7. *Architecture civile et domestique au Moyen Age et à la Renaissance,* 2 vols., Paris

VIGOUREUX, J.-J. 1972. *La Baronnie de Creully,* Bayeux.

VIOLLET-LE-DUC, E.-E. 1858-68. *Dictionnaire raisonné de l'Architecture française du XIe au XVIe siècle,* 10 vols., Paris

WEST, J. 1981. 'Acton Burnell Castle, Shropshire', in *Collectanea Historia: Essays in Memory of Stuart Rigold,* (ed. A. Detsicas), Kent Archaeological Society, 85-92, Maidstone

WOOD, M.E. 1935. 'Norman domestic architecture', *Archaeol. J.,* 92, 167-242

——, 1965. *The English Mediaeval House,* London

Notes sur l'Habitat Noble Rural dans le Nord et l'Est de l'Ile-de-France du XIIe au XVe Siècle

Jean Mesqui

L'HABITAT NOBLE RURAL AU MOYEN AGE: UN DOMAINE DIFFICILE A DÉFINIR

Prétendre appréhender de façon exhaustive les caractères de l'habitat noble rural au Moyen Age dans une région serait une forfanterie, sans l'appoint d'une recherche longue et très approfondie. Je n'aurai donc pas la prétention de présenter aujourd'hui des conclusions définitives; il n'existe pas, en effet pour l'Ile-de-France d'équipe analogue à celles, plus ou moins étoffées, qui travaillent sur la Bretagne, la Normandie ou d'autres régions. Les quelques propositions que je m'autoriserai à faire résultent tout au plus de la confrontation entre des recherches historiques menées il y a quelques années, et l'analyse architecturale de quelques uns des monuments conservés.

La base de ces recherches très partielles est un dénombrement de fiefs effectué en 1374-8 pour l'apanage royal de Valois, comprenant au nord et à l'est de Paris l'ancien comté de Valois, enrichi de châtellenies démembrées du comté de Champagne et du domaine royal direct; pour les cinq châtellenies, ce dénombrement énumère l'ensemble des fiefs nobles relevant directement du comte de Valois, autorisant une approche horizontale (fig. 1).

Il va de soi que ce dénombrement ne fournit nullement une liste complète, puisqu'il ne répertorie que les fiefs directs, n'évoquant pas les arrière-fiefs, qui purent être nombreux; mais il a l'énorme avantage de donner un instantané garantissant l'existence de certaines résidences nobles rurales en 1378.

A l'opposé, la recherche sur le terrain est extrêmement complexe si l'on cherche, ce qui est mon cas, à se limiter au Moyen Age. La première raison en est le nombre important de résidences nobles rurales qui ont disparu durant la première Guerre Mondiale, sous les bombardements. Une seconde raison est la fréquente transformation des anciennes

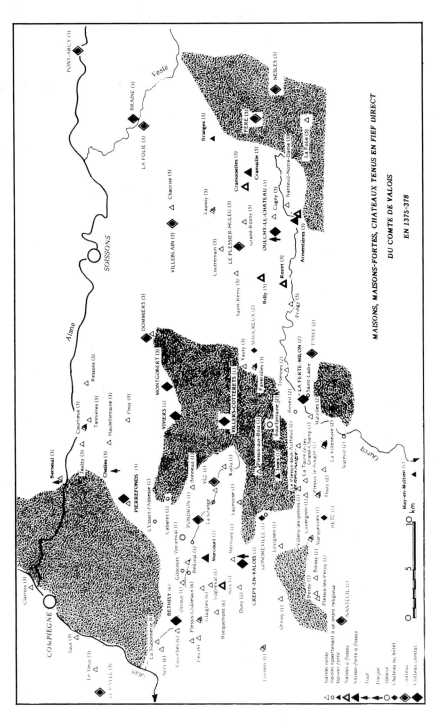

1. *Carte de la région étudiée*

demeures pour s'adapter aux exigences du confort moderne, dans une région à l'agriculture riche. La troisième raison, ce n'est pas la moindre, est la confusion qui existe aujourd'hui entre maisons médiévales transformées, maisons des XVe et XVIe siècles implantées en des sites jusque là vierges, enfin maisons plus récentes encore.

Qu'on me permette ici la plus grande humilité: je ne présenterai qu'un modeste défrichement d'un domaine qui, pourtant, est porteur de vues rénovées sur l'occupation rurale au Moyen Age, et sur la présence noble.

Dans ce défrichement, j'ai voulu mettre en correspondance les habitats ruraux mis au jour avec leurs modèles mieux connus, ceux développés par les strates les plus hautes de l'aristocratie: roi, princes, évêques, seigneurs châtelains. Cette démarche, pour artificielle qu'elle soit, permet de valoriser une certaine typologie des habitats.

LE MODÈLE URBAIN: LE PALAIS ET LA SALLE

Je commencerai par le modèle sans doute le moins connu, pourtant l'un des plus prégnants au niveau de l'histoire urbaine: celui du palais.

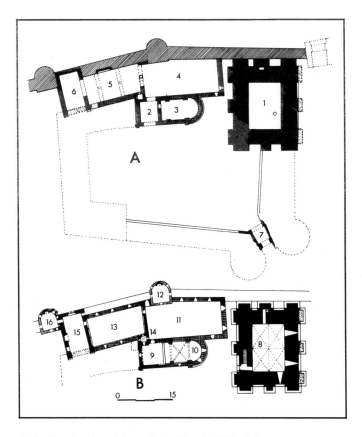

2. Senlis: plan du palais royal du début du XIIe siècle

Palais urbains

Balayons rapidement les quelques palais urbains médiévaux qui peuvent donner les grandes orientations de l'habitat noble à caractère 'civil'. De tous, le palais de Senlis est sans doute le plus expressif: ce palais royal du début du XIIᵉ siècle bâti à côté d'une tour maîtresse remarquable, possède une structure tout à fait claire (fig. 2).

On y trouve, en effet, un ensemble formé par deux grandes salles en prolongement l'une de l'autre. La chapelle à deux niveaux est accolée à la première de ces deux salles, qui sert visiblement de salle publique. La seconde grande salle, joliment décorée d'arcatures romanes, est la salle d'apparat; elle est mise en communication avec la chambre royale, elle-même prolongée par une tour de l'ancienne enceinte gallo-romaine aménagée en chapelle privative. L'ensemble possède deux niveaux, le niveau inférieur étant le niveau d'accès, avec cuisines et dépendance, chapelle pour le commun; un escalier intérieur donnait sur les salles nobles décorées. On trouve ici la trilogie, tout à fait classique, salle-chapelle-chambre; le caractère du maître des lieux explique que la fonction de la salle ait été dédoublée.

Il est, à vrai-dire, peu d'exemples où la structure soit aussi claire. Le palais épiscopal de Beauvais a révélé récemment l'existence d'une grande salle, avec chapelle accolée, sans que la chambre ait été mise au jour. A Provins, l'ensemble palatial est un conglomérat datant des années 1170–1250; on y trouve au moins une grande salle (XIIIᵉ siècle), une chapelle des années 1170 à deux niveaux, comme à Senlis, enfin un édifice à grandes baies résidentielles de la fin du XIIᵉ siècle qui était peut-être la chambre. Dans la première moitié

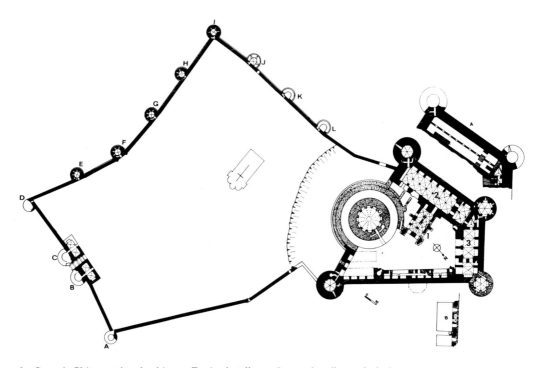

3. *Coucy-le-Château: plan du château. En 1, chapelle; en 2, grande salle; en 3, logis*

du XIIIe siècle, le château de Coucy offre un schéma palatial du même type, avec la salle flanquée par la chapelle, et le corps de logis (fig. 3). Quoiqu'il en soit, le modèle palatial urbain affirme la notion de trilogie *aula–camera–capella.* Voyons maintenant comment ce modèle put être décliné dans le monde de l'aristocratie rurale.

Demeures à salle simple

L'élément de base de cette trilogie est évidemment la salle. Dans les palais décrits, elle est mono-fonctionnelle, dans la mesure où elle est élaborée pour servir exclusivement aux fonctions ostentatoires.

Dans la petite maison rurale, la salle est fréquemment multifonctionnelle. Unique édifice seigneurial, elle accueille à la fois les fonctions ostentatoires et résidentielles. On en trouve un exemple, parmi les plus anciens (début du XIVe siècle?), à la maison de Feu, fief de la châtellenie de Béthisy. Ici, la salle rectangulaire, abondamment ouverte en ses murs gouttereaux, presqu'aveugle sur ses murs pignons, semble avoir été une salle multi-fonctionnelle (fig. 4). Le rez-de-chaussée était accessible par deux portes défendues par de curieuses bretèches: l'une, de grandes dimensions, ouvrait vers la cour intérieure, alors que la seconde, de plus petites dimensions, donnait sur le parc. Au-dessus d'un rez-de-chaussée réservé sans doute au stockage, le premier étage était doté d'une grande cheminée dont subsiste un piédroit (fig. 5).

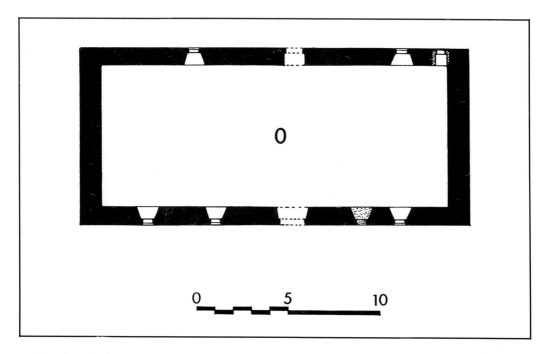

4. *Néry: ferme de Feu. Plan du rez-de-chaussée*

5. *Néry: ferme de Feu. Porte du rez-de-chaussée surmontée de sa bretèche*

6. *Rocquemont: ferme du Plessis-Châtelain. Vue du logis*

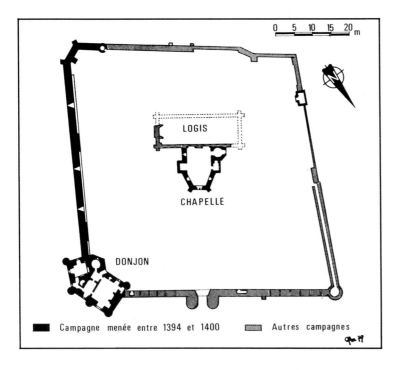

0 5 10 15 20 m

LOGIS

CHAPELLE

DONJON

■ Campagne menée entre 1394 et 1400   ▨ Autres campagnes

7. Vez: plan de l'ensemble fortifié

La maison du Plessis-Châtelain, également fief de la châtellenie de Béthisy, était plus fruste encore; sans doute aménagée au XIIIe siècle, elle ne possédait qu'une salle sans mur de refend, dotée d'une cheminée sur le mur pignon dès le rez-de-chaussée. Au-dessus, au premier étage, prenait place au moins une grande fenêtre à coussièges. Les combles étaient éclairés par deux petites fenêtres encadrant le conduit de cheminée (fig. 6).

Un exemple très intéressant de salle multi-fonctionnelle de ce type se trouve à Vez. C'est à partir de 1360 que fut édifiée la salle rectangulaire à échauguettes dont ne demeurent malheureusement que deux pans. Cette salle possédait dès le rez-de-chaussée une cheminée, d'ailleurs monumentale; mais l'étage noble était au-dessus, au premier, avec une cheminée superbement ouvragée (fig. 7).

Demeures à salle et chambre

Une progression consista à distinguer, dans le complexe de la salle, les fonctions ostentatoires des fonctions résidentielles. Ceci ne fut sans doute pas le plus courant: on sait, en effet, que la promiscuité n'était pas, au Moyen Age, ressentie comme elle l'est aujourd'hui.

SALLE ET CHAMBRE JUMELÉES. Cette solution était la plus évidente, découlant d'ailleurs de modèles palatiaux tels que Senlis. On la trouve exprimée par exemple à Armentières au XIIIe siècle d'une façon remarquable.

Ici, le logis rectangulaire flanqué par des tours circulaires est assis sur l'entrée de la cour intérieure. Cette disposition curieuse s'explique par le fait que la maison-forte comprenait en son sein, dès le départ, deux résidences distinctes attribuées à deux descendants de la même famille. Toutes deux regardaient une petite cour intérieure, mais il fallait passer sous la première pour accéder à la seconde (fig. 8).

La seule conservée en élévation est la première. Le passage d'accès divise l'édifice en deux parties inégales. Au rez-de-chaussée, on trouvait à gauche la cuisine, à droite une salle commune. Pour accéder au premier étage, on devait entrer dans la cour, et emprunter un escalier externe longeant la façade (à moins d'emprunter l'un des escaliers intérieurs aux tours). A ce premier étage, on trouvait la grande salle noble, dotée d'une cheminée monumentale, avec sa chapelle ménagée dans l'une des tours flanquantes. Au-dessus de la cuisine se trouvait la chambre proprement dite, communiquant par une porte avec la grande salle.

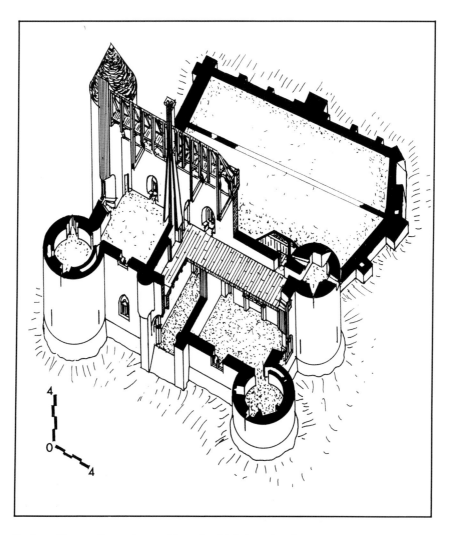

8. *Armentières-sur-Ourcq. Axonométrie en écorché de la maison forte*

9. *Berzy-le-Sec: vue de l'ensemble résidentiel du XVᵉ siècle*

Ce schéma de fonctionnement se retrouve, de façon quasi identique, à la maison de Berzy-le-Sec, plus tardive. Le logis est ménagé au-dessus du passage d'entrée, et il est divisé en salle et chambre (fig. 9).

SALLE ET CHAMBRE DISTINCTES. Un tel schéma de fonctionnement pouvait être sophistiqué à loisir. Le cas de Thiers-sur-Thève, château bâti dans le dernier quart du XIIIᵉ siècle par l'évêque de Beauvais, est très instructif de ce point de vue. Ici, l'on a repris la notion de salle sur l'entrée, avec beaucoup de similitudes avec Armentières. Mais le statut du constructeur a permis de ménager, sur la totalité de la façade, une ou plutôt deux salles en prolongement l'une de l'autre, alors que la chambre était très certainement ménagée dans un édifice indépendant, au centre du château (fig. 10).

LE TROISIÈME ÉLÉMENT DE LA TRILOGIE: LA CHAPELLE. Ainsi peut-on retrouver, dans les demeures rurales, les éléments de base du palais urbain princier, non sans simplifications. La chapelle n'est pas le dernier de ces éléments.
Certes, bien souvent l'on ne la trouve plus, preuve sans doute qu'elle n'a existé que sous forme moins solide que le reste des édifices. Citons cependant le cas du Plessis-Châtelain. Malgré le caractère assez fruste de la salle multifonctionnelle, on trouve une petite chapelle gothique indépendante tout à fait remarquable, voûtée sur ogives, avec ses peintures d'origine.

10. *Thiers-sur-Thève: vue de la façade de la salle palatiale des évêques de Beauvais (vers 1275)*

11. *Rocquemont: chapelle du Plessis-Châtelain*

Il est probable que l'indépendance de la chapelle par rapport à la salle s'explique par le fait que le fief du Plessis-Châtelain était, dès le XIIIe siècle, partagé en deux: la chapelle avait donc à desservir les deux maisons nobles dont existe encore la structure à travers les deux fermes rurales (fig. 11).

On a vu qu'à Armentières, la chapelle est également présente; cette fois, les maîtres des lieux ont profité des défenses du site, les tours flanquantes, qui constituaient autant d'appendices au complexe salle-chambre. La chapelle était donc ménagée dans l'une des tours, en communication directe avec la grande salle. A Thiers, dans le château épiscopal, la chapelle fut également ménagée dans une tour flanquante, cette fois avec un grand luxe: voûtée sur ogives, elle était accessible par une grande arcade gothique bordée par deux oratoires ménagés en encorbellement.

Vez présente également un cas remarquable. Après la construction de la salle multifonctionnelle déjà évoquée, les seigneurs de Vez entreprirent de bâtir une grande chapelle perpendiculaire, tout en coupant la salle par un mur de refend permettant d'y séparer les fonctions. A Berzy enfin, ce n'est que postérieurement à la construction de la salle que l'on songea à construire une chapelle à deux niveaux accessible depuis la salle; faute de place, elle fut ménagée dans le fossé.

LE MODÈLE CASTRAL: LA TOUR

A l'opposé du palais urbain, la tour maîtresse castrale fournissait un modèle intéressant pour la demeure rurale. Intéressant, du fait de son caractère prégnant dans le paysage féodal; mais difficile d'usage, tant était réservé aux plus grands l'usage du symbole de la tour.

Les grands modèles

Il est frappant de constater à quel point les 'grands modèles' de tours maîtresses purent être eux-même conditionnés par la structure palatiale. Bien qu'il ne ressortisse pas de la région étudiée, le cas de la tour d'Ivry, daté du début du XIe siècle, est suffisamment intéressant pour qu'on s'y arrête. Il révèle un programme proche du programme palatial, mais aggloméré dans une bâtisse rectangulaire; on y trouve deux grandes salles superposées, une chambre dotée de son antichambre, ainsi qu'une chapelle à chevet débordant (fig. 12).

Cet exemple, dont on retrouve les caractères à la tour de Grez, au sud de Paris, est caractéristique des exigences résidentielles des grands seigneurs du temps. Au sein même de la tour, on retrouve la trilogie horizontale salle/chambre/chapelle; on trouve également la structuration verticale donnant au rez-de-chaussée une fonction servile, alors que le premier étage est l'étage noble.

Tours rurales

A vrai-dire, la descendance directe dans le monde de la noblesse rurale de tels exemples fut limitée. J'en citerai deux exemples. Le premier est en soi contestable: il s'agit de la tour d'Ambleny. Certes, jamais cette tour n'eut le moindre statut châtelain: il s'agissait bien, en théorie, d'une maison rurale. Pour autant, le caractère de son constructeur, seigneur de Pierrefonds dans la première moitié du XIIe siècle, tend à relativiser le caractère commun de la construction: les seigneurs de Pierrefonds comptaient à cette époque parmi les plus

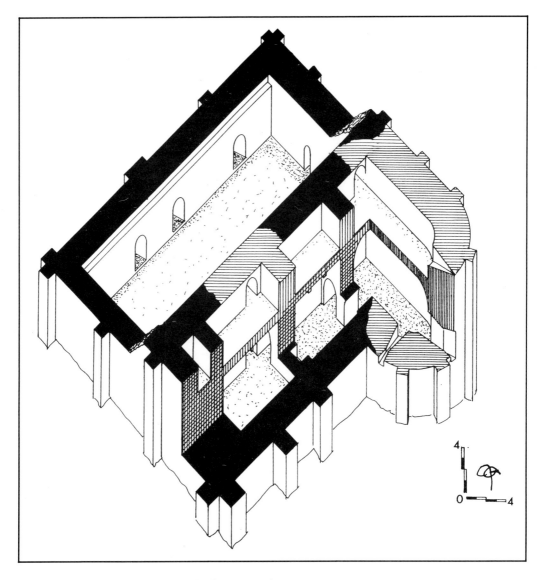

12. *Ivry-la-Bataille: axonométrie en écorché de la tour maîtresse*

puissants du nord de Paris.

Il n'en reste pas moins que la tour d'Ambleny mérite l'intérêt. Cette tour à quatre niveaux fut disposée de telle manière qu'au niveau trois, le niveau noble, on trouvait une structuration avec salle au centre, chambre dans une tourelle, possédant sa latrine reliée par un couloir intra-mural, l'une des deux autres tourelles accueillant selon toute vraisemblance la chapelle (fig. 13). Il est frappant de constater que dans un édifice d'aussi petite taille que la tour d'Ambleny, la trilogie ait été respectée; et l'on ne peut douter qu'elle ait été concue pour le seigneur lui-même.

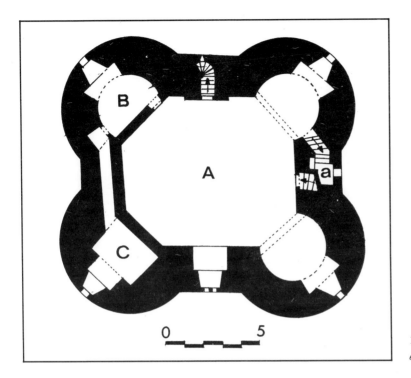

0 ———— 5

13. *Ambleny: plan du second étage de la tour*

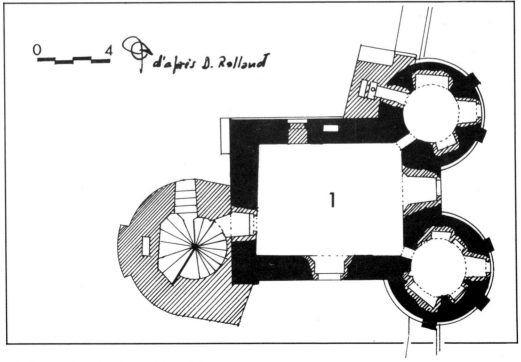

0 ———— 4   d'après D. Rolland

14. *Vic-sur-Aisne: plan du second étage de la tour*

Un second exemple est celui de la tour de Vic-sur-Aisne, sans doute également contestable, puisqu'il s'agissait du chef-lieu d'une châtellenie de l'abbaye Saint-Médard de Soissons. Pourtant, la tour rectangulaire à deux tourelles, malgré son aspect externe très impressionnant, a des murs étonnamment minces par rapport aux édifices contemporains (fig. 14). Sa structure interne est tout à fait remarquable: dans le corps rectangulaire prend place la salle, alors que l'une des deux tourelles circulaire abrite la chambre, l'autre la chapelle. On retrouve ici un programme similaire à celui d'Ambleny.

SALLES-TOURS ET TOURS-SALLES

Mais, à vrai-dire, si le programme externe, hautement symbolique, de tour maîtresse, ne put être retenu par la majorité des seigneurs ruraux, un concept hybride fit son apparition, mélangeant la symbolique de la tour avec les nécessités de la résidence. Les édifices qui virent le jour, dans cette série, furent apparemment extrêmement nombreux. Malheureusement, beaucoup d'entre eux ont disparu du fait de destructions diverses. Je distinguerai, sans doute assez arbitrairement, les 'tours-salles' des 'salles-tours', selon que le programme privilégiait la fonction symbolique, ou au contraire la fonction résidentielle.

Les salles-tours

On retrouve, pour les 'salles-tours', la distinction qui existe entre salle simples et salles à chambres. Commençons par les premières.

SALLES-TOURS SIMPLES. On trouve deux superbes exemples de salles-tours simples dans la région. La première est celle de Montmélian, du début du XIIIe siècle (fig. 15). La salle possède, au-dessus d'un niveau bas éclairé par de simples meurtrières, deux niveaux éclairés par de grandes baies, l'accès s'effectuant au niveau 2. Le niveau 3 était le niveau noble, doté d'une grande cheminée, sans qu'apparaisse le moindre signe de partition interne.

Un autre très bel exemple est celui de la salle Saint-Louis du château épiscopal de Septmonts, de la seconde moitié du XIIIe siècle. Au-dessus d'un niveau largement ouvert par de grandes baies, et doté d'une cheminée, prenaient place deux niveaux résidentiels destinés aux évêques, reliés par un escalier en vis externe (fig. 16). On ne peut manquer de mettre en relation ces salles-tours avec des édifices tels que la salle du château de Mez-le-Maréchal, dans le Loiret.

SALLES-TOURS A CHAMBRE. Au début du XIIIe siècle, deux édifices attestent de cette forme de programme. Le premier, le plus prestigieux, n'est à vrai-dire pas rural; il s'agit du 'donjon' de Crépy-en-Valois, édifice châtelain (fig. 17). Sa forme néanmoins permet de l'assimiler: il s'agit d'une vaste salle à trois niveaux amplement éclairés, rappelant le cas de la tour de Montmélian, à laquelle s'accroche une tour rectangulaire abritant les chambres résidentielles. Au surplus, une chapelle plus ancienne complète cet édifice remarquable.

La structure des communications internes ressemble de près à celle d'une tour maîtresse du XIIe siècle: l'accès est ménagé au premier étage, donnant sur un grand escalier droit conduisant à la grande salle noble, au-dessus de la salle commune. Mais l'originalité réside dans le caractère très ouvert de l'édifice, ainsi que dans la présence d'une fonction chambre matérialisée dans la tour accolée.

15. *Saint-Witz: axonométrie de la tour de Montmélian*

Moins noble de par son occupation, la maison de Sainte-Luce offre une structure tout à fait équivalente. Ici, l'édifice comprend un bâtiment principal formé de deux niveaux superposés, le niveau bas voûté alors que le niveau supérieur est celui d'une salle noble amplement éclairée de superbes fenêtres. A ce corps principal est accolé un long bâtiment abritant l'escalier, et vraisemblablement la chambre seigneuriale. Il n'est pas sûr que cet édifice n'ait pas été siège d'une seigneurie abbatiale (fig. 18).

SALLES-TOURS A TOUR MAÎTRESSE. De façon dérivée, la maison de Crouy-sur-Ourcq, bâtie à la fin du XIVe siècle, offre une structure de salle à chambre; mais ici les chambres prennent place dans une tour formant véritable tour maîtresse. La structure n'en est pas moins totalement identique à celle mise en évidence à Crépy: salles à grandes cheminées (ici, l'on ne trouvait pas moins de quatre salles superposées), chambres dotées de facilités (latrines) (fig. 19).

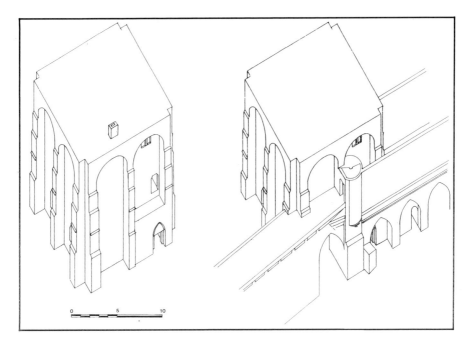

16. *Septmonts: axonométrie de la salle Saint-Louis, avant et après le travaux du dernier quart du XIVe siècle*

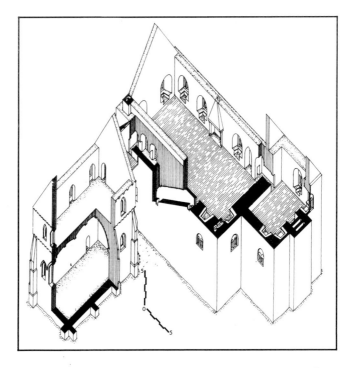

17. *Crépy-en-Valois: axonométrie en écorché de l'ensemble tour-chapelle*

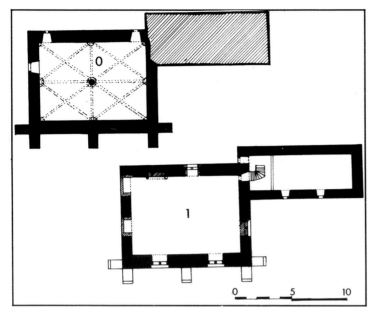

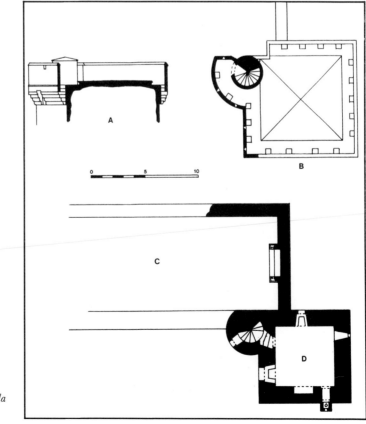

18. *Béthisy-Saint-Martin: plans de la ferme de Sainte-Luce*

19. *Crouy-sur-Ourcq: plan de la maison avec salle et tour*

Tours-salles

On terminera en évoquant les 'tours-salles', édifices où le caractère symbolique de tour l'emporte sur le caractère résidentiel de salle. A vrai-dire, cette distinction est souvent arbitraire, et demeure assez subjective. Deux très beaux exemples en demeurent dans la région, sans doute contemporains. Le premier existe à Morancy, près de Beaumont-sur-Oise, avec une tour rectangulaire flanquée par une tour à archères remarquable. La tour-salle est percée de très belles fenêtres géminées; mais l'aspect défensif prime ici (fig. 20). A Marizy-Saint-Mard, seigneurie abbatiale, la tour-salle, de très petite dimension, est pourvue de trois tourelles sur contreforts, et d'une tourelle d'escalier. A chaque niveau de la tour n'existe qu'une chambre, s'ouvrant par de superbes baies sur l'extérieur.

20. *Morancy: vue de la tour-maison*

CONCLUSION

Cette brève évocation aura permis de mettre en évidence certaines formes architecturales conservées. Il reste que l'interprétation en demeure toujours hasardeuse, du fait de la disparition vraisemblable d'une partie des bâtiments: lorsque demeure un édifice médiéval, rien ne certifie, en l'absence de fouilles, qu'il n'ait pas été accompagné à l'époque de sa construction par d'autres édifices aujourd'hui disparus. On évitera ainsi d'attribuer un trop grand poids à la traditionnelle distinction entre la salle, le *hall* anglais, et les parties résidentielles: les édifices conservés nous montrent en général la salle privée seigneuriale, celle affectée à sa vie familiale. Lorsque le rang du seigneur était suffisamment élevé, il s'y ajoutait certainement un autre édifice dont, bien souvent, a disparu toute trace.

Un second point important à noter, en conclusion de cette brève évocation, tient à la disparition trop fréquente des structures essentielles de la maison noble médiévale, aujourd'hui cachée par des édifices plus modernes, parfois en d'autres sites. Un très bel exemple en est fourni par le reste d'une maison noble à Néry, dans l'Oise, constitué par une tour à arcades ogivales qui formait très certainement une partie de la maison primitive (fig. 21). La ruine, et la reconstruction des dépendances, empêche aujourd'hui de lire en quoi que ce soit la fonction de cet édifice; pourtant, il est certain qu'il existait ici un ensemble important au Moyen Age, abandonné dès la Renaissance.

21. *Néry: vue du reste de la maison noble médiévale*

La recherche des caractéristiques des maisons nobles du Moyen Age passe donc par une analyse extrêmement approfondie sur le terrain, qui doit, en de nombreux cas, laisser de côté les implantations plus tardives dont demeurent les restes monumentaux. Il s'agit ici d'une approche à laquelle ne sont peut-être pas préparés les esprits, tant l'existence de structures anciennes est souvent considéré comme témoignage d'un enracinement ancestral.

RÉSUMÉ

NOTES SUR L'HABITAT NOBLE RURAL DANS LE NORD ET L'EST DE L'ILE-DE-FRANCE DU XIIᵉ AU XVᵉ SIÈCLE

Les châteaux fortifiés, étudiés depuis longtemps en France, sont maintenant bien connus, contrairement aux habitations seigneuriales rurales, peut-être parfois trop modestes pour intéresser les historiens de l'art et de l'architecture.

En 1984, le colloque international intitulé 'La maison-forte au Moyen Age', tenu à Nancy et Pont-à-Mousson, a ouvert la voie à une nouvelle approche, plus en prise avec la vie quotidienne, au sein de leurs demeures, des chevaliers du monde rural. Dans plusieurs régions, telles que la Bretagne et la Normandie, des études détaillées et systématiques, des travaux par petits groupes, développé sous l'égide des universités, sont en cours. Le but de cet article est quant à lui moins ambitieux, faute de moyens suffisants. Il cherche plutôt à définir une typologie, à partir des habitats nobles subsistants, et fondées sur les principales structures palatiales ou castrales.

Trois éléments sont de première importance: la salle, la chambre et la chapelle. Dans chaque résidence, ces trois éléments sont fondamentaux pour la compréhension de l'architecture d'ensemble, mais il est aussi très intéressant de considérer les différences d'association qui peuvent exister entre eux, en liaison avec la position sociale du propriétaire.

ABSTRACT

NOTES ON RURAL NOBLE SETTLEMENT IN THE NORTH AND EAST OF THE ILE-DE-FRANCE FROM THE TWELFTH TO THE FIFTEENTH CENTURY

Fortified castles are now well known structures in France, having long been studied. This is not the case with the rural noble dwellings, perhaps in some cases too vernacular to be of interest to art historians and architectural historians.

In 1984 the International Colloquium 'La Maison-Forte au Moyen Age' held at Nancy/Pont-à-Mousson opened the way for a new approach, closer to the real life of the rural knights in their 'maisons'. In several regions—like Brittany and Normandy—detailed systematic studies involving research by small groups, being carried out under the aegis of universities, are in progress; the aim of the following paper is less sophisticated, because of lack of resources. Rather, it attempts to define a typology, starting from surviving rural noble dwellings, and based on the main palatial or castral structures.

Three elements are of great importance: the *salle* (hall), the *chambre* (the chamber or solar), and the *chapelle*. In each dwelling these three elements are fundamental to an understanding of the architecture; however, it is also very interesting to consider the variation in the combination of these three basic elements, depending of the social position of the owner.

Les Manoirs du Perche

Elisabeth Gautier-Desvaux

Entre Habitat Médiéval Fortifié et Résidence Champêtre du Grand Siècle Un Chef-Lieu Seigneurial à Vocation Économique

La province du Perche, au contact des marges orientales du Massif armoricain et du Bassin parisien, abrite dans son paysage bocager une densité assez remarquable de manoirs, habitat seigneurial rural auquel nous avons eu l'occasion de consacrer une thèse de l'Ecole nationale des Chartes.[1] La présente étude, reprenant des éléments de cette recherche, s'attache à cerner la genèse, la typologie et les facteurs de décadence d'un modèle architectural dont l'essor se situe entre la fin de la guerre de Cent ans et les troubles religieux de la deuxième moitié du XVIᵉ siècle.

Formé à compter de premier tiers du XIᵉ siècle, le comté du Perche dont le territoire correspond à l'actuel arrondissement de Mortagne-au-Perche, dans l'Orne, grossi de possessions limitrophes dans les départements contemporains de l'Eure, de l'Eure-et-Loir, du Loir-et-Cher et de la Sarthe, connaîtra toujours, malgré son rattachement à la couronne royale, en 1226, une indépendance relative; l'usage d'une coutume propre, plus proche du droit parisien que du droit normand, consacrera ce particularisme jusqu'à la Révolution française.

L'emploi du terme 'manoir' pour désigner cet habitat fonctionnel ne procède pas d'une restitution artificielle. Ce vocable, familier aux archéologues anglais, figure en effet régulièrement dans les 'aveux et dénombrements' rendus par les hobereaux percherons au comte du Perche avant d'être transmis à la Chambre des Comptes de Paris; ces documents, dont les préambules sont souvent stéréotypés, mentionnent parfois sur la longue durée le 'chief manoir' ou le 'manoir principal du lieu', comme à Courteraye[3] où figurent en 1409[4] et à la fin du XVᵉ siècle,[5] 'le manoir avec les jardins, le bois et plessays joignant à icelluy', au Chesne dont le 'manoir seigneurial et domaine' se trouve composé, en 1639, de 'court cloze à murailles, dans laquelle sont bastis et ediffiés les logis et bastimens dudit lieu, le jardin et yssues dudit lieu'.[6]

Les archives fiscales, comme on le voit, ont constitué l'une des sources fondamentales de cette étude. Outre les aveux et dénombrements, divers rôles d'impositions extraordinaires, des convocations du ban et de l'arrière-ban, quelques fonds de hautes-justices et fonds privés, complétés par un dépouillement systématique des plans cadastraux dits napoléoniens, par une enquête toponymique et par des relevés de terrain, ont permis de dénombrer plus de

400 lieux seigneuriaux pour la période précitée, dont un quart environ subsistent.

LE CONTEXTE DE MISE EN OEUVRE

Les lendemains de la guerre de Cent Ans dans le Perche

La prolifération de petites seigneuries rurales dont la construction de manoirs matérialise l'existence dans le paysage percheron, au lendemain de la guerre de Cent Ans, s'inscrit dans un mouvement très général de nivellement de la hiérarchie féodale. La longue période de troubles instaurée à compter des années 1330 par le conflit franco-anglais et marquée dans le Perche par deux occupations successives (1336-60 et 1417-49), se conjugue en fait avec plusieurs facteurs défavorables pour entrainer une diminution des revenus de la terre et une baisse de la rente seigneuriale; mauvaises récoltes successives, épidémies telles que la 'peste noire', climat d'insécurité, contribuent à faire régresser les cultures, abandonner des essarts et désertifier les campagnes au profit d'un habitat regroupé.

Cette évolution économique se trouve renforcée par une mutation sociologique assez brutale des cadres de la noblesse: en 1424, la bataille livrée à Verneuil, sur les marches nord-est du Perche, aux confins de l'Ile de France, décime ses rangs déjà fort entamés par la levée de l'ost royal. Un chroniqueur local, le bailli Courtin, rapporte que 'ce fust en ceste bataille que le nom de l'antique noblesse se perdit en la plus grande partie, laquelle demeura sur place; car depuis ce temps, nous trouvons la noblesse porter aultre nom que l'ancien, ce qui est arrivé par mariages des damoiselles qui demeuroient ou veufves de maris, ou héritières des maisons par la mort des gentilshommes leurs maris ou leurs frères . . . De ceste ruyne, la noblesse du Perche est longuement incommodée'.[7] Ce renouvellement lignager est constaté à la même époque par Jean Jacquart en Ile de France: 'peu de familles pouvaient faire remonter la possession de leurs seigneuries et fiefs à un passé lointain . . . A part de rares exceptions, la guerre de Cent Ans avait achevé de décimer et de ruiner la plus ancienne noblesse. Mais elle avait permis à de nouvelles familles d'écuyers ou de chevaliers, authentiquement nobles, venus d'autres provinces, de les remplacer'.[8]

La paix recouvrée et la conjoncture climatique et sanitaire propice (du moins jusqu'au dernier tiers du XVIe siècle) favorisent une reprise démographique spectaculaire, une remise en culture des terres en friches et un redémarrage des essarts, dans les zones intersticielles entre d'anciens fiefs ou en bordure de forêts. De nombreux toponymes, empruntés au vocabulaire sylvestre (la Feillette, le Breuil, les Feugerets, la Touche, l'Epine, la Ronce) ou dérivés de patronymes (La Mouchetière, l'Aître aux Riants, la Galardière, la Bretonnière, la Robichonnière) témoignent de cet essor, inédit depuis le XIIIe siècle.

L'héritage médiéval et la permanence des sites

Cette expansion ne fait cependant pas table rase de l'heritage médiéval, loin s'en faut. Nombre de toponymes dénommant les manoirs recensés, témoignent en effet du réinvestissement de sites anciennement fortifiés ou occupés par des familles d'origine militaire: soit qu'ils désignent des fortifications anciennes (la Ferté, la Frette, le Chastel), l'implantation sur des éminences naturelles (le Tertre, la Butte, le Mont), le recours à des levées de terre artificielles (la Motte), la clôture d'espaces protégés (le Fossé, le Plessis, la Haie, la Barre, les Murs), l'utilisation de dispositifs défensifs (la Bretèche, la Mouchère), soit qu'ils recourrent au vocabulaire désignant la classe chevaleresque, son armement et ses distractions (la Chevalerie, l'Ecu, le Heaume, la Daguerie, la Levretterie), ou plus généralement une vocation militaire (la Guerrière, Bellegarde).

La permanence de l'habitat seigneurial avec réutilisation de sites ou de dispositifs défensifs apparait aussi nettement dans les textes, notamment dans les aveux et dénombrements déjà cités: c'est le cas du fief de Bures dont l'aveu rendu en 1487 mentionne le 'manoir avecque mote et place de colombier',[9] de celui de l'Aunay dont l'aveu rendu en 1490 cite 'la place de coulombier a pié qui souloit estre en la mote dudit lieu ou pies d'icelle, à laquelle mote de paier sont tenus sesdits hommes cens, rentes . . .',[10] ou encore de la Motte de Prez en Ceton (fig. 1) dont le seigneur déclare, en 1654, 'la place dudit chatel et chatellerie de Ceton, nommée la Motte de Ceton dit Prez, assise près le bourg de Ceton, cloze de fossez alentour, sur laquelle antiennement y avoit chastel et bastiments qui ont esté ruinez et à présent n'y a sur icelle que de vieilles murailles et un bois taillis servant de garenne à connils, sauf que sur partie de ladite place est la maison seigneuriale dudit seigneur et basse-cour d'icelluy, enclose et fermée de tours et murailles, et à l'environ est l'estrize de la mettairie dudit lieu seigneurial de la Motte de Ceton dit Prez, où y a grange et estable, fuie, jardins, vergers et autres commodités'.[11]

Ces mottes tronconiques, commes celles de Poix à Sainte-Ceronne ou de la Mesnière à Longpont ne jouxtent toutefois qu'un nombre restreint de manoirs. Plus fréquentes

1. *La permanence du site: le logis du manoir de la Motte de Prez en Ceton s'élève en contrebas de l'ancienne motte seigneuriale, régulièrement citée dans les aveux et dénombrements*
M. Ganivet

apparaissent les dispositions de *moated sites* similaires à ceux étudiés par Madame Le Patourel,[12] éminences légèrement surélevées, ceintes de fossés quadrangulaires, comme au Grand Clinchamps à Chemilly ou au Grand Boulay à Feings. Ces aménagements plus tardifs semblent bien dans certains cas, avoir été destinés à 'mettre l'habitat à l'abri d'une montée des eaux, soit de la nappe phréatique, soit d'une rivière voisine'[13] (c'est le cas de la Guerdière en Marchainville, dans une zone d'étangs, et du Plessis en Dancé). Les remblais de terre de ces *Wasserbürger,* selon la typologie décrite par Müller-Wille,[14] s'avèrent cependant souvent trop modestes pour parer à une inondation saisonnière et caractérisent certaines installations à flanc de coteau telles que Monpoulain en Bubertré. Il peut s'agir alors d'aménagements défensifs sommaires, incrits dans la tradition militaire du fossoiement, et emblématiques du prestige seigneurial.

La permanence de l'habitat seigneurial se manifeste également dans les nombreuses réutilisations de structures maçonnées, tours rondes ou carrées contre lesquelles vient s'appuyer le logis construit à la Renaissance (fig. 2): des exemples spectaculaires en sont offerts à la Fresnaye en Saint-Germain-de-la-Coudre où une élégante galerie Renaissance s'appuie contre les parois massives d'un fort donjon tronqué, à l'Angenardière en Saint-Cyr-la-Rosière, au Royau et à la Tarennière en Préaux, aux Chaponnières en Saint-Cyr-la-Rosière. Le souci d'intégration du neuf dans l'ancien se manifeste d'aillleurs dans la plupart de ces exemples, par le recours décoratif aux galeries, aux tours accolées, aux corniches moulurées, et illustre bien les précepts de Philibert de l'Orme qui recommande 'd'accomoder le vieil bastiment avecques le nouveau, soubz une telle grâce et dextérité que tous les membres de la maison s'y puissent trouver bien à propos et sans aucune subjection'.[15]

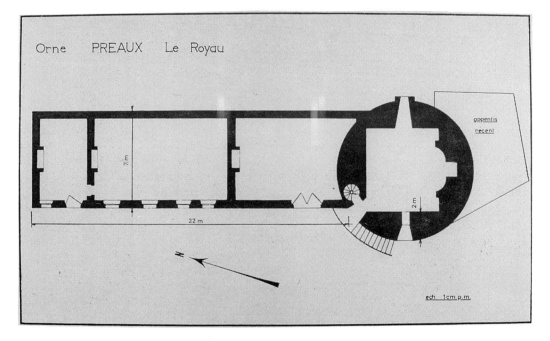

2. *La réutilisation des structures défensives anciennes: la grosse tour ronde du Royau sert de point d'ancrage à la demeure seigneuriale*
E. Gautier-Desvaux; A. Morin

Les innovations: la 'maison rustique' du XVIᵉ siècle

Le propos de Philibert de l'Orme et ses références aux exigences du confort et du décor soulignent bien les préoccupations nouvelles des bâtisseurs de 'maisons rustiques' chères à l'agronome Charles Estienne,[16] et dont la plupart des manoirs du corpus percheron s'avèrent représentatifs. Les critères d'implantation relèvent à l'évidence de l'ordre économique: il suffit pour s'en convaincre d'examiner la densité remarquable de manoirs dans les vallées fertiles de l'Huisne et de ses affluents, selon une disposition linéaire caractéristique que ponctuent de très nombreux moulins; à l'inverse, les terres d'argile à silex, occupées en grande partie par des forêts, notamment au nord et au nord-est du territoire, s'avèrent particulièrement peu propices à de tels établissements seigneuriaux. Un autre facteur de regroupement consiste dans les voies de communication (d'ailleurs souvent implantées dans les vallées): nombre de manoirs, aux noms évocateurs tels que 'le Gué', 'le Pont', 'les Planches', se trouvent ainsi édifiés dans des sites stratégiques pour la perception de péages ou de tonlieux. On notera par ailleurs quelques concentrations sur des sites métallurgiques exploités dès les années 1480, aux environs de Boissy-Maugis, Longny-au-Perche et Tourouvre.

La primauté des facteurs d'implantation d'ordre économique sur les facteurs d'ordre défensif se manifeste également dans l'assiette même de ces manoirs, dictée par la possibilité de captage d'eau potable et d'extraction de matériaux de construction, pierre calcaire et marne, généralement offerte à mi-hauteur des collines du Perche, entre les bas-fonds alluviaux et les hauteurs argileuses: cette disposition est attestée à Courboyer en Nocé, la Moussetière en Boissy-Maugis, Pontgirard en Monceaux, Boiscordes en Rémalard. Semblable parti exclut naturellement toute vocation strictement guerrière, l'approche d'éventuels assaillants pouvant être occultée par les surplombs voisins.

LES CARACTERISTIQUES DU MANOIR RENAISSANCE DANS LE PERCHE

L'environnement

La disposition même des abords du 'chastel et manoir principal' obéit à des principes consignés dans la coutume du Perche, rédigée en 1505 puis 1558, et qui visent à garantir l'intégrité économique et symbolique du manoir: 'appartient aussi audit aisné le bois de haute fustaye estant près et à la veüe de ladite maison . . . Et où près ladite maison y aura plusieurs bois de haute fustaye, ledit aisné sera tenu de prendre et se contenter du plus prochain'.[17] Ce petit bois dont l'existence est traduite par l'appellation de plusieurs manoirs (la Touche, le Breuil) assure en effet la disponibilité de 'merrain' indispensable à l'entretien des charpentes; il signale et garantit l'existence d'un chef-lieu seigneurial, comme le recommande Charles Estienne: 'n'oubliez pas la partie du midy ny aussi du septentrion à l'endroit duquel ferez la touche de bois pour la marque et la défense de vostre lieu'.[18] Il est à noter par ailleurs que les fourches de la justice seigneuriale se trouvent parfois erigées dans ce bois ou à proximité, comme le mentionnait l'aveu de Courtheraye en Saint-Aubin-de-Courteraie: 'le bois et plessays à toutes bestes, quatre setiers de terre en un tenant en laquelle sont assises les fourches de la haute justice dudit lieu'.[19]

La garenne, réserve giboyeuse, et les étangs, réserves poissonneuses, sont donc également mentionnés par de nombreux aveux et dénombrements et figurent dans les livres de raison comme des sources de profit non négligeables du domaine direct. Il en est de même pour les multiples moulins à blé, à tan, à foulon, à fer, à papier dont la production complète les revenus agricoles et dont les bâtiments s'inscrivent à proximité parfois immédiate du logis manorial, comme à l'Aunay en Ceton ou Cherperrine en Saint-Maurice-sur-Huisne.

Le 'pourpris' manorial

La coutume du Perche déjà citée réserve au fils ainé d'une famille noble, outre le bois de haute futaie, 'la haute et basse cour, avec le circuit, estans dedant ledict circuit grange, estables et autres édifices, pressoirs, douves et fossez'.[20] Ce 'circuit' ou périmètre fortifié est encore appelé 'estrize' ou 'pourpris' et protège tant le logis que les bâtiments agricoles et divers bâtiments annexes sur lesquels nous reviendrons.

Dans quelques spécimens du type *Wasserburg*, comme le Grand Boulay à Feings, Clinchamps en Chemilly, La Ventrouse en La Ventrouse, la Pellonnière en Pin-la-Garenne, des douves en eau garantissent ce pourpris. De hautes murailles renforcées de tours d'angle, comme à l'Angenardière en Saint-Cyr-la-Rosière, Vaujours en Rémalard, en matérialisent l'emprise; l'élévation des murailles reste cependant modeste dans la plupart des cas, comme à Boiscordes en Rémalard ou la Moussetière en Boissy-Maugis, où les parements extérieurs de bâtiments agricoles assurent la continuité de l'enceinte (fig. 3).

3. *Le pourpris manorial de la Moussetière en Boissy-Maugis alternativement délimité par des murailles et des bâtiments agricoles, renforcé par des tours d'angle rondes*
M. Ganivet

4. *Une porte charretière, surmontée de créneaux symboliques et doublée d'une porte piétonne, donne accès à la cour de la Moussetière en Boissy-Maugis*
E. Gautier-Desvaux

La porte charretière permettant d'accéder à la cour est généralement doublée d'une porte piétonne plus basse dont l'entrée du manoir de la Moussetière déjà cité, couronnée de créneaux décoratifs, offre un exemple savoureux (fig. 4). Dans certains cas, comme à La Ventrouse, deux tours renforcent la sécurité de ce passage qui peut même prendre l'allure d'un petit châtelet, selon la disposition attestée à Chanceaux en Saint-Jouin-de-Blavou. Malheureusement, les progrès du machinisme agricole ont particulièrement dégradé ces accès; la porte cochère de l'Epinay en Saint-Hilaire-sur-Erre a ainsi disparu, seule subsistant la porte piétonne surmontée d'un écu.

Le quadrilatère ainsi délimité dont la surface moyenne représente environ un arpent, soit 5000m^2,[21] se trouve souvent divisé en deux parties par le logis seigneurial disposé perpendiculairement à son grand côté. Donnant sur l'entrée principale, la cour agricole bordée de bâtiments fonctionnels, grange, écurie, étable, charretterie, pressoir, fournil et autres appentis indispensables à l'exploitation (fig. 5); de l'autre côté, le jardin réservé aux cultures potagères, plantes médicinales et d'agrément. Il est à noter que la façade principale du logis, généralement ouverte sur cour, donne le plus souvent vers l'est selon les conseils formulés par Pierre de Crescens dans son *Livre des prouffitz champêtres et ruraulx* édité en 1530:[22] 'des deux orientations habitables, devons scavoir que la cité, qui est ouverte vers orient

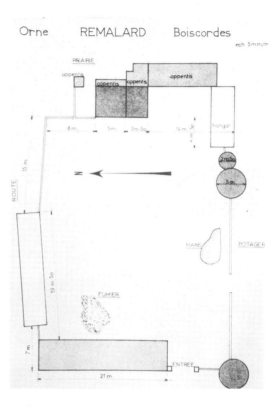

5. *Le pourpris manorial de Boiscordes en Rémalard*
E. Gautier-Desvaux; A. Morin

et qui de droit le regarde en opposite est saine et de bon air, car le soleil au commencement du jour s'eslève au-dessus et clarifie l'air': c'est le cas du Gué en Monceaux, de La Lubinière en Préaux, du Montgâteau en Ceton. Ainsi se trouvent conjugés les impératifs sanitaires et la nécessaire surveillance de la main d'oeuvre agricole.

Dans ce 'pourpris' s'élèvent également des bâtiments dont l'existence est liée à des prérogatives seigneuriales: le colombier et la chapelle. Quelques exemples de colombiers inclus dans le logis même sont attestés au Chêne en Saint-Ouen-de-la-Cour, à Courboyer en Nocé ou aux Rosiers en Réveillon. Mais il s'agit là, semble-t-il, d'exceptions, la disposition la plus fréquente consistant en une tour distincte, parfois une tour d'angle de l'enceinte comme à l'Angenardière ou à Boiscordes (manoirs déjà cités), le plus souvent un édicule éloigné du logis et proche de la mare, afin d'éviter un voisinage malodorant et de permettre aux pigeons de se désaltérer (fig. 6). La présence d'une chapelle liée à l'exercice du droit de patronage est plus rare et ne caractérise que les seigneuries les plus importantes, souvent déjà détentrices du droit de haute justice. Alexandre de La Vove avoue ainsi tenir, en 1579, son 'manoir de Saint-Gilles-de-La-Brière, clos allentour de fossez avec les bois taillis, domayne et dépendances . . . auquel lieu y a une chapelle fondée de Saint-Gilles, en ma présentation et patronage'.[23] Un siècle plus tard, le seigneur du Haut-Montgoubert déclarera 'la chapelle Sainte Catherine avec le droit d'y présenter, construite dans la cour et jardin dudict Montgoubert, plus une fuye à pigeons dans les circuits de la mesme court'. Les manoirs de La Vove en Corbon, Chanceaux en Saint-Jouin-de-Blavou, Vauvineux en Pervenchères

6. *Le colombier du manoir de la Pellonnière en Pin-La-Garenne: les bandeaux circulaires sont destinés à interdire l'accès des rongeurs aux 'boulins'*
E. Gautier-Desvaux

7. *La chapelle seigneuriale de Courboyer en Nocé, incluse dans l'enceinte manoriale (extraite de* La Normandie Illustrée, *Nantes, 1854)*
A. Morin

ont ainsi conservé la chapelle, à la différence du manoir de Courboyer-en-Nocé,[24] malheureusement amputé de son sanctuaire en 1947 (fig. 7).

La vocation proprement agricole du manoir est manifestée en outre par la proximité immédiate de bâtiments d'exploitation, encadrant la mare et le fumier, composantes indissociables de cet ensemble. La grange seigneuriale, de proportions imposantes puisqu'elle doit permettre de resserrer les produits du domaine direct aussi bien que les redevances en nature du domaine indirect, constitue la pièce maîtresse de cet environnement bâti et sa charpente à la forte déclivité, domine nettement les autres appendices tels qu'écuries, étables, hangars, pressoirs, fournil. On notera le souci de décor même modeste qui confère à ces édifices utilitaires une note de rustique élégance.

Le logis

Selon que le manoir a réinvesti un site défensif ancien ou qu'il a été construit d'une seul jet, le plan-masse du logis connait une grande variété d'interprétations. Le type le plus simple est illustré par le Plessis en Dancé ou l'Aunay en Ceton, simples bâtiments rectangulaires que signalent des croisées moulurées protégées par des grilles ouvragées en fer forgé, des cheminées monumentales et des épis de faîtage.

Tout aussi réduits de proportions mais plus emblématiques du prestige seigneurial, La Barre en Ceton (fig. 8), La Mare en Mauve, Courboyer en Saint-Cyr-la-Rosière s'enorgueillissent d'une tour ronde accolée à la façade principale; à la tour ronde peut se substituer une tour octogonale plus élaborée, selon le schéma adopté au Gué en Monceaux ou au Grand Montgâteau en Ceton (figs. 9 et 10).

8. *La modestie du logis manorial de La Barre en Ceton*
E. Gautier-Desvaux

9. *Au manoir des Rosiers en Reveillon,*
une tour octogonale demi-hors-oeuvre
assure la desserte du logis
E. Gautier-Desvaux

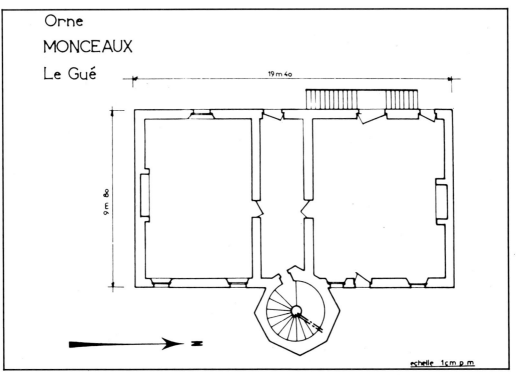

10. *Un schéma traditionnel de distribution interne de la demeure: le manoir du Gué en Monceaux*
E. Gautier-Desvaux; A. Morin

11. *A la Lubinière en Préaux, une disposition plus complexe des tours confère à l'ensemble une savoureuse harmonie: une tour octogonale flanque la façade principale, tandis que deux tours rondes confortent les angles du pignon sud*
E. Gautier-Desvaux

A partir de ces modules de base, bâtiment rectangulaire, tours rondes et polygonales, échauguettes, de nombreuses variantes sont attestées (fig. 11). La plus fréquente consiste en un plan en 'T', dans lequel deux corps de bâtiments, parfois de dimensions identiques, comme à Boiscordes en Rémalard, s'assemblent pignon contre façade. Autre variante, la disposition en 'L' adoptée à La Mare déjà citée ou à La Pelleterie en Bivilliers, dont l'angle intérieur devait être renforcé par une tour. La disposition cruciforme apparaît aussi à Courboyer en Nocé où les tours flanquant symétriquement les façades du logis sont reliées selon un axe perpendiculaire à la ligne de faîtage.

Les matériaux utilisés pour la maçonnerie proviennent généralement de carrières voisines du manoir: le plus souvent, petits moellons calcaires assemblés à l'aide d'un mortier à chaux et à sable (rares sont en effet les exemples de recours au calcaire de gros appareil, tels que Chanceaux en Saint-Jouin-de-Blavou). La brique n'apparait que vers le nord; le seul spécimen d'utilisation de ce matériau que nous connaissions est celui de La Ventrouse. De même, l'utilisation de colombage pour les parois extérieures n'est attestée qu'à l'Epinay en Saint-Hilaire-sur-Erre. Les assises, fort réduites, ne se distinguent que rarement des murs proprement dits; dans certains cas, le grès dit 'roussard' ou 'roussier' est employé, comme au Pontgirard en Monceaux; dans d'autres, au voisinage de terres argileuses, le silex s'y substitue. Les matériaux de couverture consistent généralement en tuile plate sur les toits à deux pentes et sur les tours rondes de fort diamètre; l'ardoise couvre les tours rondes de section restreinte et les tours polygonales; aucun spécimen de dôme en pierre, tel qu'en présentait La Lubinière en Préaux au siècle dernier, ne subsiste aujourd'hui.

Les élévations restent cantonnées à l'échelle modeste de l'habitat étudié: dans bien des cas, deux travées de croisées sur deux niveaux, séparées par la tour de façade qui assure et protège la desserte horizontale et verticale du logis. Dans les bâtiments les plus importants, tels que Courboyer en Nocé, un troisième niveau, réservé à la domesticité, surmonte le premier étage, sur rez-de-chaussée surélevé. Les proportions et le décor des croisées se restreignent souvent en fonction de leur élévation. Il convient néanmoins de noter la qualité de lucarnes éclairant les combles de plusieurs logis, comme au Gué en Monceaux, ou aux Rosiers en Réveillon déjà cités.

Le parti de décor est souvent réduit à sa plus simple expression, corniches ou bandeaux moulurés, encadrements des portes et fenêtres, culots des tourelles, souches de cheminées. Il procède pour une bonne part d'une transposition symbolique des éléments défensifs, tels que créneaux (La Moussetière en Boissy-Maugis), bretèches (La Tarennière en Préaux) ou échauguettes (La Mare en Mauves). Dans les manoirs plus importants, comme La Vove en Corbon, Courboyer en Nocé, l'Angenardière en Saint-Cyr-la-Rosière ou Le Montgâteau en Ceton, des détails sculptés à décors variés, géométriques, végétaux ou figurés, rehaussent la distinction du bâtiment (figs. 12 et 13). Les escaliers et cheminées constituent des supports privilégiés du décor intérieur (escalier hélicoîdal de La Vove, cheminées peintes du Plessis en Dancé et des Rosiers en Réveillon, au même titre que les solives moulurées (Chanceaux) et parfois peintes (le Plessis); on notera en outre quelques spécimens de pavages décorés, gravés de motifs géométriques (La Revaudière en Dancé).[25]

12. *Dans un ensemble héterogène comme celui de l'Angenardière en Saint-Cyr-La-Rosière, une galerie reliant l'une des tours d'angle au logis constitue un élément de confort et de décor; ce dispositif est également attesté à la Fresnaye en Saint-Germain-de-la-Coudre*

E. Gautier-Desvaux

13. *Un spécimen de décor sculpté: le culot de la tourelle accolée
à la tour octogonale de Montgâteau en Ceton*
E. Gautier-Desvaux

VERS DE NOUVEAUX MODELES

Les regroupements fonciers des XVIIe et XVIIIe siècles

Comme nous l'avons mis en évidence, l'extrême densité des manoirs dans le paysage percheron du XVIe siècle, coïncide avec un morcellement caractéristique de la propriété seigneuriale qu'attestent les aveux et dénombrements de l'époque. Une étude menée à partir de ces documents sur cinq manoirs permet de situer autour de quinze hectares la moyenne dc leurs domaines directs, gage d'une indépendance économique même modeste.

Divers facteurs se conjuguent néanmoins dès 1560 pour modifier cet équilibre fragile au profit d'un important mouvement de regroupement foncier. D'une part, les revenus du domaine indirect, déjà érodés depuis la fin du XVe siècle, s'amenuisent très sensiblement à partir de cette date et ne permettent plus d'abonder le produit de la réserve; d'autre part, la croissance démographique de l'après-guerre de Cent Ans, au terme d'une phase de 'rattrapage', aboutit à une surcharge de population sensible; enfin, de 1500 à 1594, diverses épreuves liées aux troubles religieux se trouvent accentuées par des désordres climatiques qui engendrent de mauvaises recoltes successives. Face à une petite noblesse rurale directement atteinte par cette conjoncture de crise, se dessine l'ascension d'une bourgeoisie de robe anoblie par des charges de judicature et de finance ou par des offices municipaux, et d'une bourgeoisie commerçante: la possession d'un fief et des droits honorifiques y afférents constitue pour ces dernières catégories sociales la sanction d'une véritable promotion.

A côté d'une élite aristocratique suffisamment nantie pour surmonter les difficultés conjoncturelles, et d'ordres religieux bénéficiaires du climat de piété et de charité de la Contreréforme, de nouveaux seigneurs rassemblent les terre dont ils entreprennent la mise en valeur raisonnée: en l'espace de cent ans, de 1600 à 1699, la moyenne des domaines 'avoués' à la Chambre des Comptes progresse régulièrement jusqu'à atteindre soixante-quinze hectares. Rassemblés au sein d'un même ensemble territorial, plusieurs manoirs perdent de ce fait leur vocation de chefs-lieux de seigneuries pour celle de simples fermes, ainsi qu'en témoignent les nombreux baux conclus à partir du premier quart du XVIIᵉ siècle.

Selon les cas, le 'principal manoir' du nouveau fief peut se trouver purement et simplement rasé pour faire place à une vaste demeure ordonnée à la manière des modèles de Philibert de l'Orme où basse-cour et résidence se trouvent soigneusement distinctes; plus fréquemment une série 'd'embellissements' permet d'habiller, voire de maquiller au goût du jour le vieux logis; les résultats en sont parfois étonnants et disparates (La Fresnaye en Saint-Germain-de-la-Coudre, La Vove en Corbon).

L'abandon au simple statut de ferme a le mérite d'assurer la sauvegarde de la plupart des bâtiments agricoles et d'une partie de l'enceinte, le logis n'étant plus que partiellement occupé par des fermiers qui en cloisonnent les espaces habités et y stockent, le cas échéant, grains et fruits.

Cette évolution, un peu simplifiée pour les besoins d'une brève synthèse, met néanmoins en évidence le rôle charnière du manoir, en tant que maillon d'une chaîne dont l'habitat médiéval fortifié et la résidence occasionnelle du grand siècle, constituent les liens les plus directs: un habitat à vocation économique, fonctionnel, encore héritier des traditions de défense, mais déjà précurseur d'une recherche de bien-être et d'esthétique, parfaitement intégré dans son environnement naturel.

RÉSUMÉ

LES MANOIRS DU PERCHE

La province du Perche, située aux confins du massif armoricain et du bassin parisien, compte un nombre remarquable de manoirs. Malgré son rattachement à la France en 1226, elle conserva une large indépendance. La coutume du Perche réserve au fils aîné non seulement le bois de haute futaie mais aussi le pourpris: les cours et toutes les dépendances—y compris les murs d'enceinte et les fossés qui protègent l'ensemble—ainsi que les bâtiments étroitement associés aux prérogatives seigneuriales comme la chapelle et le pigeonnier.

La toponymie révèle l'ancienneté de nombreux sites avec des noms qui témoignent de fonctions défensives, de la construction d'ouvrages en terre, d'activités propres à la classe chevaleresque ou encore d'une vocation militaire. La permanence de l'implantation de l'habitat seigneurial apparaît dans les sources écrites comme à travers la réutilisation et l'adaptation de bâtiments plus anciens.

La guerre de Cent Ans a entraîné la destruction de nombreux ensembles et a contribué au déclin et à l'extinction d'un grand nombre de lignages anciens. C'est à la phase de reconstruction qui suivit que l'on doit la plupart des manoirs existants.

Le développement des idées de la Renaissance fut source de changement. Le goût pour la symétrie du plan et la recherche d'un plus grand confort commencèrent à se manifester. Des facteurs économiques, tels qu'une véritable organisation et gestion du manoir, sont mis en lumière par la publication de manuels influents; le maintien de l'unité économique et symbolique du manoir demeure essentiel.

Les XVIIe et XVIIIe siècles apportèrent une plus grande rationnalité. De nombreux manoirs furent rasés pour faire place à de plus grandes constructions édifiées selon les nouvelles modes architecturales; d'autres furent seulement modifiés et agrandis. Beaucoup furent réduits au niveau d'une simple ferme, état dans lequel ils sont parvenus jusqu'à nous.

ABSTRACT

THE MANOIRS OF THE PERCHE

The province of the Perche, on the margins of the Armorican massif and the Paris Basin, contains a remarkable number of *manoirs*. Notwithstanding its attachment to the French crown in 1226 it maintained considerable independence. The custom of the Perche reserves to the eldest son, not only the woodland, but the manorial *pourpris*—the courtyards and all dependent buildings including the enclosing walls and moats—as well as those buildings closely linked to seigneurial prerogative, the chapel and the dovecot.

Place-name evidence demonstrates the antiquity of many sites: names that testify to defence, to the building of earthworks, to the activities of a knightly class or of a military vocation. The permanence of the seigneurial habitat and continuity of site is borne out by documentary evidence; it is also evident in the reuse and adaptation of earlier buildings.

The Hundred Years' War was responsible for much destruction of the fabric of buildings; it also contributed to the decline and extinction of many an ancient family. In the aftermath came a rebuilding to which we owe most of the extant *manoirs*.

The advent of Renaissance ideas led to change. Symmetry of plan and a move to greater comfort begin to appear. Economic factors, with the proper ordering and management of the estate, are highlighted by the publication of influential manuals; the maintenance of the economic and symbolic integrity of the *manoir* remains paramount.

The seventeenth and eighteenth centuries brought change as estates were rationalized. Many *manoirs* were razed to make way for larger structures in the new styles of the period; others were simply adapted and enlarged. Many were reduced to the status of a farm in which form they have survived to the present day.

NOTES

[1] Gautier-Desvaux 1973.
[2] Bourdot de Richebourg 1727.
[3] Commune actuelle de Saint-Aubin-de-Courteraie.
[4] Arch. nat., P 276[1], fol. 23bis.
[5] Arch. nat., P 275[2], fol. 312, n.d.
[6] Arch. nat., P 874[1], fol. 58.
[7] Courtin 1904.
[8] Jacquart 1974, 72.
[9] Arch. nat., P 275, fol. 318.
[10] Arch. nat., P 289[3], fol. 373.
[11] Arch. nat., P 842, fol. 102.
[12] Le Patourel 1972.
[13] De Boüard 1967.

14 Müller-Wille 1966.
15 De l'Orme 1567, LI, chap. I.
16 Estienne 1564.
17 Bourdot de Richebourg 1727, 678.
18 Estienne 1564, 4.
19 Arch. nat., P 275[3], fol. 312, s.d. [fin XVe siècle].
20 Bourdot de Richebourg 1727, 647.
21 Sur 32 'pourpris' avoué entre 1600 et 1700: 19 ont une surface comprise entre 1/2 et 2 arpents; 11 entre 2 et 6 arpents; 2 atteignent 12 arpents (6ha).
22 De Crescens 1486, chap. I, 10.
23 Arch. nat., P 314[1], fol. 21.
24 Arch. nat., P 873[1], fol. 1.
25 Voir l'exemple du domaine de Landres étudié par La Jonquière 1803, 304 et seq.

BIBLIOGRAPHIE

BOÜARD, M. de. 1967. 'Recherches récentes sur les mottes de Rhénanie', *Annales de Normandie*, 17, 359-64

BOURDOT DE RICHEBOURG, J. 1727. *Coutumes des pays, comté et baillage du Grand Perche et des autres terres et seigneuries régies et gouvernées selon iceux, dans: Nouveaux coutumier général ou corps des coutumes générales et particulières de France*, Paris

COURTIN, R. 1904. *Histoire du Perche*, publiée par le vicomte de Romanet et M.-H. Tournoüer, Mortagne

CRESCENS, P. de. 1486. *Le Livre des Prouffitz champestres et ruraux*, Paris

ESTIENNE, CHARLES. 1564. *L'Agriculture et Maison rustique de Monsieur Charles Estienne, en laquelle est contenu tout ce qui peut estre requis pour bastir maison champestre, nourrir et médeciner bestiail et volaille . . .*, Paris

GAUTIER-DESVAUX, E. 1973. 'Les manoirs du Perche'; thèse soutenue pour l'obtention du diplôme d'archiviste paléographe, Paris: École nationale des Chartes

JACQUART, J. 1974. *La crise rurale en Ile-de-France*, Paris

LA JONQUIERE, X. 1884. 'De la division de la propriété territoriale dans le Perche (fief de Landres)', *Mémoires de la Société hist. et archéol. de l'Orne*, t. III, 304-39, Alençon

L'ORME, Philibert de. 1567. *Le Premier Tome de l'Architecture*, Paris

LE PATOUREL, J. 1972. 'Moated sites of Yorkshire', *Château Gaillard, Etudes de castellogie médévale*, 5, 121-32, Caen

MULLER-WILLE, M. 1966. *Mittelalterlichen Burghügel (Motten) in nördlichen Rheinland*, Köln

The Seigneurial Domestic Buildings of Brittany, 1000–1700

Gwyn Meirion-Jones, Michael Jones and Jon R. Pilcher[1]

The primary aims of the project are to identify the elements of the Breton *manoir;* to trace and explain the evolution of the 'manor-house' and its attendant buildings, including their number and function; to establish the function of rooms within the house and their degree of specialization; to establish a typology and chronology of house-type from the point of 'descent from the motte' down to *c.* 1700; to study the changing social position, economic and legal status of the owners of seigneurial residences over the period under investigation; to investigate the extent and nature of fortification; and to establish an evolutionary and chronological sequence for the site-plans of the seigneurial ensembles.

The secondary aims of the project are also important: to date as many buildings as possible; to identify and date the sequence of decorative detail and ornamentation including doorways, windows, chimney-pieces, chimneys and other features; and to establish a chronology and typology of roof-structure using absolute dating techniques, chiefly those of dendrochronology.

These primary and secondary aims are being achieved through extensive and intensive fieldwork; by examination of archive material in both public and private archives; and by the application of dendrochronological dating techniques to selected buildings.[2]

THE HISTORICAL BACKGROUND

Seigneurial domestic buildings can only be fully understood in the context of the totality of rural settlement of which they are an integral part. Much has already been written about the settlement patterns of Brittany; the province is essentially a land of dispersed settlement in which isolated farms and hamlets are the chief elements. By the twentieth century the hamlet was the dominant form of settlement; throughout most of historical time the parish centre, or *bourg,* was no more than a group of a few farms, a *presbytère* and perhaps a smithy, close to the parish church. It was not until the nineteenth century that most Breton *bourgs* grew, with the addition of a school, a *mairie,* shops and other services, accompanied by the building of storeys on to what had previously been predominantly single-storey dwellings. Very few *bourgs* have survived in more or less their original form, witnesses to this earlier period. Although the dispersed rural habitat survives it has been the subject of considerable change since the 1950s with agrarian restructuring and rural out-migration. Hamlets are everywhere apparent; they comprise groups of small farms, from two or three to twenty or more. The long-house—the one-room house with an adjacent byre under the same roof— was the normal form of dwelling until the twentieth century for most of the rural population owning livestock; those without animals inhabited one-room single-storey houses. Farms were small, often very small, rarely exceeding ten hectares. Families—husband, wife and ten or more children—lived their complete life-cycle from birth to death in a single room; cattle and other animals were confined to the lower end of the small rectilinear house, originally without physical separation. Only from the mid-nineteenth century onwards were wooden partitions inserted to separate man and beast.[3] It must not be supposed that the rural poverty which characterizes nineteenth-century Brittany, reaching its nadir in the years before and after World War I when rural out-migration remained high, was always prevalent in earlier centuries. But house-types were little different in earlier times; a family can hardly live in less than one room. It is against this picture of the life and economy of the vast bulk of the rural population that the seigneurial life-style and the dwellings of the upper classes must be measured.[4]

The generic title 'seigneurial residence' is preferred to the more ambiguous *château* and *manoir*. The latter, from the Latin *manere,* is used in Brittany as elsewhere to mean both the *domaine* and the chief dwelling-house itself. There can be no sharp divide between the *manoir* and the *château.* In medieval documents they are often used synonymously, whereas in both popular imagination and oral tradition the two are very different, distinguished in general by size; this distinction is entirely subjective. Except for a few rare cases, every château and its *domaine* may correctly be described also as a *manoir,* but only a minority of *manoirs* are of that scale which leads to their being commonly termed *châteaux.* The great fortresses certainly stand out and there are many smaller *châteaux,* less strongly fortified, which merge into the fortified *manoir.*

Defence may be said to begin only when there is provision for flanking fire, when the defenders are able to protect their own outside walls by lateral fire. Where such provisions are absent, walls and towers are best regarded as being for security rather than defence. After the end of the War of Succession (1341–65) so-called defensive features became increasingly symbolic in many new-built residences, notably so in the smaller houses of the sixteenth and seventeenth centuries.

By the fifteenth century there were upwards of 10,000 noble families in Brittany, distributed unequally in about 1,300 parishes. Some parishes had as many as twenty-five or more noble families.[5] It follows that the density of seigneurial dwellings also shows an uneven distribution, with large numbers in some areas and fewer in others. In general, the denser the pattern of seigneurial residences, the poorer were the noble occupants and the smaller their estates. At least 10,000 seigneurial residences would have been required. Noble families are most numerous in the north, conspicuously so in the Penthièvre, the Trégor and Léon; they are fewer along the poorer southern littoral, in the areas on both sides of the Loire and, in general, along the eastern Marches.[6] Many a *manoir,* especially in northern Brittany, consisted of only a small manor-house, a home farm or *métairie* and an estate often as small as twenty hectares; the *métayer* worked the land and the noble owner usually took half the produce.

The processes by which such a seigneurial regime emerged in Brittany are still little understood. Davies has recently provided a persuasive study of the origins of one powerful early ecclesiastical lordship, that of the abbey of Saint-Sauveur (35 Redon).[7] Within a few years of its foundation in AD 832, free men were entering the abbey's allegiance, handing over their land and submitting to various forms of service. In later centuries these would be described as feudal: labour services, corvées, suit of court, and the payment of a whole array of customary rents. An earlier, highly fragmented, largely self-regulating society—of peasant villages and hamlets in which the leading figures were machtierns, who exercised a curious combination of judicial and social functions—is caught in its last phases. After AD 875 machtierns almost entirely disappear from the record; in their stead it is the abbot of Saint-Sauveur who now acts as lord of the parishes, *plebes,* in which the abbey held land. Superior authority—that of the 'king' or 'princes' of ninth-century Brittany—was little felt at a local level.

Then followed the Viking attacks on the province and the disintegration of the Carolingian *regnum.* Documentary evidence fails; when it once again becomes adequate we are in a world socially and politically dominated not only by many ecclesiastical lords, abbots and bishops, but even more obviously, by secular counts and powerful castellan lords. Between *c.* 970 and 1066 it is the counts of Rennes who exercise a more general hegemony as dukes of Brittany; after 1066 the counts of Nantes and Cornouaille gathered ducal powers into their hands, chiefly through the accidents of succession. In their entourage were many castellan lords *(domini),* whose hold on military and political power is as evident in Brittany as it is in many other parts of France in this period. Some undoubtedly held their positions by delegation of ducal or comital authority. But in most cases we can only speculate on the circumstances in which seigneurial families came to hold the castles from which they dominated the surrounding countryside.[8] Their gradual usurpation of public authority for their own private interests is, however, a process which may be traced in Brittany during the eleventh and twelfth centuries. By 1200 there were some forty or so major castellanies in the province; most survived intact till the seventeenth century, some to the Revolution. The evolving military architecture of their major castles is a fascinating subject; it is not one which can be seriously treated here.[9]

During the period when castellan lordships developed, a larger social group consisting of knights—*milites*—is to be found in the service of both dukes and castellans. They performed garrison duties and fought for their lords on campaigns, though levels of service remain modest in comparison with those exacted in the Anglo-Norman realm. Some of these knightly families were cadet branches of more aristocratic lineages. Charter evidence reveals many of them possessing not only estates but considerable political and economic freedom, owing only the loosest allegiance to feudal superiors. These families are, in the main, the ancestors of the numerous late medieval Breton *noblesse.*

But what of their origins? Were they, for instance, the descendants of the machtierns of Celtic Brittany? Is there an even longer perspective? Many seigneurial sites of later periods are associated with evidence of earlier phases of occupance as M. Meuret has recently observed with regard to some Merovingian and Carolingian sites.[10] Continuity between Gallo-Roman villas and even earlier periods may be suggested in some cases as at Les Fossés (22 Plélan-le-Petit), or Coadélan (22 Prat).[11] Many ancestors of the medieval and early modern *noblesse* may, however, have simply been men who took advantage of disturbed times to establish a local hegemony. A partial answer for their success is provided by archaeological evidence: motte-and-bailey castles. In the obscure post-Carolingian period in Brittany, apart from great castellan lords, the *milites* are the men who own these primitive early private fortifications.

Over six hundred mottes have already been discovered in the province. Such dating evidence as there is confirms that they developed from the tenth century onwards, whilst a study of their siting shows that, as elsewhere, it is economic factors every bit as much as military reasons which explain their distribution. Many are closely connected with the great colonization of virgin lands which occurred in this period.[12] It is with the petty 'lords' who directed this movement and their dwellings that we are principally concerned.

In the course of two or three centuries this embryonic *noblesse* not only continued to expand rapidly in numbers, but was brought into formal feudal relationship with the great castellan lords and the duke himself.[13] In this way a strong tenurial framework was formed that endured to the end of our period. Furthermore, it is from the records—*aveux, minus, hommages*—generated by these feudal relationships that the vast bulk of our documentary evidence for *manoirs* and other seigneurial buildings is derived.[14] Before passing to a review of the archaeological and architectural evidence for these buildings, however, something may be said on the question of nomenclature.[15]

Castrum/castellum, mota/motte and other terms usually associated with medieval fortified buildings or sites—*fortericia, haie, plessis, roche*—are encountered frequently in Brittany. Most of them occur widely in place-names. Some, like *haie* or *plessis,* have a distinct regional distribution; others appear to be general in usage, though their appearance in charter evidence may be tardy. The first *mota* mentioned specifically in such a source is in 1208 when mottes had long existed in the duchy.[16] No examples of *dongio/donjon* in an early Breton context have been discovered and only a few of *turris.* The combination of many of these elements with a proper name—Châteaugiron (35), La Motte Glain (44), La Roche Bernard (44), Le Plessis Balisson (22)—is a particularly well marked feature of the early period in which important castellan lordships were founded. But the habit was one which persisted. It influenced the formation of estate- or lordship-names for the rest of the Middle Ages: a presumption that such elements or names indicate early seigneurial authority is legitimate. But each case requires investigation before that presumption can be properly authenticated.

In addition to elements indicating some degree of fortification, personal names compounded with topographical or vegetal descriptions—*tertre, touche, launay, noë, bois (coët* in Breton-speaking regions)—are also frequently found in a seigneurial context. Many may be associated closely with the main wave of medieval colonization. Although older in origin, *villa/ville* is likewise very common in medieval place-names in both its Romance and Breton form (*ker*). Unfortunately, in so far as there has not been as much rigorous study of Breton toponyms in this period as there has been of those of the early Middle Ages, little can be said with certainty about chronological or evolutionary patterns.[17]

The earliest written evidence for buildings of seigneurial status in medieval Brittany comes from the Cartulary of Redon.[18] This contains one of the most significant surviving collections of Carolingian charters (some 350 in all) for the period from around AD 800 to AD 920 (in eleventh-/twelfth-century copies). These show that the machtierns usually inhabited residences which, when not simply described as houses (*domus*), were called *aulae (lis/lez (-iou)* in Breton). *Lis/lez* is a very common element in Breton place-names and there is clearly an analogy with the medieval and modern Welsh *llys,* court or aristocratic dwelling.[19] The cartulary makes plain that some *aulae* contained several chambers and that, besides their domestic usage by men of high status, public functions were occasionally performed at them. [20]

It is probable that some *lezioù*, especially those located in open country, were also protected by a surrounding enclosure, ditch, hedge or palisade. However, so far, since most literary descriptions are cryptic and it has proved difficult to identify *aulae* in archaeological contexts, we are largely ignorant about their real form. A possible exception is la Montagne du Prieuré (29 Locronan) where recent excavations have revealed a complex in which, among other activities, there was working of gold in the early tenth century. This site has been identified by Philippe Guigon as seigneurial and he has further speculatively linked it with a *chastel* mentioned in the late twelfth-century *Chanson d'Aquin* or the *aula* of King Gradlon cited in the *Vita Ronani*, compiled around 1230. [21] Unfortunately, La Montagne is not a Breton equivalent of Doué-la-Fontaine (Maine-et-Loire); [22] by the mid-eleventh century the site was deserted, though a later name, Les Salles en Locronan, is suggestive. Elsewhere it seems likely that some *lis/lez* sites subsequently developed as early motte-and-bailey castles.

Aulae are specifically mentioned at some castles at a relatively early date; at Rennes (35), Josselin (56), Châteaubriant (44) or Fougères (35), for example. [23] At the latter the remains of an impressive thirteenth-century seigneurial hall may still be seen. The dwellings of those of knightly, rather than baronial, rank were normally termed *domus* in the central Middle Ages. This is, however, a particularly flexible term in medieval Brittany. Charter evidence shows that it was applied to peasant homesteads and town houses as well as to the dwellings of the nobility. Analogy with other regions suggest that when used in this latter context *domus* normally signifies the existence of a *donjon* (keep) or tower, the most characteristic feature of a *maison-forte*. [24]

Although the terms are not very frequently encountered in conjunction in Brittany, *fortericia, domus* and *maison* do suggest some local examples of this type: a tower, with or without an attached hall, chamber-block and outbuildings. Moreover, simple early towers of this type can be identified archaeologically, incorporated in later surviving buildings (22 Hac en Le Quiou, 22 Coadélan en Prat). The fullest excavation of a Breton *maison-forte* so far undertaken is that of Sainte-Geneviève (56 Inzinzac-Lochrist). [25] Here a moated and fortified enclosure of the thirteenth century was replaced by a three-unit *manoir* during the fifteenth century. [26] Whilst it is likely that many such *maisons-fortes* developed in Brittany after 1200, as they did elsewhere, both written and archaeological evidence currently remains scanty.

The descriptions discovered in early Breton charter evidence for seigneurial dwellings—*aula, domus, turris, palatium*—fade rapidly after 1200 with the exception of *domus*. Indeed *palatium* was always very rare: that which Étienne de Fougères, bishop of Rennes, built at Rannée (35) around 1170 appears to have had many characteristics associated with later manors. It is described as a stone building some one hundred feet long, with appurtenances, enclosed by a wall and surrounded by fruit orchards. [27] It has been suggested that the place-name Le Pallet (44), where an impressive natural motte with the remains at its foot of an early quadrangular keep, testifying to the importance of the *castellania Palatio* in the twelfth century, derives from *palatium*, a reference to an earlier Roman villa in the locality. [28] *Thalamus*, a chamber, perhaps one sometimes used for storing money and other valuables, is also a very rare usage in Brittany; a charter of 1172 was dated *in thalamo Vitreii*, whilst a few years earlier in 1166 Duke Conan IV confirmed a grant to the abbey of Savigny *in thalamo iuxta turrim*, in all probability at Rennes. [29]

The origins of the manor in Brittany are particularly obscure: the institution existed long before the term *manerium/manoir* was used to describe it: an estate held by someone of superior social status, divided between a demesne with a reserve, usually worked by a dependent peasantry, and other tenures and rights. In the early eleventh century there is mention in charters of such estates with *medietariae/métairies,* home farms that were an integral component of all late Breton manors.[30] But the term *manerium/manoir* itself is only present from the early thirteenth century. Its use spreads from provinces lying to the east of Brittany just as other feudal terminology and practices had done in an earlier period. Moreover, as it crosses the duchy during the century it is accompanied by two other terms: *herbergementum/herbergement* and *maison/mansion.*[31] In all three instances they may simultaneously represent both the ensemble of buildings constituting the seigneurial residence and also the demesne and financial or juridical rights attaching to manorial lordship. They are not mutually exclusive; they are parcel of a much larger vocabulary relating to degrees of seigneurial authority.

By the later Middle Ages, the vernacular was predominant in Breton manorial terminology: *manoir, herbergement* and *maison* were commonly joined after 1400 by *salle* and *hôtel.* Whilst it would be true to say that each of these descriptions may be attached to particular forms of seigneurial residence and that some consistency (or hierarchy) of usage is observable, hence a crude typology could be constructed, as in earlier times the various categories are by no means exclusive. The same building or complex of buildings can be described (even in the same document) in several ways: we also have many cases of what literary scholars term synecdoche, a part standing for the whole and vice versa. Just as in the earliest period *aula* might represent a single hall or a series of buildings, even a whole castle, so in the late Breton Middle Ages, *salle* may refer to the major building of a seigneurial site, the hall, or to the total manorial complex. Attempts still occasionally made to distinguish *châteaux* from *manoirs* are similarly doomed to failure in Brittany unless the most rigorous chronological and temporal distinctions are observed.[32]

An early example is provided by documents summarizing arrangements made in 1248 when the viscounty of Porhoët was divided between heiresses. They survive in both Latin and French versions. Where *herbergamentum* serves in one, *manoir* appears in another.[33] A few years later the manor of Bodegat (56 Mohon) is similarly described as both *manerium* and *herbergamentum.*[34] It was the centre of a small lordship, which survived to the end of the Ancien Régime; for a couple of centuries it was owned by the Sevigné family. Its site is a low platform within a curve of the River Ninian, surrounded by still visible ditches and water-meadows.[35] In some charters it seems that a distinction is being made between the actual residence (*manoir*) and the estate (*herbergement*) but ambiguity persists. Without archaeological investigation or more explicit written evidence we can seldom say, on the basis of nomenclature alone, what form the actual buildings of a *herbagementum, manerium* or *château* took.

To take a later example, Travers (22 Erquy) was called an *hôtel, manoir* and *maison* in successive fifteenth- and sixteenth-century *aveux.*[36] Many other contemporary *manoirs,* without any apparent addition to their architectural ensembles became *châteaux* in the sixteenth or seventeenth centuries. On the other hand some terminological changes do reflect architectural developments. Reference to the 'new castle' at Quintin (22) in 1202—if it is not a new work *ab initio*—suggests the replacement of an earlier structure with a new stone fortress, itself ultimately replaced in the seventeenth century.[37] The 'new manor' of Kerdéozer (29 Pleudaniel), referred to in an *aveu* of 1481, was built in the early fifteenth century if an inscription with the date 1418 still visible on a chimney-piece may be accepted.[38] The site of Le Bois Orcan (35 Noyal-sur-Vilaine) was a *masure* or *herbregement* in the late fourteenth century; *la meson neuffve* is mentioned in 1407; an *aveu* of 1458 first refers to *la salle* and one of 1460 to the *manoir;* in 1583 the seigneury was erected as a castellany; a *minu* on the death of Joseph de Morais, comte de Brezolles, who died in Savoy in 1692, begins *'Et premierement, le chateau et seigneurie du Boisorcan . . . '.*[39] By linking the documentary evidence with the architectural and archaeological we obtain some certainty: it is more than time to turn to the rich architectural evidence.

THE PERIOD *c.* 1000 TO THE FOURTEENTH CENTURY

Evidence of the earliest-known medieval buildings, meagre though it is, derives from three sources: archaeology, archival material and the iconography of the Bayeux Tapestry. Unfortunately for our research, medieval archaeology has made relatively little progress in Brittany; we lack, for example, the high-quality excavations of rich sites, often patiently carried out in campaigns of many seasons duration, that have so illuminated our knowledge of medieval England and Germany. Only at Leskelen (29 Plabennec) and Sainte Geneviève (56 Inzinzac-Lochrist) have excavations relevant to our interests been of real quality, yielding significant results.

We have already drawn attention to the large number of mottes in the province.[40] They vary considerably in size and, for the most part, their dates must remain a matter of speculation. Three Breton mottes are illustrated on the Bayeux Tapestry—those of Dinan, Dol and Rennes—as substantial mottes bearing timber *donjons,* though with what degree of real accuracy we cannot say. As the late Allen Brown writes of the Bayeux Tapestry, 'making due allowance for possible ignorance, for artistic licence, and for the inevitable lack of perspective and proportion, we may surely expect it to provide an idea of the overall appearance of these different sorts of building, if no more'.[41] The more important domestic buildings, palaces and manor-houses, are represented on the Tapestry by their halls alone, confirming the central role of the great hall in medieval domestic architecture. Of the ten halls in the tapestry, three are in Normandy, all ground-floor halls.[42] None of the halls illustrated shows any internal division; all are free-standing buildings without either chamber-blocks or service rooms adjoining. The hall in which Duke William holds his council before the invasion shows, in the centre of its roof, what looks like a louvre for a central hearth. It is also evident from the buildings depicted that both stone and timber construction techniques were then current in northern France, though the nearest examples to Brittany are in the adjacent province of Normandy.

The motte-and-bailey castle is portrayed five times on the Tapestry. At all three Breton sites illustrated—Dinan, Dol and Rennes—the ditch and counterscarp about the base of the motte are clearly shown. All display a timber bridge, fitted with wooden steps, crossing the ditch and rising to the summit of the motte. At Dol there is a gate at the top of the bridge; at Dinan the gate stands at the foot. At Rennes a palisade circles the flat top of the motte. This iconographical evidence is particularly valuable for the representation of the timber towers standing upon the mottes, within the palisade, smaller versions perhaps of the great timber-frame *donjon* described by a twelfth-century chronicler, Lambert of Ardres, upon the motte of Ardres.[43] The obviously timber tower at Dinan appears to stand on stilts on top of its motte, an arcaded structure—evidence that in the *donjon* the principal room is at first-floor level—and also providing more room for movement on the restricted summit of the motte. An interesting comparison has recently been brought to light in the excavation of the site of the original *donjon* of the *château* of Fougères where the earliest evidence is of a ring of large post-holes; these might plausibly be interpreted as having accommodated an open arcade similar to that illustrated on the tapestry at Dinan. [44] The structure on top of the motte at Rennes is more massive with a domed roof and a porch—perhaps a *logis porche*—at the head of the timber bridge. At Dol a crenellated tower is shown with a chequered pattern in the upper stages, the latter interpreted by Brown as a covering of plates of hide, wood, tile or metal, to protect against fire and missiles. [45] That these are timber buildings is dramatically highlighted by the rendering of the siege of Dinan where the tower is being set on fire. The Bayeux Tapestry thus testifies to three points important to our understanding of mid-eleventh-century Brittany: the existence of the motte-and-bailey castle in a well developed form; the presence of a fully established timber-frame tradition; and the development of the tower to provide storeyed accommodation.

Breton mottes vary considerably in size. Some are ten metres or so in height, others rise only a metre or two above the surrounding land and are constructed in the form of a truncated cone with a platform capable of supporting several buildings, presumably encircled by a palisade. Others, whilst being of considerable height, have smaller platforms which could have supported only a *donjon,* or tower, and little else. Archaeological and documentary evidence show that some mottes continued in use until the fifteenth century. Only at Leskelen have excavations been of a quality and scale sufficient to enable significant conclusions to be drawn about the number of buildings, their function and form. [46] Here the motte is a magnificent stone-revetted structure ringed by a deep ditch. A stone-built *chapelle* stands in the *basse cour.* In the eleventh century a large house of wood and clay, roofed with thatch, was constructed and defended by a wooden palisade. The motte reached its final form at the end of the eleventh, or the beginning of the twelfth, century when stone ramparts protected the summit, the wooden house by then having been replaced by a stone tower designed as much as a seigneurial residence as for defence.

Here is indisputable evidence of a seigneurial building of timber and clay pre-dating the construction of the ?eleventh-/twelfth-century motte, with a stone *donjon* serving as a seigneurial residence; the ground-floor room of the *donjon* measures 5.55m by 6.50m internally (the size of the hall of the single-cell peasant house, or the long-house, of later centuries). This room, under which there was a subterranean *cave,* appears to have been relatively high—in excess of 4m—and an oven, presumably a bake-oven, contrived in the wall of one of the angles. A kitchen function for this ground-floor room is thus entirely plausible, the *cave* serving as a store for drink. There is evidence to suggest that this stone-built ground-floor unit supported a timber-frame structure containing upper chambers. [47] If this interpretation is correct then we have here a complete seigneurial residence in the form of a simple tower-house—a type which recurred in medieval Brittany—with accommodation arranged vertically, kitchen and service functions below, private hall immediately above and chambers above the hall. There can be no essential difference between such an arrangement additionally fortified as a *donjon* and the solar tower of many a *manoir.* The motte of Leskelen appears to have been abandoned, *c.* 1400, in favour of a *manoir* built in the *basse cour.* Subsequent evolution involved the transfer of the seigneurial residence to the small *manoir* of La Salle nearby, at the end of the sixteenth, or beginning of the seventeenth, century. [48]

It is not only the sheer numbers of mottes—over six hundred have already been identified in the historic Duchy—but their site and situation which suggests that their function was not entirely, nor necessarily primarily, defensive. Some are sited in impressive defensive locations; others occupy valley sites. Indeed, many motte sites are exactly where one would expect to find most of the later medieval *manoirs,* in choice locations with an assured supply of good water, juxtaposed between the arable fields and the meadow. These are the prime agricultural sites and the question of continuity of occupance from much earlier periods is immediately raised. Although evidence for most manorial sites is at present tantalizingly absent, it is difficult to believe that in a region where the best soils have for so long been densely settled, many *manoirs* are not the lineal descendants of Gallo-Roman *villae.* We suggest that administrative and economic considerations, as well as the well-being of the seigneur conscious of his status and desirous of enhancing his *domaine,* were at least as important as defensive considerations. Social position, the desire to increase wealth and the need to produce enough food to feed a retinue were prime considerations. Thus the location of Quillimadec (29 Ploudaniel), on the flood-plain of a small but rich and well watered valley, is entirely consistent with the need to manage an estate to maximum profit and at the same time be well placed for the exercise of administration and justice. Quillimadec became the seat of a marquisate in the seventeenth century but its medieval history is completely unknown before the fifteenth century. [49]

Mottes were designed for war, certainly, but they were also—and more importantly—the seat of seigneurial power and authority. The number of instances in which a motte may be associated with a nearby and later—and often relatively small—seigneurial house is remarkable. We have previously cited the example of Le Châtellier (22 Saint-Samson), where a tiny motte survives at the end of the *allée d'honneur,* opposite the *chapelle,* and on the edge of the *basse cour* in which the fifteenth-century *manoir* stands to this day, the whole on the edge of arable land in a dominant position overlooking the valley of the Rance. The natural motte of Brélidy (22 Brélidy) dominates the surrounding countryside, clearly an example of a well chosen defensive position, but nevertheless of paramount economic and administrative importance (fig. 1). The earliest mention of 'le chastel de Brelledi' so far discovered is in letters of 13 June 1342 by which Charles de Blois, duke of Brittany, granted it to Antonio (or Ayton) Doria, a Genoese in French and Breton service, following its confiscation from Eon de Trésiguidy. In the fifteenth century a cadet line of the Rostrenen family held Brélidy and it passed at the beginning of the sixteenth century to the Du Parc, sires de Locmaria. The estate was finally split up and sold in the mid-eighteenth century. [50] The magnificent and largely natural motte of Le Pallet (44 Le Pallet) provides a similar example, the Romanesque choir and apse of its former *chapelle castrale* surviving to function as a mortuary chapel for the adjacent cemetery. [51]

A motte was, by its very presence, size and situation, a symbol of seigneurial prestige, power and wealth. Like the *château* which superseded it, it was the ultimate status symbol of its period to which every seigneur might aspire. Its construction and enhancement was consequently a desirable objective for any lord, whether its defensive qualities were effective or not or even whether they were ever to be put to the test. In the same way, at a later stage, that the defensive features of the late medieval *manoir* were often—too often—largely symbolical of seigneurial position and power, and of only limited practical use in the event of conflict.

From this evidence two threads emerge which are to run continuously through Breton seigneurial building tradition: the co-existence of a timber-frame tradition with that of building

1. *Brélidy (Brélidy, Côtes-d'Armor): the natural motte with the later residence below*
Photograph: Gwyn Meirion-Jones

in stone; and the provision of *chambres,* often stacked in a tower, in seigneurial residences. The ground-floor hall is everywhere present and from at least as early as the twelfth century the upper hall makes its appearance. The *donjon* is only a tower-house adapted for defence, in its simplest form consisting of several rooms stacked one above the other. As we have seen with the timber-frame *donjon* at Dol, the ground-floor can take the form of an open arcade, whereas at Leskelen there is a true ground-floor room, with stone walls, having a kitchen function. The room immediately above must, by its very position, be the most public of the tower rooms—the hall, albeit sometimes a private hall—and one may reasonably suppose increasing privacy with height, the most private room in a tower being the uppermost.

Sites such as Leskelen and Brélidy also provide evidence of the use of stone as a building material in the eleventh and twelfth centuries. The extent to which the use of stone for walling—and the knowledge of stone construction techniques—has been continuous since Roman times is difficult to assess. As we shall see, the probability is that most building in the eleventh and twelfth centuries, when the first known surviving seigneurial buildings came into existence, was of wood. Stone construction certainly existed, both in domestic and ecclesiastical architecture, but timber construction was dominant. The earliest description of a *manoir* relates how Étienne de Fougères, bishop of Rennes (1169–79), constructed a *palatium* of stone at Rannée, Ille-et-Vilaine: *Nos vero ibi palatium lapideum fere centum pedes habens in longitudine, et appendicia et murum in circuitu, propriis sumptibus reedificavimus . . . et viridarium quod adjacet palatio proprio sumptu emimus, et in eo plures propriis manibus inseruimus surculos.* All nine Breton bishops possessed at least one *manoir* in the later Middle Ages, those of Rennes and Nantes usually maintaining three or four simultaneously.[52]

Of the seigneurial *ensembles* we have studied in detail, several have elements to which twelfth- or thirteenth-century dates may be ascribed on stylistic grounds, dates confirmed in several cases by dendrochronological dating of oak timbers. We have already drawn attention to the first-floor hall with a rear ground-floor kitchen unit, at Dol-de-Bretagne, stylistic details of which suggest a twelfth-century date.[53] It must be emphasized that the upper, or first-floor, hall is a well known phenomenon in twelfth-century France. Our recent fieldwork in Cluny, in collaboration with French colleagues,[54] suggests that in that one Burgundian town alone there are in excess of one hundred Romanesque houses of this type surviving, mostly behind later façades; Cluny is still a Romanesque town, substantially unchanged since the early thirteenth century. If these figures are grossed up for those French towns with surviving early houses known to us, then it may not be an exaggeration to suggest that a total of some two thousand twelfth-century houses may now survive in France. The upper hall, as the focus of family life for the established bourgeois or the rural seigneur, is a well-established fact in twelfth-century France and we should therefore not be surprised to find it even on the Atlantic fringes of Europe.

Not far away from Dol, in the *commune* of La Boussac, on the edge of a north-facing escarpment, with wide views across the bay of Mont Saint-Michel, stands the *manoir* of Le Brégain, once a *prieuré* of the abbey of Saint-Florent-lès-Saumur. What we see today is the somewhat mauled former ground-floor hall with a stair-turret, on the western wall of which the roof-crease outlines the presence of the former upper-hall roof-line; a pair of doorways at ground and mezzanine levels suggests that there was once an eastern continuation of this building. A water-leaf capital on the solitary surviving jamb of the chimney-piece suggests a late twelfth-century date for the ground-floor hall. Stubs of former tie-beams, surviving within the masonry of the present stone walls, at what we believe to have been tie-beam level of the twelfth-century ground-floor hall, give a dendrochronological date within the range 1171–90, according with the typological dating suggested by the chimney-jamb (fig. 2a).[55] That Le Brégain at this date consisted of only a ground-floor stone hall is suggested by the fact that these surviving stub tie-beams are of relatively small scantling, too small to have been load-bearing in a hall of such width. We can only speculate about the nature of the roof structure at this date, but the probability—based on our knowledge of twelfth-century French roof-types—is that it was of the collar-rafter type, trussed with periodic tie-beams marking the bays. Thus we postulate an open hall with a lateral chimney-piece, rather than with the open hearth so common at this date in other parts of the Anglo-Norman world. As yet we have not a shred of evidence for the open hearth at this social level in any part of Brittany, although it is difficult to believe that it did not exist. Indeed, at the lowest social level, it survived until the 1950s in the impermanent dwellings of the rural poor.[56]

It may be significant that when this hall was rebuilt about a century later, massive floor beams with heavy cambered braces were inserted, at a slightly higher level than that of the stub tie-beams to carry the (new) floor of the upper hall. Unfortunately, both hearth and chimney-piece of this upper hall were destroyed, presumably at the time when the upper storey was demolished to create the present farm buildings. The earlier roof structure is also lost. Only the two massive ceiling beams (fig. 2b) are thus available for dendrochronological analysis, yielding a date '1272 + ',[57] which accords well with the architectural details and style, not only of the massive Savoyard windows, but of the ogee-headed doorway with its roll-moulding and the detailing of the stair-turret. The position of the twelfth-century

2. *Le Brégain (La Boussac, Ille-et-Vilaine): (a) remains of the late twelfth-century chimney-piece; (b) the late thirteenth-century arch-braced tie-beams*
Photographs: Gwyn Meirion-Jones

its roll-moulding and the detailing of the stair-turret. The position of the twelfth-century entrance to this ground-floor hall is not certain; it may have been on the site of the present doorway, but examination of the masonry suggests that this late thirteenth-century doorway was inserted into a pre-existing wall at this time; this evidence, taken with the fact that the stub tie-beams embedded into this same walling yield a late twelfth-century date, are sufficient to confirm that the twelfth-century hall was built with stone walling. Accommodation at Le Brégain at this early date thus consisted of a stone-built ground-floor hall with a lateral chimney-piece and such other seigneurial *chambres* as have now disappeared; there is no evidence to suggest whether there was a chamber-block and, if so, whether it was contiguous or detached. By the end of the thirteenth century a second, first-floor, hall had been added above the earlier ground-floor hall, together with a stair-turret, containing in its uppermost part three superimposed cells—two *chambres* and a small *chapelle*. Of a kitchen and *chambre seigneuriale* at this date there is no trace; the only clue to their former existence may be the two doorways in the tower unit, opening on to the east; the kitchen presumably stood here, with the *chambre seigneuriale* above.

In the heart of the Trégor the *manoir* of Coadélan (22 Prat) stands in a classic seigneurial location in a shallow valley, a stream dammed to form a pair of lakes/fish-ponds with subsidiary ponds; it is a classic spring-point site (fig. 3). Whilst the question of continuity of occupance can be a vexed one, with absolute proof elusive, it is certainly suggested here.

3. *Coadélan (Prat, Côtes-d'Armor): the early tower lies at the rear of the house to the left. The entrance doorway opens into the* salle basse, *above which is the upper hall. The kitchen is to the left of the stair turret*
Photograph: Gwyn Meirion-Jones

At the entrance to the former walled enclosure stands a *chapelle,* only twenty metres or so from a large *menhir,* positioned over a spring which issues from its base to feed one of the smaller ponds. The present house is of several builds; a full analysis of this complex building is to be published elsewhere. [58] For the moment we should note a pair of superimposed halls, an embryo cross-passage, a kitchen and a pair of towers, one of which has a very early look about it. As ceiling beams in the kitchen and the cross-passage have yielded dates of 1304–16 and 1365–81 respectively [59] it is reasonable to suppose that the tower is of thirteenth-century date or earlier. A similar primitive tower of the 'tower-house' type survives at Suscinio (56 Sarzeau), almost certainly part of the ducal building works of Pierre Mauclerc (1213–37) from 1218 onwards (fig. 4). [60]

The Coadélan tower has all the appearance of a thirteenth-century or earlier date. It is the solar tower *par excellence* containing a ground-floor store and two heated *chambres* above, each provided with a latrine. Whether this was a solar tower associated with a detached timber-frame ground-floor hall, or whether the present stone-built halls unit was preceded by an early hall of stone attached to the tower, is a matter of speculation. For the moment we simply do not know. It is clear, however, that in the early fourteenth century the present structure was either constructed, or reconstructed, with a first-floor hall open to the roof, over a ground-floor hall. Perhaps it was at this date that an open hall with central hearth was replaced by the superimposed halls with chimney-pieces; for the moment we can only speculate. There is reason to believe that this upper hall may have been furnished with

4. *Suscinio (Sarzeau, Morbihan): the early thirteenth-century tower rises behind the modern footbridge*
Photograph: Gwyn Meirion-Jones

speculate. There is reason to believe that this upper hall may have been furnished with projecting galleries, front and rear, linked by internal galleries; surviving corbels on the outside walls of the building are difficult to explain unless they served as support for timber galleries (the walls were lowered in the sixteenth century); furthermore, internal doorways in the upper hall gables can only be satisfactorily explained if they provided access to internal galleries overlooking the upper hall. We know that the building was the subject of extensive reconstruction in the years following 1659 when the upper hall was ceiled; not only do its timbers yield dendrochronological dates, which suggest a felling date of *c.* 1660 for the main beams, but we have recently discovered the building contract of that year which lists not only the dimensions of all the timbers used, but also the costs.

The excavated seigneurial site of Sainte-Geneviève (56 Inzinzac-Lochrist) provides evidence of a *maison forte,* perhaps of late thirteenth- or early fourteenth-century date, protected by ditch and bank, completely rebuilt towards 1450 to form a three-unit house with rear kitchen, bakehouse and other offices. This appears not to be a particularly well endowed site although it continued to be occupied until the mid-sixteenth century when it was abandoned.[61] Another complex *manoir* to which we refer in more detail, below, is Le Bois Orcan (35 Noyal-sur-Vilaine) where at the rear of the present building there is clear evidence of a reused fourteenth-century doorway. At the highest seigneurial levels, particularly in the inhabited castles, there is much evidence of stone building construction in the thirteenth and fourteenth centuries. The great inhabited *donjons* of Largoët (56 Elven)—the tallest surviving seigneurial *donjon* in France—and Grand-Fougeray, of Fougères, the Tour Solidor (35 Saint-Servan) and of the now sadly degraded Coëtmen (22 Tréméven), are constant reminders of the power and status of their builders.

Attention must be drawn to two aspects of the ground-floor hall in France. There is never a physically-bounded cross-passage at the lower end as there nearly always is in late medieval English manor-houses. In a few houses where stone partitions occur these can be shown to have been inserted later. Whilst there may well be a pair of opposed doorways at the lower end of the hall, marking what we call an embryo cross-passage, the visitor entering by one of these not only has an unrestricted view of the whole hall as far as the hearth, usually in the gable wall, but may also be immediately seen by all in the hall. It may be that non-permanent timber screens were present in some houses but no evidence of such has yet come to light. In some seigneurial houses the visitor may also discover that the [ground-floor] hall floor slopes upwards from the lower to the upper (hearth) end, irrespective of the ground slope outside, emphasizing the status of the upper end of the hall. Such is the case, for example, at La Salle (22 Plurien), Coadélan (22 Prat), Le Bois Orcan (35 Noyal-sur-Vilaine) and Le Plessis Josso (56 Theix). The gently rising floor level subtly impresses upon the visitor the high social status of the owner, his power and position expressed, in his absence, by the elaborate chimney-piece, almost invariably bearing his arms on the bressumer; the eyes of the peasant are elevated to the presence of his earthly lord (represented by the hearth and chimney-piece) in the same way that in church—where not infrequently the nave rises gently towards the east—his eyes gaze upwards to the presence of his heavenly Lord in the Eucharistic sacrifice upon the altar.

THE FIFTEENTH CENTURY

It is to the fifteenth century that many *manoirs* largely owe their present appearance, having been built, or rebuilt, during the century. Whilst there is evidence of building activity during the long period of the Wars of Succession and the Hundred Years' War, there was also much destruction. Rebuilding became increasingly common from *c.* 1400 onwards and many, if not most, Breton *manoirs* owe something to the spirit of renewal and reconstruction of the period.

Mottes, as we have seen, were already well developed by the mid-eleventh century, passing their apogée in the fourteenth century; some continued to be used—and inhabited—throughout the Wars of Succession into the fifteenth century, after which they ceased to be viable. They provided only limited accommodation and restricted movement; the arrival of artillery and the improvement of fire-power in the later fourteenth, and especially the fifteenth, century also led to the need for much stronger stone fortifications, something the dukes of Brittany were to provide in a vigorous burst of castle-building.

We have referred elsewhere to the rebuilding of Bien Assis (22 Erquy),[62] for which there is documentary evidence' of considerable importance.[63] Geoffroy de Quelennec held Bien Assis from *c.* 1412 and showed himself to be a model landlord. He was concerned not only with rebuilding the house itself, but also with improving the estate. He had 'fait de belles mesons et grandes reparacions oudit manoir de Bienassis et fait de beaux amenagemens'. Among the latter he had brought land back into cultivation, planted orchards and woods, enclosed and drained fields (*fosser*) and created meadows so that where previously there had only been five days mowing there were now thirty. The description of Geoffroy's building activities is just as interesting. Several witnesses to legal proceedings of 1434, in which his paternal uncle Jean, vicomte de Fou, claimed possession of 'lostel et manoir de Bienassis', confirmed that when Geoffroy entered the lordship there was no suitable place for him to live and how 'ledit manoir estoit mal loge et y avoit une ancienne salle gaste et vide laquelle led. Geoffroy [de Quelennec] a fait tresbien reparer et ediffier'. The former *manoir* consisted of only 'une vieille salle fondee sur postz de boays ou maniere de cohue'. As a result of his improvements Bien Assis had been turned into 'un des beaux manoirs du pais et deparavant ny avoit qune veille salle gaste de lancienne faczon' as he had built there 'une meson neufve' where he had painted 'chambres et salles', which several witnesses described as 'bien amenagées' (the oldest, eastern, part of the present *manoir*) (fig. 5).

5. *Bien Assis (Erquy, Côtes-d'Armor): the early fifteenth-century rebuilding*
Photograph: Gwyn Meirion-Jones

This evidence is of the utmost importance for establishing beyond doubt the existence of the timber-frame tradition at the beginning of the fifteenth century. That timber-framing is regarded as being of some antiquity is confirmed by the hall's having been built in 'lancienne faczon'; the implication is that not only was the timber-frame hall an 'old' type, but also normal and therefore widespread. *Cohue,* a term widely used and understood in Brittany, derives from an original verb meaning 'to make a noise', 'a hubbub'; it was transferred to the location of the 'hubbub', and came to mean the market hall itself, particularly a timber, aisled, market hall. Several of these survive in Brittany—at Clisson, Le Faouët, Plouescat and Questembert, for example—and many more have been lost since the nineteenth century. Whilst we cannot be certain that the timber-frame hall of Bien Assis was aisled, it does seem probable, both from the reference to 'posts of wood', and by the analogy with the *cohue;* these market halls are always aisled structures. This is the first categorical statement for the existence of the timber hall in fifteenth-century rural Brittany at the level of the manor-house and there is the further implication that such a constructional form was ubiquitous.

Other evidence of timber-framing in Brittany is not wanting. Vestigial timber-framing, at the lowest social levels, is known in certain areas during the nineteenth and early twentieth centuries; timber-frame construction from the fifteenth and sixteenth centuries survives in many of the towns. Urban evidence is insufficient by itself, however, to establish the former presence of the technique in the countryside. Only in the east of the former Duchy, around Fougères and Rennes, is there a significant quantity of timber-framing in surviving rural buildings, forming a true region of timber-framing. Some manorial buildings retain vestiges of this tradition; it occurs frequently in Ille-et-Vilaine and is by no means absent further west. It is particularly known in gatehouses (as in the former gatehouse of the abbey of N.D. des Anges (29 Landéda) and at Tréhorenteuc (56 Tréhorenteuc)), as well as for the construction of galleries which must have been common to judge from surviving evidence. The field-worker has the distinct impression, as he observes that region of eastern Brittany where the tradition is still strongly represented, that he is observing a zone in regression and that it must once have been much more extensive. There is the further, negative, evidence for this period of rebuilding of the fifteenth century. Many *manoirs* display no trace whatsoever of stone construction that can be ascribed to a period earlier than 1400; these stone houses may not be just reconstructions of earlier stone residences, but—as in the case of Bien Assis— reconstructions in stone of former timber-frame dwellings. In Finistère the rebuilding is later in many instances, being of sixteenth- and seventeenth-century date. This evidence, coupled with that of the Bayeux Tapestry, above, is sufficient to establish the existence of a widespread timber-frame tradition in the province before the fifteenth century. That many of the largest *châteaux* and *manoirs* were stone-built from an early date is not in dispute; the fifteenth century was not just a rebuilding of stone structures damaged by war and neglect, it was very much a great rebuilding in stone of a ravaged countryside in which timber-frame construction was common and in which it had for centuries co-existed with stone construction techniques.

It is only in the fifteenth century that the full range of the buildings of the manorial complex becomes clear. This is partly because so much building survives from that date and partly because documentary evidence is then more abundant. The *manoir* generally occupies a choice agricultural site, frequently located at, or close to, the junction of arable land and meadow, a point where the water-table is high and springs break forth. Here at the edge of a gentle valley we have the optimum location as, for example, at Les Fossés (22 Plélan-le-Petit), Le Plessis Josso (56 Theix), Hac (22 Le Quiou), La Bourbansais (35 Pleugueneuc), Kergroadès (29 Brélès) and Goulaine (44 Haute-Goulaine); not all of these are moated sites, but all display most of the attributes of the fully developed manorial ensemble. Nevertheless, the moated *manoir* exists in very large numbers and moats were certainly an established form of defence before the fifteenth century, although we are not yet able to say when they first came into fashion. Protection is also provided in many cases by a seigneurial lake, serving also as a fish-pond, formed by damming the valley; such is the case at Coadélan (22 Prat), at Kervéatoux (29 Plouarzel), at Le Plessis Josso (56 Theix), at La Bretesche (44 Missillac) and at Le Rocher Portail (35 Saint-Brice-en-Coglès). Where the relief so permitted, such a lake may have been only one of several fish-ponds; the fine series at Le Rocher Portail is an excellent example. Fish-ponds may be associated also with *viviers* or fish-tanks; a magnificent series, constructed in stone, is to be seen at Beaulieu (22 Languédias), once a monastic property, where the seigneurial lake provides power for a mill and the dam carries a causeway, or *chaussée*. Such multiple functions are common: water from the outlet of the lake at Le Plessis Josso serves also to drive a mill-wheel and the dam carries the main approach road, the *chaussée*. These examples are repeated at Kervéatoux, at Le Rocher Portail, at Hac and many other locations. Woods, gardens, orchards and the *allée d'honneur* are conspicuous elements of the manorial landscape. Although stables for horses often form part of the manorial ensemble, farm animals are almost always a little distance away, at the *métairie*, usually sited outside the manorial enclosure, be it walled, moated or both; the *métairie* of Trécesson (56 Campénéac), alongside the *chaussée*, just before the drawbridge, is a very good example. The manorial enclosure is characterized by the residence itself, by ancillary buildings, by an enclosing wall and sometimes a gatehouse which may be integrated into the *enceinte*. Access to the walled courtyard is via the gatehouse and there is rarely a secondary entrance.

Many a *manoir* displays evidence of fortification; arrow-loops may occur in a few very early buildings, and gun-loops are found in many structures. Some sites are obviously defensive and effectively so. Kerouzéré (29 Sibiril) and Kerjean (29 Saint-Vougay) were built with serious defence in mind. Other residences may more accurately be described as *maisons fortes*, built for security rather than serious defence. We agree with the view that defence *sensu stricto* only begins when there is provision for flanking fire, i.e., the enclosing walls can be covered by flanking fire from within.[64] This puts Plessis Josso, for example, on the borderline between security and defence (fig. 6). Many *manoirs* in the middle and lower ends of the scale, could scarcely have held out against attack for more than a few minutes! Their 'defences' might have been a deterrent to cattle rustlers, but their walls were both too low and too long to have been effectively held. Most of the 'defensive' features to be seen today in the majority of *manoirs* are a reflection of seigneurial pretentions and symbolic of seigneurial power; they do not seriously contribute to defence.

Two building types frequently draw attention to themselves by the prominence of their architecture and by the fact that they are often free-standing: the dovecot, or *colombier*, and the *chapelle*. Both are ubiquitous. The dovecot is usually free-standing but occasionally incorporated into one of the buildings of the manorial ensemble as in the tower of the *logis porche* at Mesedern (29 Plougonven) or in the upper gable of Le Chêne (22 Trévron). The *chapelle* may be some distance from the manoir, located at an ancient holy site, long predating the seigneurial residence. More generally, the place of family (and community) worship forms part of the manorial *ensemble*, free-standing either inside or outside the courtyard. It sometimes forms part of the walled enclosure as at La Haye (35 Saint-Hilaire-des-Landes) or at Kerjean (29 Saint-Vougay), or is incorporated into the house itself as at Hac (22 Le

6. *Le Plessis Josso (Theix, Morbihan): the largely fifteenth-century house, to which a sixteenth-century* pavillon *was added. The ensemble is provided with walls and a corner tower for protection: here we see provision for security rather than serious defence*
Photograph: Gwyn Meirion-Jones

Quiou), La Roche Jagu (22 Ploëzal), Kerouzéré (29 Sibiril). At Coadélan (22 Prat) there is both a chapel within the house and another close to the entrance.

HALL AND CHAMBER

The concepts of 'hall' and 'chamber' are evident from the earliest identifiable seigneurial buildings, as we have seen. It is the presence of an upper *chambre* in addition to the ground-floor hall, or *salle basse,* which distinguishes the seigneurial residence from that of the peasant who lived entirely in one ground-floor room. The lord's *chambre* might be at mezzanine level over a semi-sunken *cave,* or it might be at full first-floor level over a kitchen. Such an arrangement—*salle basse, chambre* and *cave*/kitchen—we have termed the 'seigneurial minimum' accommodation. Occasionally where the *chambre* lies over a *cave,* a kitchen is located in a rear outshot. Where a specialized kitchen is altogether absent, cooking must have been done in the hall; we have no evidence yet for the former presence of outside cooking arrangements or detached kitchens.

The *salle basse* served not only as a common hall for the lord's household; it was also the general meeting place for both the estate and the community at large. Gossips were to be found hanging around the *manoir* every day as is reported at Bien Assis;[65] people came to the *manoir,* to talk about their problems and exchange news. The hall was frequented by villagers, neighbouring gentry and visitors on a daily basis, not just on high days and holidays; hospitality was provided, and tables kept ready, to feed any newcomer to the seigneurial hall, at least at the upper end of the social scale, as is demonstrated by the *manoir* of L'Hermitage (22 Lorges) in 1468 where four tables 'qui se dresoint touzjours en la salle dud. lieu de premiere assiepte a digner et a souper de dresouer en taxes, couppes, eguieres et petiz potz dargent'.[66]

In the fifteenth century many a *salle basse* must have been of the 'open hall' type, its roof trusses visible, in those *manoirs* where an upper hall had not then been constructed. A number of open ground-floor halls survive to this day little altered, save for the insertion of a ceiling to create a loft-space (we shall return to this phenomenon below, p. 183), witnesses to the two classic roof-types: the 'double' roof with king-post trusses, and the collar-rafter truss 'single' roof, with a third, hybrid, type occasionally found in which king-posts have been introduced into the collar-rafter system. It must be stressed that there is no trace of former open hearths in these open halls; chimneys were placed generally in the upper gable wall, but lateral chimney-pieces are sometimes found. One has the impression that the sight of the bare bones of the roof structure was considered unacceptable, if not downright vulgar, and the finer quality roofs are often barrel-vaulted—boarded (*lambrisée*)—leaving only the tie-beams and king-posts visible. The *chambre seigneuriale*, too, was likely to be open to the roof, almost invariably has its own chimney-piece and frequently a latrine; other common fixtures are a window with shutters and *coussièges* and an *évier*. Chimney-pieces are generally of good quality and often very fine indeed. The splendid late sixteenth-century chimneypiece now displayed in the castle of Pontivy (56) comes from the *manoir* of Coët Candec.

A number of *manoirs* have survived from this period almost unmodernized though sometimes modified and frequently damaged in the process, to serve today as farm buildings. Examples include the subsequently extended La Salle (22 Plurien) where the *chambre seigneuriale* stands over service rooms with a pair of service doorways on the English model; the kitchen here stood at the rear and was provided with a serving hatch. Other examples are Les Vergers (22 Hillion); Le Carpont (22 Trédarzec), a house of three-unit form with the *chambre seigneuriale* at the lower end over the kitchen, and a second pair of *chambres,* one above the other at the upper end; Le Boberil (35 L'Hermitage), where additional accommodation was added to the rear during the sixteenth century (fig. 7); Le Téhel (35 Saint-Symphorien) and La Ville Andon (22 Plélo), both *manoirs* of three-unit form. Carjégu (22 Yffiniac), although much modified, is a very good example of the seigneurial 'minimum' with a *chambre* over the kitchen, the latter connected to the hall by both a doorway and a *passe-plat,* as is La Ville aux Fèvres (22 Plélo).

A striking phenomenon is the persistence of the inhabited, or solar, tower in the architecture of the fifteenth century to which attention has been drawn elsewhere.[67] We have referred (above, p. 170) to the early-looking tower of Coadélan (22 Prat), and the pre-1448 solar tower of Hac is now well known.[68] To these may be added the early tower incorporated into later work at Suscinio (56 Sarzeau) and a possible early solar tower now forming the lower end of the *manoir* of Le Plessis Josso (56 Theix). These surviving solar towers are not just a Breton phenomenon, many examples may be cited over the length and breadth of France.

A second, persistent, feature of Breton seigneurial residences is the phenomenon of the upper hall, or halls, for as many as three—and occasionally four—are found in the grandest buildings, superimposed to form a veritable 'hierarchy of halls'. A pair of superimposed halls is relatively common in the larger *manoirs,* as we have noticed at Le Brégain (35 La

7. Boberil (L'Hermitage, Ille-et-Vilaine): an open ground-floor hall, with the seigneurial chamber raised over a cellar
Photograph: Gwyn Meirion-Jones

Boussac). Hac (22 Le Quiou) has three, the uppermost contained partly within the roof-space and having a fine barrel-vaulted roof structure; L'Etier (56 Béganne) has three, the uppermost, like that of Hac, being partly accommodated in the roof-space; the gatehouse of Suscinio (56 Sarzeau) boasts four storeys, the uppermost hall again being carried into the roof-space. This arrangement for the uppermost hall is very common and is to be found in buildings of the highest quality, witness that at Josselin (56 Josselin) where dormer windows—the usual method of admitting light to such a hall—are fashioned with all the extravagance of the late Flamboyant style. This hierarchy of halls can pose certain problems of interpretation; where there are two there can be no doubt that the ground-floor hall performed its time-honoured function, whilst some form of social selection limited those invited up to the first-floor hall; it can be no accident that at both Hac and Kerouzéré, to cite but two instances of many, the second hall still functions as a *salon*, the latter-day equivalent of the medieval upper-hall. It is more difficult to explain why at Hac, the *chapelle* opens on to the third, uppermost, hall, whilst at Kerouzéré and La Roche Jagu it opens on to the first-floor hall; at Suscinio it is related to the second-floor hall.

Hierarchy is also evident in the arrangement of *chambres*. We have noted that the *chambre seigneuriale* is always raised up to at least mezzanine level and its presence is usually announced externally by window dressings finer than those of any other window, save possibly that of the *salle basse*. Internally, a fine chimney-piece, window-seats, a latrine and an *évier* are usual. Other *chambres* also have such fittings, although usually characterized by a quality which just fails to reach that of the *chambre seigneuriale*. These additional *chambres* may be located above the *chambre seigneuriale,* as in a solar tower, or at the other end of the building (upper or lower end of the hall as the case may be), or as is not infrequently the case, particularly later in the century, in an outshot which might contain a kitchen on the ground floor and *chambres* above. There is evidence from several widely dispersed sites that the *chambre* allocated to the seigneur was always on the first raised level and that the private accommodation of his lady was that *chambre* immediately above his own; this seems to be the case when each spouse has an 'apartment' of several *chambres,* in many cases related to an adjacent hall, just as much as when each has only one room at his or her disposal. We shall return to this theme.

The presence of a ground-floor hall, open to the roof, i.e., not ceiled, was a considerable impediment to circulation in a house with chambers at both ends; such an arrangement required, as is seen at Le Carpont (22 Trédarzec) and La Ville Andon (22 Plélo), two stairways, one at each end. The advantage of an arrangement in which halls were stacked· vertically, one above the other, is that lateral circulation is possible at each floor level, only one stairway being required, although access to some rooms might involve passing through others. Since the staircase is the most expensive item in a house of this kind, the saving is considerable; it is probable that 'open' ground-floor halls continued to be built, however, throughout the fifteenth, and probably into the sixteenth, century. It is only at the end of the fifteenth century that new houses, at the highest social level, are built with ceilings from the outset.

8. *La Touche Brandineuf (Plouguernast, Côtes-d'Armor): the former presence of a timber gallery along the façade at first-floor level is evident from the surviving corbels*
Photograph: Gwyn Meirion-Jones

Circulation within the house was also facilitated by the presence of galleries, usually of wood. Evidence for their former existence at Coadélan has already been cited; interpretation of the façades of several houses strongly points to the former existence of a gallery, such as at La Caillibotière (22 Saint-Aaron), La Touche Brandineuf (22 Plouguernast) (fig. 8), and L'Etier (56 Béganne). At La Roche Jagu there can be no possible doubt; the rear gallery survives and the front gallery has left all too obvious traces. As well as adding to the defensive capabilities of the house, it served to provide access from the stair turret to the twin doorways of the upper-most hall, presumably when the latter was temporarily subdivided to make two *chambres* for guests. Both upper halls at Hac were also provided with two hearths. Although each of these halls is sufficiently large to benefit from two hearths for heating purposes, such an arrangement does make occasional temporary subdivision, with curtains or moveable screens, much easier. The hearth, with its fine chimney-piece, is as much a status symbol as a practical consideration; a hearth is an essential prerequisite if a room is to be designated a *chambre,* worthy to receive a guest. Hence the need for more than one hearth if a larger space is to be subdivided to create even temporary *chambres.* Shorter galleries are also found linking a *chambre* of some importance with a latrine tower; examples may be cited at La Grand'Cour (22 Taden), La Ville Daniel (22 Plaine-Haute) and Le Bois Orcan (35 Noyal-sur-Vilaine). Such galleries, whilst they might make for chilly nocturnal perambulations, also added to 'defensive' capabilities and, more practically, provided a vantage point from which to view the gardens and the landscape in fine weather.

The survival of so-called manor-houses whose ground-plans do not conform to the norm raises questions of their true original function. Le Fretay (35 Pancé), which we have dated by dendrochronology to 1441-2—a date consistent with documentary evidence for the reconstruction of the adjacent castle—consists of two upper *chambres* above a byre; there is no trace of a *salle basse,* of cooking facilities or service rooms. [69] The fullest early description of Le Fretay dates from 1619:

> 'Arrivés au chasteau du Fretay l'aurions veu environné de fossez à fond de cuve, fermant de pont-levis avec double fossé par le devant . . . consistant iceluy chasteau en trois corps de logix, le grand desquels est composé par embas d'une grande salle de quarante pieds de long et vingt-quatre de large, ayant cuisine à l'une des costières de ladicte salle vers le couchant et à l'autre une petite chapelle au dedans de l'une des tours, sans armes ny escussons; et à l'autre bout de ladicte salle tirant vers le soleil levant est une grande chambre et office ayant cave au-dessous, et trois grandes chambres et greniers au-dessus avec un grand et petit degrez à vis faicts de grison par où on monte esdictes chambres et cinq grosses tours flanquées ès environs dudict corps-de-logix ayant galleries par lesquelles on va des unes aux aultres, dans trois desquelles sont chambres et garde-robes, l'une desquelles chambre est appelé la Chambre au Duc'.

The document adds that: 'les deux autres corps de logis moins importants se trouvaient dans le même cour, l'un à l'est où demeurait le métayer, l'autre à l'ouest "ayant chambres haultes", the same disposition that we find today. [70] A briefer description of 1603 is more formal:

> 'le lieu, chasteau, manoir et maisons du Fretay avecques le portal, doufves et fossez sittue en la paroisse de Pance, avecques les jardrins et piece de terre ou entiennement y avoiet de la vigne et place de fuye et colombier de tout de la terre arrable et non arrable, jardrins, vergiers, garainnes, boys de haulte fustaye et taillis en ce quest de la retenue du chasteau il y en a en tout quatre vingtz journaulx aincy les garannes. . . .' [71]

Marc'hallac'h (22 Plestin-les-Grèves) is similar. At Kernac'hriou (22 Pleudaniel), three doorways give access to a series of *chambres* well provided with latrines; there is no trace here of the normal arrangements of the medieval manor, the structure being more reminiscent of the 'staircase' arrangement of an Oxford college. Here probably lies the clue: these are chamber-blocks designed and built either for senior members of the seigneurial family, or for guests, or both. Where then were the ground-floor halls and other manorial buildings? At Le Fretay the nearby *château* may provide the answer; in the other two cases the most plausible explanation is that there were free-standing buildings in some other part of the *ensemble.* The strong possibility that they might have been of timber may also explain their disappearance and non-replacement. If a *manoir* had been abandoned by its owner to his *métayer,* content to live like any other peasant in one room, there would have been no incentive to rebuild a decaying timber hall.

The above examples are not the only ones where the all-important ground-floor hall is absent. At Kerandraou (22 Troguéry) and La Grand'Cour (22 Taden), as well as at other locations, we have gatehouses which provide access to a courtyard in which nothing is to be found but the dependent buildings of the present farm. These gatehouses provided very fine quarters, not only for the seigneurial family, but for servants too. Nevertheless, neither possesses that essential mark of the manoir, the common ground-floor hall. Here again it is reasonable to postulate the former existence of a detached hall, probably of timber, in the courtyard.

Thus in the fifteenth century we see a culmination of the medieval tradition with renovation and rebuilding in stone on a considerable scale after wars which had caused much destruction. The ground-floor hall remains the centre of manorial life; seigneurial families enjoyed private accommodation at first-floor level and above. Multi-period buildings result from the improvement and upgrading of earlier structures. Solar towers with superimposed *chambres* are incorporated into some rebuilds, as at Hac, Le Plessis Josso and Coadélan. Some buildings were conceived as entities but only partly built; all too common tusking betrays to this day the ambitions of former owners whose intentions were never fulfilled. The straight stairway survives from earlier periods, but in all new building the newel stair, usually in stone, but occasionally wholly or partly in wood, is the norm. Decoration is dominated by the Flamboyant style with octagonal sections for posts and columns.

THE RENAISSANCE

Renaissance styles appear towards the end of the fifteenth century as Flamboyant-gothic ornament becomes noticeably decadent in its expression but it is in the sixteenth century that the Renaissance idiom makes its impact. By mid-century it is in full flood. These new styles have long been sub-divided into 'first' and 'second' Renaissance. Reality is more complex: in Renaissance France as a whole eight clearly-defined periods have been recognized.[72] Much more research is needed before a similar degree of refinement can be applied to the classification of Renaissance building in Brittany.

During the sixteenth century the Duchy continued to enjoy that economic prosperity which had its origins in the later Middle Ages but which blossomed after the ending of the wars. Closer political relations with France, expressed in the marriages of Duchess Anne successively to two French kings and culminating in the Union of 1532, were but one expression of a greater well-being. In an age when the New World was being discovered and sea voyages attempted on a scale previously unknown, the position of Brittany—a major Atlantic peninsula—gave it that advantage which, not for the first time in history, it was able to exploit. Wealth—from commerce, trade and the land—found its expression in building.

Superficially, the sixteenth century marks the advent of classical motifs and detail. The appearance of a degree of symmetry, albeit imperfect, may be noted. The addition of a tower at Coadélan, containing an indoor chapel (affording greater privacy and dispensing with the need to cross the yard in wet weather), to give balance if not symmetry, is one such example. The century saw the complete rebuilding of houses of which all previous trace is now lost, a process which continued into the next century. In some cases new houses were built alongside the old residence, the latter being later relegated, only to be occupied by the *métayer,* or by a junior member of the family. In some instances, as at Goulaine (44 Haute-Goulaine), a fine new house completely supersedes whatever preceded it.

Regional variations occur; the large number of Renaissance houses in Finistère, for example, suggests that the west may not have witnessed the fifteenth-century rebuilding so evident further east. There is a continuing upgrading of earlier stone structures. The century saw the building of halls ceiled from the outset, leaving only a *grenier* above the uppermost level, as well as the upgrading, by the insertion of a ceiling, of ground-floor halls previously open to the roof. With the advent of ceiling in all rooms the need for multiple stairways is reduced; circulation through the halls is possible for the first time in many houses. With the insertion of ceilings into former open halls, internal galleries disappear. Circulation consequently becomes less of a problem; one stairway can serve all floors and all rooms, although the convenience of a secondary 'back' stairs, particularly for service purposes may lead to duplication. Secondary stairways may also exist, as at Le Bois Orcan, to link the private chambers of lord and lady. The popularity of the L-shaped house, a feature already noted in the fifteenth century at Bien Assis and other locations, is furthered by the building of a single newel stairway in the angle. The economy of having a single stairway (the most expensive single element by far in the construction of a house) to serve all rooms is apparent. The arms of the L-plan are usually differentiated by function, further emphasized by the hierarchy of doorway and window details; at La Ville Daniel, superimposed halls are accommodated in one arm, kitchen with *chambres* above in the other, the *cave* in the angle.

Chambres may be arranged in apartments in the larger houses, providing the occupants with a sequence as at La Ville Daniel, Le Bois Orcan, and Kerouartz (29 Lannilis). By the end of the century the new modish stairways are rectilinear in plan although the newel stairway remains, often as a secondary stairway at the rear, chiefly with a service function (*v.* Kerouartz).

That some open free-standing timber halls may still have existed at this period is suggested by the building of the detached chamber-block at Kernac'hriou (22 Pleudaniel) for which we have a date by dendrochronology of 'after 1554'.[73] The 'open' hall was not entirely extinct. The uppermost hall at Kerouzéré (29 Sibiril) dates from the very end of the sixteenth century, rebuilt after the house had been sacked; it may, however, have served a rather utilitarian purpose as a guard room as it leads directly on to the wall-walk. The ceiled upper hall had already made its appearance at Bel Air (29 Brélès), *c.* 1600,[74] and the ceiled ground-floor hall much earlier, as at La Guéhardière (35 Bazouges-sous-Hédé), where the hall ceiling beams fall within the date-span 1494–1513.[75]

Whilst single-storey ground-floor halls were now constructed with ceilings from the outset, and upper halls similarly provided with ceilings, many earlier halls remained open to the roof. Some have survived in this state, no doubt in part because they ceased to be inhabited by the noble families who owned them. In many cases such halls were ceiled purely in response to fashion, partly as a recognition of the greater warmth and comfort the new arrangements would bring. In many houses it is possible to detect that new ceilings were inserted into the earlier 'open' halls, thus upgrading the accommodation. This is the case, for example, at Le Téhel (35 Saint-Symphorien), Le Carpont (22 Trédarzec), La Salle (22 Plurien), La Grande Goublaie (22 Saint-Aaron), Boberil (35 L'Hermitage) and many others. The significance of this development for the evolution of the stairway and the freedom of circulation is of fundamental importance to the understanding of the plan evolution of the Renaissance house: it is a phenomenon that can be broadly—and provisionally, pending further research—ascribed to the period 1500–1660. The degree of privacy became enhanced and, in consequence, room function eventually became more specialized. The accommodating of extended families was made easier, as was the providing of rooms for guests. Servants quarters could now, at least in principle, be contrived in the roof-space although it was often not until the nineteenth century that this became at all common.

A corollary of these changes is that the 'public' function of the *manoir* is diminished. Towards 1600 the *salle basse* is no longer open to the view of the visitor standing in the doorway. An original stone partition wall separates it from what has now become the entrance vestibule, usually housing also the main staircase. The evolution of the *salle basse* into what was to become the *salon* of the eighteenth century has begun. In some houses (Kerouartz, 29 Lannilis; Kerbabu, 29 Lannilis; Kerjean, 29 Saint-Vougay) this ground-floor hall is raised over a semi-sunken cellar which runs the whole length of the room, and sometimes beyond. Access to the vestibule is now up a short flight of steps, further distancing the *salle basse* from the common visitor. Thus is privacy still further enhanced.

Two other developments deserve notice. The open ground-floor gallery is already established by 1600; examples occur at Guernachanay (22 Plouaret), *c.* 1600, at Kerjean (29 Saint-Vougay), half a century earlier, and at Crénan (22 Le Foeil). Galleries appear both as open arcades and as closed features and, whilst in some cases they represent merely a response to fashion, poorly integrated with the building, in others they perform a significant linking function, a vital element in the planning of the courtyard and in the linking of constituent buildings. One of the earliest and most beautiful is that of the château of Châteaubriant. That at Kergroadès is simpler (fig. 9). The need for further, and more private seigneurial accommodation is satisfied in many earlier houses by the building of a seigneurial *logis* at the rear of the house, usually with a pleasant outlook across fields. Of the latter, La Ville Geoffroy (22 Plélo) provides a good example.

Long before the dawn of the seventeenth century Gothic mouldings and details have been superseded by the classical idiom. There is ever increasing evidence of symmetry although at the beginning of the century the eccentric juxtaposition of Renaissance dress and medieval plan forms is still to be found, as at Kerouartz and Kerbabu (29 Lannilis) where new houses were constructed alongside existing ones making symmetry imperfect if not comic. The hall survived as the main common room, albeit partitioned off from the entrance vestibule; the result was sometimes an asymmetry scarcely concealed by classical forms. The main entrance doorway now sometimes open into the stairwell so that the hall is closed by a wall at the lower end with access by a doorway. Thus the visitor no longer crosses the threshold to find himself in the lower end of the hall (Kerbabu; Kerouartz; Bel Air is an exception,

9. *Kergroadès (Brélès, Finistère): the gallery links the two wings at ground-floor level whilst the walkway above links the* chapelle *and the chaplain's lodging*
Photograph: Gwyn Meirion-Jones

having two entrances with doorways expressing hierarchy, the larger giving access to the hall, the smaller to the upper hall and *chambres*). Increasing emphasis on privacy is seen with an increase in the number of *chambres* and latrines. A *logis seigneurial* makes its appearance in some houses, to one side (Le Plessis Josso) or at the rear (La Ville Geffroy en Plélo; Boberil en L'Hermitage).

With the arrival of the eighteenth century the 'traditional' *manoir* gives way to an architecture that reflects national taste rather than local traditions. Plan forms change radically and ground-floor living again becomes acceptable: salon, dining room, library and study reflect new styles of living detached from the immediate needs of running a country estate. With the general improvement of transport and communications new styles and fashions are more quickly diffused. The pull of Paris and the concentration of power in the capital increase, accompanied by a decline of regional power. Many *manoirs* and *châteaux* become summer residences—some were probably never otherwise—or only occasionally used; others—large numbers—are relegated to the status of farms to be occupied by peasants who live in them largely in one room as they would in a vernacular farmhouse, using the remaining rooms, if at all, for storage. Neglected by their owners, many have thus survived to the late twentieth century when it has once again become fashionable to possess a *manoir* and much renovation and restoration is currently is progress.

ACKNOWLEDGEMENTS

The success of this project is in no small way owing to the help and support of numerous friends and colleagues in the many French institutions we visit; thanks are particularly owing to the directors and staff of official agencies, government and regional departments, the libraries, museums, archives and similar institutions where we are unfailingly received with courtesy, interest and sometimes more than a little curiosity. We have on previous occasions singled out Madame Le Louarn, former Conservateur Régional des Monuments Historiques, for special mention; she took a great interest in our work and was a never-failing source of information and assistance during her time as Conservateur Régional. We are most grateful to her. We would wish also to thank Alain-Charles Perrot, Architecte en chef des Monuments Historiques for the *départements* of Ille-et-Vilaine and Côtes-d'Armor, for the interest he shows in our work and for the opportunity to collaborate with him at Le Bois Orcan. Our informal contacts with the Architectes des Bâtiments de France, and their staffs, have also been helpful and informative; we should particularly like to mention Monsieur Pierre Monerie (Côtes-d'Armor) who has taken an interest in our work for several years.

Once again we are deeply in debt to the many owners to have allowed us access to their properties; in many instances our visits have been only a reconnaissance, but some buildings have been selected for detailed study, requiring access to all rooms as well as roof spaces; in numerous cases we have made repeated visits always to be received with courtesy and helpfulness and often not a little hospitality. In addition to those owners and occupants whose help has already been acknowledged in previous publications, we should like, in particular, to emphasize our gratitude to Monsieur and Madame Blanchard (L'Etier), Dr and Madame Boudier (La Ville Balin), Dr and Madame Boutbien (La Noë Verte), Monsieur and Madame Boulmer (Le Brégain), the Comte and Comtesse de Calan (La Touche Trébry), the Comte and Comtesse Olivier de Calan (Kerouzéré), Monsieur and Madame Cocu (La Gaudesière), Monsieur and Madame Isidor Corbel (La Ville Andon), the Comte and Comtesse de la Goublaie de Nantois (La Grande Goublaie), Monsieur and Madame Guillaume (La Ville aux Fêvres), Madame Huet (La Roche Jagu), Mademoiselle de Kergos (La Touche Brandineuf), Monsieur and Madame Kermanac'h (Kernac'hriou), Madame de Kerjégu (Bien Assis), both Monsieur and Madame Landon and Monsieur and Madame Colleu (Le Bois Orcan), the Comte and Comtesse Lionel de La Haye Saint Hilaire (La Haye Saint Hilaire), Monsieur and Madame Lenaff (Pouldu), Monsieur et Madame Loiselet (Kerbabu), Monsieur Nielsen and Monsieur Machenaud (Hac), the Mesdames de Sagazan (Tronjoly), the Comte and Comtesse Henri de Saint-Pierre (Beaumanoir), Monsieur and Madame Salmon-Legagneur (Le Plessis Josso), Madame Studler (La Ville Daniel), Monsieur and Madame Suire (Toul an Gollet), Mademoiselle de Taisne (Bel Air), Monsieur and Madame Tardival (La Ville Geffroy); we are also most grateful to those many, too many to name individually here, to whose homes we have so far paid only brief visits but to which we may return.

Research projects need finance. Much though we regret the fact that our dendrochronology programme is no longer regarded as 'new science' deserving of funding in the sense of that term, given the current difficult financial climate, we nevertheless continue with our dating programme albeit at a lower level of intensity than we would wish; it continues to be fruitful. The following bodies have provided us with support, either of money or in kind, since the start of the project and it is with considerable gratitude that we once again acknowledge their assistance: The British Academy; the Science and Engineering Research Council; the

Leverhulme Trust; the Centre National de la Recherche Scientifique; the London Guildhall University (formerly the City of London Polytechnic); the University of Nottingham, the Queen's University of Belfast; and the Society of Antiquaries of London.

ABSTRACT

THE SEIGNEURIAL DOMESTIC BUILDINGS OF BRITTANY, 1000–1700

The evolution of the seigneurial residence is traced from the earliest known sites, the motte-and-bailey castles, to the Renaissance. Many of the elements known in adjacent parts of western Europe are found also in Brittany: the free-standing ground-floor hall, the chamber-block, the inhabited tower with its ascending hierarchy of rooms, both undefended and in its fortified form, the *donjon*. Hall and chamber are the recurring common elements which, together with the kitchen and *cave,* form the 'seigneurial minimum' accommodation. The *chambre* is always raised above ground level. Emphasis on height—and domination—is a recurring theme. From the thirteenth century multiple halls become common, stacked above each other; two superimposed halls are frequent, four not unknown. Veritable apartments appear—each with hall and chamber—on several levels. Although the open hall is ubiquitous, no evidence of a former open hearth has yet come to light in the buildings studied. Many of the smaller *manoirs* retain their open roofs until the fifteenth century or later. The period 1500–1660 is one of modernization of medieval halls by the insertion of ceilings, rationalizing internal communication. With the Renaissance come new decorative styles, although the medieval plan usually survives. Peace, greater wealth and prosperity following the Union with France lead to much new building and the rebuilding of earlier residences.

RÉSUMÉ

LES CONSTRUCTIONS SEIGNEURIALES EN BRETAGNE, 1000–1700

L'évolution de la résidence seigneuriale est retracée à partir des plus anciens sites connus, les châteaux à motte, jusqu'à la Renaissance. La plupart des types recensés dans les régions voisines d'Europe de l'Ouest apparaissent aussi en Bretagne: le *hall* à charpente apparente, le *chamber-block,* la tour, fortifiée ou non, caractérisée par la hiérarchie ascendante des pièces et enfin le donjon.

Le hall et la chambre sont les éléments permanents qui, avec la cuisine et la cave, constituent la forme minimale de l'habitat seigneurial. La chambre est toujours à l'étage et l'accent mis sur la hauteur—et la domination—est un phénomène constant. A partir du XIIIe siècle, la superposition de plusieurs salles devient fréquente: souvent deux et jusqu'à quatre. De véritables appartements apparaissent alors, sur plusieurs niveaux, chacun avec un *hall* et une chambre. Bien que le *hall* à charpente apparente soit omniprésente, aucun indice de foyer ouvert n'a encore été mis en évidence dans les bâtiments étudiés. Beaucoup de petits manoirs conservent leur charpente lambrissée jusqu'au XVe siècle, voire plus tard.

La période 1500–1660 voit la modernisation des *halls* d'origine médiévale par l'insertion d'un plafond, ce qui rationalise la circulation intérieure. Avec la Renaissance, de nouveaux modes décoratifs apparaissent, bien que le plan médiéval perdure en général. La paix et la plus grande prospérité qui suivent le rattachement de la Bretagne à la France entraînent une forte activité de construction ou de transformation des résidences antérieures.

NOTES

The origins of the seigneurial domestic buildings project are explained in Jones *et al.* 1989, 104, below; it is the principal current project of a small group of senior academics drawn from different institutions, working together as the European Vernacular Architecture Research Unit. Based at London Guildhall University (formerly the City of London Polytechnic), EVARU is under the direction of Professor Meirion-Jones (Professor Emeritus and Honorary Research Fellow, LGU); the other main contributors to the Brittany project are Professor Michael Jones (Professor of Medieval French History, University of Nottingham) and Professor Jon Pilcher (Professor of Palaeoecology, The Queen's University of Belfast). Although the present authors are responsible for the greater part of the work so far accomplished, mention must be made of the considerable contribution to the dendrochronology programme by Dr Frédéric Guibal, now of the CNRS Besançon, whilst he was SERC Post-doctoral Research Assistant (a joint appointment, City of London Polytechnic/Queen's University of Belfast). Our work would have been much more difficult and less effective without the excellent technical support provided by Don Shewen, Chief Technician in the Department of Geography, London Guildhall University. Both he and Graeme Coston, before the latter's departure to take up another post, have given much support in both laboratory and field, contributing significantly to the rapid progress made in dendrochronology, especially in the early stages. Since autumn 1989, Andrew Moir (Laboratory Technician) has taken up the laboratory aspects of the dendrochronology and we are enormously grateful to him for the preparation and preliminary analysis which he has made of the oak cores deriving from our 1989 dendrochronology field season. We have continued to enjoy the services of the Cartographic Unit at LGU and thanks here are owing to Gareth Owen and Andrew Ellis. Among our other colleagues, Dr Philip Dixon has assisted with fieldwork, notably in north Finistère, and Pierre Corbel and Roger Bertrand have contributed to our informal field seminars held during a weekend in September in certain years.

Se: Bibliography for details of publications arising from the work of EVARU: Guibal 1987;

1988; Guibal *et al.* 1987a; 1987b; Guibal and Pilcher 1988; Jones *et al.* 1986; 1987; 1989; Meirion-Jones and Jones 1991a; 1991b; 1992a; 1992b; 1992c; Meirion-Jones *et al.* 1990; forthcoming.

[3]   For a summary of research on rural settlement in Brittany, see Meirion-Jones 1982, 21-44 and 191-249 for a full account of the Breton long-house.

[4]   Agrarian restructuring, greatly accelerated after the founding of the European Economic Community, had a profound effect. The last forty years in France have witnessed the greatest agricultural revolution in European history and, with it, the passing of an agrarian civilization. Along with these changes there has been much destruction of 'traditional' building at all social levels but peasant buildings have suffered most as farmers have sought to modernize rapidly and all that was representative of the older way of life, poverty and toil, tools, implements as well as buildings, was cast aside in the all-important struggle to evolve. Vast quantities of evidence valuable to the ethnologist and historian of rural life has been lost for ever.

[5]   Jones *et al.* 1989, 74-9.

[6]   Meirion-Jones and Jones 1992b.

[7]   Davies 1988.

[8]   Chédeville and Tonnerre 1987, 113-220 provides the fullest recent treatment of these developments; cf. Jones 1988, 24-31.

[9]   cf. Meirion-Jones and Jones 1991a; 1992a for profusely illustrated accounts.

[10]   Meuret unpublished communication, Brest 1992, but cf. Brand'honneur 1990, 17.

[11]   Below, p. 170.

[12]   Sanquer 1977; Chédeville and Tonnerre 1987, 179-93; Jones 1988, 68. In private conversation at the Colloquium, Brian Davison expressed scepticism about dates prior to the late eleventh century for the construction of mottes: that of La Garnache (85) has allegedly and variously been dated by 14C to AD 1000 x 1050 (*Bull. Soc. archéol. Finistère,* 109 (1981), 79) or AD 990 x 1010 (Chédeville and Tonnerre 1987, 191), but it is not clear whether these dates have been properly calibrated so that we are dubious about their apparent precision. The whole question of the dating of Breton mottes deserves more rigorous investigation in the light of the latest scientific advances.

[13]   Gallet 1983, 79 *et seq.* provides a good regional account of 'feudal' relations.

[14] cf. the classic discussion of *aveux* by Sée 1906, 77-82.

[15] The following discussion is based on a documentation too extensive to be cited in full here.

[16] Geslin de Bourgogne and De Barthélèmy 1855-79, VI, 149, no. xli, *Capellam de Mota de Guingampi* [22 Guingamp]; Bernier 1977; *plessis* appears to be limited to Bretagne *gallo,* a point made in conversation at the Colloquium by Monsieur Emmanuel Salmon-Legagneur.

[17] For some pioneering remarks, see Chédeville and Tonnerre 1987, 295-310.

[18] Aurelien de Courson 1863; our remarks owe much to Davies 1988.

[19] Davies 1988, 36, 137.

[20] *Ibid.,* 140-1.

[21] Guigon 1989; Chédeville and Tonnerre 1987, 135-8, provides a recent suitably cautious account of the value of the Chanson d'Aquin.

[22] De Boüard 1973-4.

[23] Morice 1742-6, I, 507, *Actum Redonis in camera aulae ipsius ducis* (9 October 1100); *ibid., 774, Actum in aula Filgeriarum* (1199); *ibid., 834, in aula nostra* (Châteaubriant, 1219); Rosenzweig 1895, no. 193, *in aula sua* (Josselin, 1118).

[24] cf. Bur 1986.

[25] Bertrand 1985, 274-5; 1985-6, 29-42; 1986a, 53-4; 1986b, 221.

[26] See also below p. 171.

[27] See below p. 167 and note 52.

[28] Du Berthou 1910, 414-19 is the best account of the lordship of Le Pallet; a charter of 1084 x 1089 names 'Daniel de Palatio' as a witness (Morice 1742-6, I, 431). A charter mentioning the *castellania Palatio,* dated by Du Berthou to 1066, should however be dated 1116 x 1141 (Guillotel 1973, no. 161). The castle was largely destroyed during the wars of the later Middle Ages; a brief description is provided in an *aveu* of 1533 (Du Berthou 1910, 15, 418).

[29] Morice 1742-6, I, 657 and 666. The use of *camera* is also infrequent; for an early example cf. *ibid., 507, in camera aulae ipsius ducis* [Alan IV] at Rennes (1101), whilst one is mentioned at Vitré in 1156 (*ibid.,* 574).

[30] *id est unam medietariam in Conburn* [35 Combourg], *duas in Planafilice* [35 Pleine-Fougères]. . . .' (Bigne de la Villeneuve 1876, no. XII; Guillotel 1973, no. 29, with the date 1024 x 1034); *duas medietarias apud villam que nuncupatur Piriccus* [35 Piré-sur-Seiche] (*Mém. Soc. Hist. Archéol. Bretagne,* 61 (1984), 64, dated 1040 x 1060; Planiol 1981-4, IV, 221-3).

[31] For the earliest Breton example of *manerium* see Jones *et al.* 1989, 107 n. 27; for *herbergementum* cf. Duparc 1964, esp. 26-7. There is a charter of *c.* 1080 which contradicts Duparc's view that the word is first used in a Breton context in the early thirteenth century (Morice 1742-6, I, 772, *Herveus butellarius dedit . . . unum arbergamentum in ipso cymiterio ubi domus patris sui antea fuerat* [35 Roz-sur-Couesnon], cf. *Mém. Soc. Hist. Archéol. Bretagne,* 52 (1972-4), 14), though Duparc seems correct in thinking that its more general adoption only occurs after 1200. For *maison/mansion* cf. Morice 1742-6, I, 980 (1262); 1214 (1307); Blanchard 1898-1900, I, cxlii (1329).

[32] There is a curious gap between the last charter usages of *aula* in the early thirteenth century and the appearance in the late fourteenth century of *salle* to describe the major component of most manors: the hall. A detailed study of the distribution of the place-names La Salle or Les Salles in Brittany would prove most instructive. For a sensible discussion of terminology in another region see Héliot 1955, 574-83.

[33] Morice 1742-6, I, 933-5; Rosenzweig 1895, no. 275.

[34] Morice 1742-6, I, 960-1.

[35] Le Mené 1891-4, I, 547-8 for Bodegat; *aveux* of 1640 (rendered by Henry de Sevigné) and 1735 survive in Arch. dép. du Morbihan, E 2741.

[36] Arch. dép. Côtes-d'Armor, E 126, E 241 and E 246.

[37] Geslin de Bourgogne and De Barthélèmy 1855-79, IV, 51; Morice 1742-6, I, 944, 959-60 for the 'new castle' of Quintin; it was erected into a separate castellany *c.* 1227 and the *donjon* is mentioned in 1379 (La Borderie 1889, 241, 257-8). For contracts and accounts for the extension of the castle in the late fifteenth century see Arch. dép. Ille-et-Vilaine, 1 F 1252-5.

[38] Meirion-Jones 1986, 19. The main archival sources are Arch. dép. Côtes-d'Armor, E 1008, E 2660, E 2708-14; Chantilly, Musée Condé, série F. Registre 158.

[39] Arch. dép. Loire-Atlantique, B 2141/1 is the principal archival source for the history of Le Bois Orcan.

[40] Jones *et al.* 1989, 80.

[41] Brown 1965, 76; Wilson 1985, 213-15.

[42] Brown 1965, 79.

[43] Mortet 1911, t. I, 183-5.

[44] Cucarull 1990, 67-90. Champagne and Cucarull 1988, 2-6. Champagne 1988, 357-8.

[45] Brown 1965, 83.

[46] Irien 1981.

[47] *Ibid.,* 115.

[48] *Ibid.,* 118.

[49] On the death of Morice de Kerasquer, sire de Quillimadec, in 1473 his son, Morice, succeeded. Arch. dép. Loire-Atlantique, B 1713.

[50] Arch. dép. Loire-Atlantique, E 154 no. 1; Arch. dép. Côtes-d'Armor, 66 J 5.

[51] See note 28, above, for Le Pallet; it is well known that Berengarius and Lucia, the parents of Peter Abelard (b. 1079) were of knightly stock and lived at Le Pallet (*Historia Calamitatum,* cap. II). Grand 1958, 364-5 attributes the chapel 'au XIe siècle avec reprise au XIIe'.

[52] Rennes, Bibliothèque municipale MS 17, edited in Morice 1742-6, I, 672-3 and commentary in La Borderie and Poquet 1896-1914, III, 253-4. Étienne de Fougères's *palatium* seems to have been rebuilt by Anselme de Chantemerle, bishop of Rennes (1390-1427): Guillotin de Corson 1880-6, I, 120. For the bishop's residence at Dol see Déceneux 1977, 232-7.

[53] Meirion-Jones 1986, 27.

[54] In preparation for publication as *La Ville de Cluny et ses Maisons,* Paris

[55] Jones *et al.* 1989, 87 and 100-4.

[56] Meirion-Jones 1978-9.

[57] Jones *et al.* 1989, 87.

[58] Meirion-Jones *et al.,* forthcoming.

[59] Jones *et al.* 1989, 83.

[60] *Ibid.,* 82.

[61] See note 25, above.

[62] Meirion-Jones 1986, 20; Jones *et al.* 1989, 82.

[63] Arch. dép. Côtes-d'Armor, E 1529.

[64] Le Patourel 1986, 17.

[65] Arch. dép. Côtes-d'Armor, E 1529.

[66] Arch. dép. Ille-et-Vilaine, I F 1225 fol. 60^r-61^r.

[67] Meirion-Jones 1986, 23-5; Jones *et al.* 1989, 82-3.

[68] Meirion-Jones *et al.* 1990; Jones *et al.* 1989, 87-90; Meirion-Jones 1986, 63-72.

[69] Jones, *et al.* 1989, 100-1.

[70] *Revue historique de l'Ouest,* 8 (1892), 232, after Arch. dép. Ille-et-Vilaine, fonds de Laillé.

[71] Arch. dép. Loire-Atlantique, B 2148, *aveu* of Regnaud de la Marzelière, chevalier de l'ordre du Roi, vicomte de Fretay, captain of fifty men-at-arms of King's ordonnances, governor of the town and castle of Fougères etc., 14 March 1603.

[72] Babelon 1988; 1989; Mussat 1979; 1991.

[73] Jones *et al.* 1989, 91.

[74] We are indebted to Mademoiselle de Taisne for copies of archival material relating to Bel Air. A firm point of departure for a history of the house is a datestone of 1599 and an inventory of goods found at the manor on the death of François Kerengarz in February 1606.

[75] Jones *et al.* 1989, 91. There is still a problem of identification here: two manoirs have been discovered with similar names at Bazouges-sous-Hedé, La Gueharderie and La Gahardière and it has not proved possible so far to distinguish between them easily (cf. Anne Duportal 1915, 292-3; Banéat 1973, I, 116). Guillotin de Corson (Arch. dép. Ille-et-Vilaine, 1 F 1724) provides the following descent for La Gueharderie during the critical period of building: 1437, Geoffroi Piedeloup; 1445, Geoffroi Piedeloup; after 1445, Raoulette Piedeloup married to Louis de Lespinay; 1524, Bonabé de Lespinay, their son; 1542, Gilles de Lespinay. For that of La Gahardière see Jones *et al.* 1989, 108, n. 50.

BIBLIOGRAPHY

AURELIEN de COURSON (ed.) 1863. *Le Cartulaire de l'Abbaye de Redon en Bretagne,* Paris

BABELON, J.-P. 1988. *Le Château en France,* Paris

——, 1989. *Châteaux de France au Siècle de la Renaissance,* Paris

BANEAT, P. 1973. *Le Département d'Ille-et-Vilaine, Histoire, Archéologie, Monuments,* 4 vols., revised edition, Paris

BERNIER, G. 1977. 'Un toponyme franc d'origine carolingienne en Bretagne: Haie', *Dossiers du Centre régionale archéologique d'Alet,* 5, 27-8

BERTHOU, P. du 1910. *Clisson et ses Monuments,* Nantes

BERTRAND, R. 1985. 'Inzinzac-Lochrist (Morbihan). Sainte-Geneviève', *Archéologie médiévale,* 15, 274-5

——, 1985-6. 'La maison-forte de Ste-Geneviève en Inzinzac', *Société lorientaise d'Archéologie, Conférences et Travaux,* 29-42

——, 1986a. 'Une fouille en cours: Sainte-Geneviève en Inzinzac-Lochrist (Moribihan)', in Bur, M. (ed.), 1986, *La Maison forte au Moyen Age,* 53-4, Paris

——, 1986b. 'Inzinzac-Lochrist (Morbihan). Sainte-

Geneviève', *Archéologie médiévale,* 16, 221

BIGNE de la VILLENEUVE, P. (ed.) 1876. *Cartulaire de l'Abbaye de St-Georges de Rennes,* Rennes

BLANCHARD, R. (ed.) 1898-1900. *Cartulaire des Seigneurs de Rays,* 2 vols., Poitiers

BOUARD, M. de 1973-4. 'De l'*aula* au donjon, les fouilles de la motte de la Chapelle à Doué-la-Fontaine (X^e-XIe siècles)', *Archéologie médiévale,* 3-4, 5-110

BRAND'HONNEUR, M. 1990. *Les Mottes médiévales d'Ille-et-Vilaine,* Institut Culturel de Bretagne/Centre Régional d'Archéologie d'Alet

BROWN, R. ALLEN, 1965. 'The architecture' in *The Bayeux Tapestry* (ed. F. M. Stenton), 2nd edition, 76, London

BUR, M. (ed.) 1986. *La Maison forte au Moyen Age,* Paris

CHAMPAGNE, F. 1988. 'Fougères (Ille-et-Vilaine). Le château', *Archéologie médiévale,* 18, 357-8

CHAMPAGNE, F. and CUCARULL, J. 1988. 'Bilan de trois années de fouilles archéologiques au château de Fougères', *Le Pays de Fougères,* 68, 2-6

CHEDEVILLE, A. and TONNERRE, N.-Y. 1987. *La Bretagne féodale, XIe-XIIIe siècle,* Rennes

CUCARULL, J. 1990. 'Le logis du château de Fougères (XIe-XVIIIe): essai d'analyse archéologique', *Les Dossiers du Centre Régional d'Archéologie d'Alet,* 18, 67-90

DAVIES, WENDY 1988. *Small Worlds. The Village Community in Early Medieval Brittany,* London

DECENEUX. M. 1977. 'La résidence des évêques de Dol à la fin du moyen âge', *Annales Soc. Hist. Archéol. Saint-Malo,* Année 1977, 232-7

DUPARC, P. 1964. 'Hébergement et abergement', *Bibliothèque de l'École des Chartes,* 122, 5-88

DUPORTAL, ANNE 1915. 'Hédé, la seigneurie', *Bulletin et Mémoires de la Soc. archéol. du Département d'Ille-et-Vilaine,* 44, 198-391.

GALLET, J. 1983. *La Seigneurie bretonne (1450-1680); l'Exemple du Vannetais,* Paris

GESLIN de BOURGOGNE, J. and BARTHELEMY, A. de (eds.) 1855-79. *Anciens Evêchés de Bretagne,* 6 vols., Paris and Saint-Brieuc

GRAND, R. 1958. *L'Art roman en Bretagne,* Paris

GUIBAL, F. 1987. 'Dendrochronology of oak in Brittany', *Dendrochronologia,* 5, 69-77

——, 1988. 'Aspects de la dendrochronologie des habitations seigneuriales de Bretagne', *Bois et Archéologie/Wood and Archaeology,* First European Conference, Louvain-la-Neuve, 2-3 October 1987, *PACT,* 22, 85-97

GUIBAL, F. and PILCHER, J.R. 1988. 'Remarques sur la comparaison des séries d'épaisseurs des cernes des Côtes-du-Nord à celles d'Ille-et-Vilaine', *Revue d'Archéométrie,* 12, 29-33

GUIBAL, F., JONES, M.C.E., MEIRION-JONES, G.I. and PILCHER, J.R. 1987a. 'Dendrochronologie de trois manoirs des Côtes-du-Nord', *Les Dossiers du Centre régional archéologique d'Alet,* 15, 63-70

——, 1987b. 'Introduction à l'architecture des habitations seigneuriales bretonnes', *Architecture vernaculaire,* 11, 45-59

GUIGON, P. 1989. 'Locronan (Finistère). Montagne du Prieuré', *Archéologie médiévale,* 19 (1989), 338-9

GUILLOTEL, HUBERT 1973. 'Recueil des actes des ducs de Bretagne, 944-1148', Paris, Faculté de Droit, thèse de doctorat

GUILLOTIN de CORSON, ABBE. 1880-85. *Pouillé historique de l'Archevêché de Rennes,* 6 vols., Rennes and Paris

HELIOT, P. 1955. 'Les demeures seigneuriales dans la région picarde au moyen-âge. Châteaux ou manoirs?' *Recueil de Travaux offerts à M. Clovis Brunel,* 2 vols., Paris, I, 574-83

IRIEN, J. 1981. 'Le site médiéval de Lezkelen en Plabennec: le castel Saint-Ténénan', *Bull. Soc. archéol. Finistère,* 99, 103-19

JONES, MICHAEL 1988. *The Creation of Brittany,* London

JONES, M.C.E., MEIRION-JONES, G.I. and PILCHER, J.R. 1986. 'Les constructions seigneuriales domestiques (manoirs) en Bretagne', *Les Dossiers du Centre régional archéologique d'Alet,* 14, 121-2

JONES, M.C.E., MEIRION-JONES, G.I., PILCHER. J.R. and GUIBAL, F. 1987. 'Bretagne: les constructions seigneuriales domestiques', *Bulletin monumental,* 145, pt. 2, 205

JONES, MICHAEL, MEIRION-JONES, GWYN I., GUIBAL, F. and PILCHER, J.R., 1989. 'The seigneurial domestic buildings of Brittany: a provisional assessment', *Antiq. J.,* 69, 73-110

LA BORDERIE, A. de 1889. 'Nouvelle généalogie des seigneurs de Quintin du XIIIe au XVIe siècle', *Mémoires de la Société archéologique et historique des Côtes-du-Nord,* 2ème série, 3, 235-84

LA BORDERIE, A. de and POCQUET, B. 1896-1914. *Histoire de Bretagne,* 6 vols., Paris and Rennes

LE MENE, J. 1891-4. *Histoire des Paroisses de Vannes,* 2 vols., Vannes

LE PATOUREL, J. 1986. 'Fortified and semi-fortified manor houses in eastern and northern England in the later Middle Ages', in *La Maison Forte au Moyen Age* (ed. M. Bur), Paris

MEIRION-JONES, G.I. 1978-9. 'Un problème d'évolution de la maison bretonne: le foyer ouvert', *Archéologie en Bretagne,* 20-21, 18-26

——, 1982. *The Vernacular Architecture of Brittany,* Edinburgh

—— (ed.) 1986. European Vernacular Architecture Research Unit, *The Seigneurial Domestic Buildings of Brittany: First Interim Report, 1983-85,* London

—— (ed.) 1987. European Vernacular Architecture Research Unit, *Newsletter,* 1, London

MEIRION-JONES, G.I. and JONES, M.C.E., 1991a. *Aimer les Châteaux de Bretagne,* Rennes. English edition, *Wonderful Châteaux in Brittany.* German edition, *Liebenswerte Schlösser der Bretagne*

——, 1991b. 'Le manoir de La Grand'Cour en Taden', *Le Pays de Dinan,* 11, 61-78

——, 1992a. *Les Châteaux de Bretagne,* Rennes

——, 1992b. 'La résidence seigneuriale en Bretagne à la fin du Moyen Age et au début de la Renaissance', in *1491—La Bretagne, terre d'Europe: Colloque international, Brest, 2-4 octobre 1991* (eds. J. Kerhervé and T. Daniel), 337-353, Brest

——, 1992c. 'Châteaux et manoirs de Bretagne: une nouvelle recherche', *Journées d'Etudes sur la Bretagne et les Pays celtiques, Kreiz,* Brest, 1, 153-94

MEIRION-JONES, G.I., JONES, M.C.E., PILCHER, J.R. and GUIBAL, F. 1990. 'Un des grands manoirs bretons: le château de Hac au Quiou', *Le Pays de Dinan,* 10, 171-207

——, forthcoming. 'Coadélan en Prat: un des grands manoirs bretons'

MORICE, DOM H. 1742-6. *Mémoires pour servir de Preuves à l'Histoire ecclésiastique et civile de Bretagne,* 3 vols., Paris

MORTET, V. 1911. *Recueil de Textes relatifs à l'Histoire de l'Architecture . . . en France au Moyen Age,* t. I, Paris

MUSSAT, A. 1979. *Arts et Culture de Bretagne: un Millénaire,* Paris

——, 1991. 'L'Héritage' in *Bretagne: Guide Bleu,* 65-94, Paris

PILCHER, J.R. and BAILLIE, M. 1988. 'Make a date with a tree', *New Scientist,* 17 March 1988, 48-51

PLANIOL, MARCEL 1981-4. *Histoire des Institutions de la Bretagne* (ed. J. Brejon de Lavergnée), 5 vols., Mayenne

ROSENZWEIG, L. (ed.) 1895. *Cartulaire du Morbihan,* Vannes

SANQUER, R. 1977. 'Les mottes féodales du Finistère, *Bull. Soc. archéol. Finistère,* 105, 99-126

SEE, H. 1906. *Les Classes rurales en Bretagne du XVIe Siècle à la Révolution,* Paris, reprinted Brionne (1978)

WILSON, DAVID M. 1985. *The Bayeux Tapestry,* London

Index

(Page references to figures in **bold**)